An Overview of Aboriginal and Treaty Rights and Compensation for Their Breach

Purich's Aboriginal Issues Series

An Overview of Aboriginal and Treaty Rights and Compensation for Their Breach

Robert Mainville, LL.L., LL.M.

Purich Publishing Ltd.
Saskatoon, Saskatchewan

All enquiries and orders regarding this publication should be addressed to Purich Publishing Ltd.
Box 23032, Market Mall Postal Outlet
Saskatoon, SK Canada S7J 5H3
Tel: (306) 373-5311
Facsimile: (306) 373-5315
E-mail: purich@sk.sympatico.ca
Web site: www3.sk.sympatico.ca/purich

National Library of Canada Cataloguing in Publication Data
Mainville, Robert, 1953–
    An overview of aboriginal and treaty rights and compensation for their breach

(Purich's aboriginal issues series)
Includes bibliographical references and index.
ISBN 1-895830-17-6
1. Indians of North America—Canada—Legal status, laws, etc. 2. Indians of North America—Canada—Treaties. I. Title. II. Series.
KE7709.M33 2001   342.71'0872   C2001-910470-7
KF8205.M33 2001

Editing, design, and layout by Page Wood Publishing Services, Saskatoon
Index by Geri Rowlatt, Victoria
Cover design by NEXT Communications, Inc., Saskatoon
Printed in Canada by Houghton Boston Printers, Saskatoon
Printed on acid-free paper

Readers will note that words like Aboriginal, Native, and Indigenous have been capitalized. In recent years, many Aboriginal people have argued that such words should be capitalized when referring to specific people, in the same manner that European and American are capitalized. I agree; hence the capitalization.
Donald Purich, Publisher

Contents

Acknowledgements

I wish to thank my wife, Johanne, for her numerous encouragements. This book would have not been completed but for her. As she is a practising lawyer herself very familiar with the subject matter discussed here, her advice has been precious to me. I take this opportunity to extend my deepest gratitude to Bill Namagoose and Brian Craik of the Grand Council of the Cree. Finally, I thank my administrative assistant, Isabelle Desbiens, who spent numerous hours preparing the manuscript. Her devotion over the many years we have worked together is greatly appreciated and deserves recognition here.

Table of Cases

Table of Authorities

Aronson, S. "The Authority of the Crown to Make Treaties with Indians" [1993] 2 C.N.L.R. 1.

Asch, M., & P. Macklem. "Aboriginal Rights and Canadian Sovereignty: An Essay on R. v. Sparrow" (1991) 26:2 Alta. L. Rev. 502.

Barnes, N. "*Delgamuukw*, Division of Powers and Provincial Land and Resource Laws: Some Implications for Provincial Resource Rights" (1998) 32:2 U.B.C. L. Rev. 318.

Bartlett, R.H. "Aboriginal Land Claims at Common Law" [1984] 1 C.N.L.R. 1.

———. "You Can't Trust the Crown: The Fiduciary Obligation of the Crown to the Indians: Guerin v. The Queen" (1984–85) 49 Sask. L. Rev. 367.

———. "The Fiduciary Obligation of the Crown to the Indians" (1989) 53 Sask. L. Rev. 301.

Barton, B. "Comment" (1987) 66 Can. Bar Rev. 145.

Binnie, W.I.C. "The Sparrow Doctrine: Beginning of the End or End of the Beginning?" (1991) 15 Queen's L.J. 217.

Brownlie, I. *Treaties and Indigenous Peoples.* Oxford: Clarendon Press, 1992.

Brun, H. "Les Droits des Indiens sur le territoire du Québec" (1969) 10 C. de D. 415.

———. *Le territoire du Québec.* Québec: Les Presses de l'Université Laval, 1974.

Challies, G.S. "Quelques problèmes d'expropriation" (1961) 21 R. du B. 165.

———. *The Law of Expropriation.* Montreal: Wilson et Lafleur, 1963.

Clark, B. *Indian Title in Canada.* Toronto: Carswell, 1987.

Clinton, R.N., N.J. Newton, & M.E. Price. *American Indian Law.* Charlotteville, Virginia: The Michie Company, 1991.

Cohen, F.S. *Felix S. Cohen's Handbook of Federal Indian Law.* Rennard Strickland *et al.,* eds. Charlottesville, Virginia: The Michie Company, 1982.

Elliott, D.W. "Aboriginal Title." In B.W. Morse, ed. *Aboriginal Peoples and the Law.* Ottawa: Carleton University Press, 1989.

Evans, J.M., & B. Slattery. "Federal Jurisdiction-Pendant Parties-Aboriginal Title and Federal Common Law-Charter Challenges-Reform Proposals: *Roberts* v. *Canada*" (1989) 68 Can. Bar Rev. 817.

Forgues, J., & J. Prémont. *Loi sur l'expropriation annotée.* Cowansville, Québec: Les Éditions Yvon Blais, 1998.

Grammond, S. "La protection constitutionnelle des droits ancestraux des peuples autochtones et l'arrêt Sparrow" (1991) 36 McGill L.J. 1382.

———. "Aboriginal Treaties and Canadian Law" (1994) 20 Queen's L.J. 57.

———. *Les traités entre l'État canadien et les peuples autochtones.* Cowansville, Québec: Les Éditions Yvon Blais, 1995.

Green, L.C., & Olive P. Dickason. *The Law of Nations and the New World.* Edmonton: University of Alberta Press, 1989.

Henderson, J.S. Youngblood, M.L. Benson, & I.M. Findlay. *Aboriginal Tenure in the Constitution of Canada.* Toronto: Carswell, 2000.

Hogg, P.W. *Constitutional Law of Canada,* 4th ed., vol. 1 (looseleaf). Toronto: Carswell, 1997.

Hurley, J. "Aboriginal Rights, the Constitution and the Marshall Court" (1982–83) 17 R.J.T. 403.

———. "Aboriginal Rights in Modern American Case Law" [1983] 2 C.N.L.R. 9.

———. "The Crown's Fiduciary Duty and Indian Title: Guerin v. The Queen" (1985) 30 McGill L.J. 559.

Hutchins, P., *et al.* "When Do Fiduciary Obligations to Aboriginal Peoples Arise?" (1995) 59 Sask. L. Rev. 97.

Knoll, D. "Treaty and Aboriginal Hunting and Fishing Rights" [1979] 1 C.N.L.R. 1.

Lajoie, A., *et al. Le statut juridique des peuples autochtones au Québec et le pluralisme.* Cowansville, Québec: Les Éditions Yvon Blais, 1996.

Lambert, Hon. D. "*Van der Peet* and *Delgamuukw:* Ten Unresolved Issues" (1998) 32:2 U.B.C. L. Rev. 249.

Lawrence, S., & P. Macklem. "From Consultation to Reconciliation: Aboriginal Rights and the Crown's Duty to Consult," (2000) 79 Can. Bar Rev. 252.

Lyon, N. "Constitutional Issues in Native Law." In B.W. Morse, ed. *Aboriginal Peoples and the Law.* Ottawa: Carleton University Press, 1989.

Lysyk, K. "Indian Hunting Rights: Constitutional Considerations and the Role of Indians Treaties in British Columbia" (1966) 2 U.B.C. L. Rev. 401.

———. "The Unique Constitutional Position of the Canadian Indian" (1967) 45 Can. Bar Rev. 513.

———. "The Indian Title Question in Canada: An Appraisal in Light of Calder" (1973) 51 Can. Bar Rev. 450.

———. "The Rights and Freedoms of the Aboriginal Peoples of Canada." In W.S. Tarnopolsky and G.-A. Beaudoin, eds. *The Canadian Charter of Rights and Freedoms: Commentary.* Toronto: Carswell, 1982.

Macklem, P. "Aboriginal Rights and State Obligations" (1997) 36 Alta. L. Rev. 97.

Maddaugh, P.D., & J. McCamus. *The Law of Restitution.* Aurora, Ontario: Canada Law Book, 1990.

Manitoba. *Report of the Aboriginal Justice Inquiry of Manitoba,* vol. 1. Winnipeg: Queen's Printer Province of Manitoba, 1991.

McMurtry, W.R., & A. Pratt. "Indians and the Fiduciary Concept, Self-Government, and the Constitution: Guerin in Perspective" [1986] 3 C.N.L.R. 19.

McNeil, K. "The Constitutional Rights of the Aboriginal Peoples of Canada" (1982) 4 Supreme Court L.R. 255.

———. *Common Law Aboriginal Title.* Oxford: Clarendon Press, 1989.

———. "Aboriginal Title and Aboriginal Rights: What's the Connection" (1997) 36 Alta. L. Rev. 117.

———. "The Meaning of Aboriginal Title." In Michael Ash, ed. *Aboriginal and Treaty Rights in Canada*. Vancouver: U.B.C. Press, 1997.

———. "Aboriginal Title and the Division of Powers" [1998] 61 Sask. L. Rev. 431.

McSloy, S.P. "Revisiting the 'Courts of the Conqueror': American Indian Claims against the United States" (1994) 44 American University L.R. 537.

Morin, M. *L'usurpation de la souveraineté autochtone*. Les Éditions du Boréal, 1997.

Morris, A. *The Treaties of Canada with the Indians of Manitoba and the North-West Territories*. Toronto: Belfords, Clarke and Co., 1880. Reprint, Saskatoon: Fifth House, 1991.

Newton, N.J. "The Judicial Role in Fifth Amendment Takings of Indian Land: An Analysis of the *Sioux Nation* Rule" (1982) 61 Oregon L.R. 245.

O'Reilly, J. "La Loi constitutionnelle de 1982, droit des autochtones" (1984) 25 C. de D. 125.

Ontario Law Reform Commission. *Report on the Basis for Compensation on Expropriation*. Toronto: Attorney General for the Province of Ontario, 1967.

Owen, D.P. "Fiduciary Obligations and Aboriginal Peoples: Devolution in Action" [1994] 3 C.N.L.R. 1.

Patenaude, M. *Le droit provincial et les terres indiennes*. Montréal: Les Éditions Yvon Blais, 1986.

Picard, E. *Traité général de l'expropriation pour utilité publique*. Bruxelles: F. Larcier, 1875.

Roach, K. *Constitutional Remedies in Canada*. Aurora, Ontario: Canada Law Book, 1998.

Rotman, L.I. *Parallel Paths: Fiduciary Doctrine and the Crown-Native Relationship in Canada*. Toronto: University of Toronto Press, 1996.

———. "Defining Parameters: Aboriginal Rights, Treaty Rights, and the Sparrow Justificatory Test" (1997) 36 Alta. L. Rev. 149.

Rouland, N., S. Pierré-Caps, & J. Poumarède. *Droits des minorités et des peuples autochtones*. Paris: Presses Universitaires de France, 1996.

Royal Commission on Aboriginal Peoples. *Partners in Confederation: Aboriginal Peoples, Self-Government and the Constitution*. Ottawa: Minister of Supply and Services, 1993.

———. *Treaty Making in the Spirit of Co-existence: An Alternative to Extinguishment*. Ottawa: Minister of Supply and Services, 1995.

Sanders, D. "The Rights of the Aboriginal Peoples of Canada" (1983) 61 Can. Bar. Rev. 314.

———. "The Application of Provincial Laws." In B.W. Morse, ed. *Aboriginal Peoples and the Law*. Ottawa: Carleton University Press, 1989.

Slattery, B. *The Land Rights of Indigenous Canadian Peoples*. Doctoral thesis, Oxford University, 1979. Available from University of Saskatchewan, Native Law Centre.

———. "The Constitutional Guarantee of Aboriginal and Treaty Rights" (1982–83) 8 Queen's L.J. 232.

———. "The Hidden Constitution: Aboriginal Rights in Canada" (1984) 32 Am. J. Comp. L. 361.

———. "Did France Claim Canada on 'Discovery?'" In J.M. Bumsted, ed. *Interpreting Canada's Past*, vol. 1. Toronto: Oxford University Press, 1986.

————. "Understanding Aboriginal Rights" (1987) 66 Can. Bar. Rev. 727.

————. "Aboriginal Sovereignty and Imperial Claims" (1991) 29 Osgoode Hall L.J. 1.

————. "First Nations and the Constitution: A Question of Trust" (1992) 71 Can. Bar Rev. 261.

————. "Making Sense of Aboriginal and Treaty Rights" (2000) 79 Can. Bar Rev. 196.

Tarnopolsky, Walter S. *The Canadian Bill of Rights*, 2d rev. ed. McClelland & Stewart, 1975.

Todd, E.C.E. *The Law of Expropriation and Compensation in Canada*, 2d ed. Toronto: Carswell, 1992.

Webber, J. "Relations of Force and Relations of Justice" (1995) 33 Osgoode Hall L.J. 623.

Weinrib, E.J. "The Fiduciary Obligation" (1975) 25 U.T.L.J. 1.

Wildsmith, B.H. "Pre-Confederation Treaties." In B.W. Morse, ed. *Aboriginal Peoples and the Law*. Ottawa: Carleton University Press, 1989.

Wilkins, D.E. *American Indian Sovereignty and the U.S. Supreme Court—The Masking of Justice*. Austin: University of Texas Press, 1997.

Wilkinson, G.A. "Indian Tribal Claims Before the Court of Claims" (1966) 55 Georgetown L.J. 511.

Williams, R.A., Jr. *The American Indian in Western Legal Thought*. New York: Oxford University Press, 1990.

Woodward, J. *Native Law*. Toronto: Carswell, 1994.

Zlotkin, N.K. "Post-Confederation Treaties." In B.W. Morse, ed. *Aboriginal Peoples and the Law*. Ottawa: Carleton University Press, 1989.

An Overview of
Aboriginal and Treaty Rights
and Compensation for Their Breach

Introduction

The explosion of Aboriginal rights claims in Canada in recent years makes the issue of compensation in cases of infringements of Aboriginal and treaty rights particularly pressing. Numerous pending and potential cases represent a substantial liability for governments; in addition, there are many development projects proposed for northern Canada and elsewhere that will potentially affect Aboriginal land or traditional Aboriginal activities.

There are as yet few guidelines to help proponents of these projects and affected Aboriginal populations determine and assess appropriate compensation when Aboriginal or treaty rights are infringed. In 1997, in the seminal case of *Delgamuukw* v. *B.C.*,[1] the Supreme Court of Canada discussed the content and nature of Aboriginal title at common law, as well as the scope of the constitutional protection afforded Aboriginal title under section 35 of the *Constitution Act, 1982*.[2] Although the Supreme Court elucidated many obscure areas of Aboriginal law in *Delgamuukw* and other cases,[3] it has yet to discuss the issue of compensation for infringements of Aboriginal rights. As stated by then Chief Justice Lamer in *Delgamuukw:*

> In keeping with the duty of honour and good faith on the Crown, fair compensation will ordinarily be required when aboriginal title is infringed. The amount of compensation payable will vary with the nature of the particular aboriginal title affected and with the nature and severity of the infringement and the extent to which aboriginal interests were accommodated. Since the issue of damages was severed from the principal action, we received no submissions on the appropriate legal principles that would be relevant to determining the appropriate level of compensation of infringements of aboriginal title. In the circumstances, it is best that we leave those difficult questions to another day.[4]

This book modestly attempts to address the "difficult questions" to which Chief Justice Lamer referred.

The questions raised by compensation in cases of infringements of common law Aboriginal title are also raised in cases of infringements of Aboriginal and treaty rights generally. On many occasions, the Supreme Court of Canada has stated that compensation is an important factor when assessing whether infringements of Aboriginal and treaty rights are justified. Yet, to date, the Court has provided no clear guidance on what legal principles should be used to determine such compensation. For example, in the 1990 case of *R. v. Sparrow,* the Court placed the issue of compensation at the heart of the justification test in cases of infringements of Aboriginal rights, but it provided no guidelines as to how such compensation was to be determined.[5] Consequently, the courts have been reluctant to directly address issues of compensation in Aboriginal cases and have preferred to return the parties to negotiations to settle levels of compensation once the main factual and legal issues have been determined at trial.

The reluctance of courts to get involved in setting appropriate levels of compensation can be attributed in part to the absence of a coherent legal theory that properly addresses the complex questions raised in such cases. For example, should the rules of compensation be the same for infringements of Aboriginal hunting and fishing rights as they are for infringements of Aboriginal title? Are provincial laws of expropriation applicable in such circumstances? How can the value of Aboriginal title be determined when this title often concerns land that has no or little market value? How does one compensate for the loss of a lifestyle and for the disruption of traditional societies brought about by economic development projects? Governments, industry, and Aboriginal communities in Canada are often faced with the task of determining appropriate levels of compensation when Aboriginal or treaty rights are infringed. Yet there is little case law or legal research they can turn to for guidance. As noted by K. Roach: "The remedies available for violations of aboriginal rights are largely unexplored."[6] In this book, I modestly attempt to provide some basic legal principles for determining compensation in cases of infringements of Aboriginal and treaty rights.

Although different approaches in discussing Aboriginal rights are justified, the simple but comprehensive legal principles developed here do not challenge the epistemological premises of traditional legal discourse. They have been developed based on the corpus of existing common law and the rules of constitutional law dealing with Aboriginal matters generally. Therefore, before we embark on our discussion of compensation, we must first review the nature of the rights involved, the fiduciary relationship between Aboriginal Peoples and the Crown and the duties this relationship entails, the legal and constitutional context in which Aboriginal and treaty rights evolve, and the legal principles governing infringements of Aboriginal and treaty rights.

The first part of this book undertakes this review and serves as a general introduction to issues of Aboriginal law. Thus, the first chapter of this book discusses the nature and content of Aboriginal rights at common law. The second chapter discusses treaty rights and how these differ from Aboriginal rights. The fiduciary relationship of the Crown, and the fiduciary duties resulting from this relationship, are examined in chapter three. The fiduciary relationship is the key to determining compensation in cases of infringements of Aboriginal and treaty rights. Chapter four discusses federal common law and Aboriginal and treaty rights. Chapter five reviews the legal principles governing infringements of Aboriginal and treaty rights, including a review of the justification test developed by the Supreme Court of Canada in order to allow such infringements to proceed in certain circumstances.

The second part of the book addresses more directly the issue of compensation by setting forth legal principles that can be applied when determining appropriate levels of compensation in cases of infringements of Aboriginal and treaty rights. Thus, the legal principles used to determine compensation in cases of expropriations unrelated to Aboriginal and treaty rights are briefly reviewed in chapter six. Although these principles are not fully applicable to cases of infringements of Aboriginal or treaty rights, they are useful for purposes of comparison. In chapter seven, a review of the American experience with compensation for the taking of Aboriginal land is carried out. Finally, chapter eight lays out principles for determining compensation in cases where Aboriginal and treaty rights have been infringed.

Part I
Defining Aboriginal and Treaty Rights

Chapter 1

Aboriginal Rights at Common Law

Introduction

No single event influenced Western European culture in the past millennium more deeply than the arrival of Europeans in the Americas. Christopher Columbus's arrival on American shores in 1492 was a moment that changed and shaped history as few others have. Through its sixteenth-century conquests in the New World, Spain became the then-dominant world power. Portugal, France, England, and the Netherlands soon joined in the pursuit of wealth, land, and power in the Americas. The arrival of Europeans was followed by one of the most important human migrations the world has ever known, a migration that was destined to almost completely overrun the Aboriginal populations that had initially occupied the continent.

The ensuing factual situation resulted in each European state with holdings in the New World developing moral concepts and political rules to incorporate Aboriginal populations and their territories into their American colonies. The way in which these moral concepts and political rules developed into legal rules has been studied extensively and is now well documented.[1] I will not dwell further on this interesting issue, save to point out that, like all other European legal systems confronted with the American experience, English common law had to adapt. Over time, a common law theory of Aboriginal title was developed. This was further developed into a common law doctrine of Aboriginal rights.[2]

Aboriginal rights are deeply rooted in the history of the relationship between Aboriginal Peoples and the Crown. In the beginning, this relationship was closely associated with the royal prerogative and dealt mainly with commerce and high political issues such as war and peace. In times of war, the Crown sought allies among the Aboriginal nations; in times of peace, it sought to trade with them. The communication between the parties was often carried out through imperial policies and through treaties between the Crown and the concerned Aboriginal nations, and the common law courts were rarely called upon to intervene. Over time, this political and commercial intercourse developed into a normative order that defined the parameters of the general relationship between the Crown and Aboriginal nations. The courts long hesitated to define or adjudicate this normative order since they were ill-equipped to challenge or to implement what was seen as a high political agenda. Moreover, neither the Crown nor the Aboriginal nations were inclined to subject their relationship to the supervision of the courts. Thus, for a long time, the relationship between the Crown and Aboriginal nations, and the normative order that resulted therefrom, was simply ignored by the courts. The reluctance of the courts to adjudicate this normative order has prevailed until very recently.[3]

In the nineteenth century, Canadian courts were slowly called upon to address the content of this normative order. For example, in *Connolly* v. *Woolrich*,[4] the validity and enforceable nature of Aboriginal customary law in regard to marriage was recognized. In these early cases, however, the courts did not directly consider the nature and content of the Crown's relationship with Aboriginal nations. It was not until the late nineteenth century that the Anglo-Canadian courts finally shelved their traditional reserve towards enforcing this normative order. It is to these court decisions that we now turn our attention.

The Marshall Decisions

A discussion of Aboriginal rights at common law begins with a review of some nineteenth-century decisions of the Supreme Court of the United States, and particularly with the opinions of Chief Justice Marshall in the seminal cases of *Johnson* v. *M'Intosh*,[5] *Cherokee Nation* v. *Georgia*,[6] and *Worcester* v. *Georgia*.[7]

In the aftermath of the eighteenth-century wars that culminated in the retreat of France from North America, vast new lands to the West opened up for potential British colonization. As these lands were under the control of the Aboriginal nations inhabiting them, just how they could be made available to British settlers and speculators was the subject of much controversy. Various political and legal arguments were put forward to justify claims to these lands. The upshot was that British imperial authorities claimed exclusive jurisdiction over the newly acquired territories and the exclusive right to control the granting of lands in these territories. This implied that the imperial authorities had a monopoly when it came to dealing with the Aboriginal nations and acquiring the Aboriginal interest in these lands. The imperial approach to the management and control of lands subject to Aboriginal interest was exemplified by the *Royal Proclamation, 1763,*[8] which reserved a large share of these new territories for the Aboriginal populations and placed strict controls on the conveyance of these territories to third parties.

The *Royal Proclamation* was not well received by colonists in the territories that were to become the United States of America. These colonists perceived the proclamation as an impediment to their western expansion and soon developed a discourse, loosely based on principles of natural law, which claimed that they had an inherent right to settle these lands and to purchase them directly from the Aboriginal nations. In this view, the Aboriginal nations were free to dispose of their lands to whomever they wished, and they could thus negotiate the terms and conditions for the acquisition of such lands directly with interested settlers. The imperial monopoly over Aboriginal land transactions was seen as an unwarranted and objectionable intrusion on the natural right of the Aboriginal nations to govern their own affairs as they deemed fit. The obvious purpose of such a discourse was to justify the direct acquisition of Aboriginal lands by settlers. It was therefore not surprising to find colonists defying the terms of the *Royal Proclamation* and setting up huge land-speculation schemes in "Indian Country."

In 1773, a trader named Murray purchased large tracts of land directly from the Illinois for $24,000, which was a large sum of money at that time. The land in question was located within the boundaries of the "Indian Country" that had been reserved under the terms of the *Royal Proclamation*. In 1823, the validity of the 1773 Murray purchase was reviewed by the Supreme Court of the United States in the case of *Johnson v. M'Intosh*.[9] The United States government had granted Mr. McIntosh land rights in the area where Murray claimed to have purchased the land from the Illinois. The resulting inconsistencies in title required the Supreme Court to adjudicate between the competing imperial and colonialist views.

In *Johnson v. M'Intosh,* Justice Marshall firmly supported the imperial view of relations with Aboriginal Peoples. He denied that the Aboriginal inhabitants had any natural right to carry out land transactions without the permission and control of the sovereign authorities, and he confirmed that in regard to land transactions, Aboriginal nations were obliged to treat exclusively with the sovereign power under whose sphere of influence they fell. This conclusion did not disenfranchise the Aboriginal inhabitants of their land rights; however, in Justice Marshall's view, such rights could not be disposed of freely by Aboriginal Peoples. In a nutshell, Justice Marshall stated

(a) that discovery of lands by a European power gave title in those lands to the discovering sovereign against adverse claims from other European powers;

(b) that this title by discovery gave the discovering European power the exclusive right of acquiring the lands from their Aboriginal inhabitants;

(c) that, notwithstanding this title by discovery, the Aboriginal inhabitants of these lands nevertheless remained entitled to the possession of the lands until such time as they were ceded by them to the sovereign of the discovering European power; and

(d) that the powers of the Aboriginal inhabitants as sovereign nations were impaired by the title through discovery in that they could not transact in regard to their rights with any authority or person other than the sovereign of the discovering European power.

These principles were derived by Justice Marshall from a pragmatic view of the role of the judiciary in reviewing and adjudicating the normative order resulting from contact between Aboriginal nations and European powers. As noted above, this normative order derived from the history of the political relationships between European powers (the "Crown" for those colonies under British rule) and the Aboriginal nations within their spheres of influence. Inequitable though they often were, these relationships left their mark on Aboriginal law. Justice Marshall was up front about unprincipled nature of his judicial approach when he stated: "Conquest gives a title which the Courts of the conqueror cannot deny, whatever the private and speculative opinions of individuals may be, respecting the original justice of the claim which has been successfully asserted."[10] In this often-quoted passage, he set out his central position:

On the discovery of this immense continent, the great nations of Europe were eager to appropriate to themselves so much of it as they could respectively acquire. Its vast extent offered an ample field to the ambition and enterprise of all; and the character and religion of its inhabitants afforded an apology for considering them as a people over whom the superior genius of Europe might claim an ascendancy. The potentates of the old world found no difficulty in convincing themselves that they made ample compensation to the inhabitants of the new, by bestowing on them civilization and Christianity, in exchange for unlimited independence. But, as they were all in pursuit of nearly the same object, it was necessary, in order to avoid conflicting settlements, and consequently war with each other, to establish a principle, which all should acknowledge as the law by which the right of acquisition, which they all asserted, should be regulated as between themselves. This principle was, that discovery gave title to the government by whose subjects, or by whose authority, it was made, against all other European governments, which title might be consummated by possession.

The exclusion of all other Europeans, necessarily gave to the nation making the discovery the sole right of acquiring the soil from the natives, and establishing settlements upon it. It was a right with which no Europeans could interfere. It was a right with which all asserted for themselves, and to the assertion of which, by others, all assented.

Those relations which were to exist between the discoverer and the natives, were to be regulated by themselves. The rights thus acquired being exclusive, no other power could interpose between them.

In the establishment of these relations, the rights of the original inhabitants were, in no instance, entirely disregarded; but were necessarily, to a considerable extent, impaired. *They were admitted to be the rightful occupants of the soil, with a legal as well as a just claim to retain possession of it, and to use it according to their own discretion; but their rights to complete sovereignty, as independent nations, were necessarily diminished, and their power to dispose of the soil at their own will, to whomsoever they pleased, was denied by the original fundamental principle, that discovery gave exclusive title to those who made it.*[11] [Emphasis added]

Chief Justice Marshall had further occasion to express his views on Aboriginal rights in *Cherokee Nation* v. *Georgia*[12] and *Worcester* v. *Georgia.*[13] At the time these cases were heard, in the early nineteenth century, the Cherokee were an organized Aboriginal nation that had founded towns, developed a form of government resembling that of the United States, and started to farm their lands. In the early 1830s, the state of Georgia passed legislation to ensure control of Cherokee lands by the state government. The ultimate purpose of this legislation was to displace the Cherokee from their lands in Georgia and to relocate them with other Aboriginal tribes west of the Mississippi. The legislation provided that it was unlawful for any person to cause the assembly of any council or legislative body of the Cherokee for purposes of legislating or for any other purpose. It made it unlawful for the tribunals of the Cherokee to sit, and it made it a crime to discourage the Cherokee from emigrating beyond the Mississippi River. The legislation also made it a crime for any white person to reside within the Cherokee Nation unless that person had a license from the state governor and had taken an oath to support and defend the laws of Georgia. The legislation also provided for the creation of an armed guard to apply these state laws within Cherokee lands. Further legislation was then passed by the state of Georgia to annul all Cherokee laws, to annex to Georgia all Cherokee lands, to extend Georgia state laws to these lands and to all those there residing, and to declare Cherokee individuals incompetent witnesses in any state court in litigation to which a white person might be a party.

It is not surprising that the Cherokee Nation sought to challenge the validity of this legislation. In order to have the Supreme Court of the United States entertain its challenge, the Cherokee Nation asserted its status as a foreign state. However, in *Cherokee Nation* v. *Georgia*,[14] the Court found that the Aboriginal nations of the United States were "domestic dependent nations" whose status as independent peoples had been severely impaired. Therefore, the Cherokee Nation could not petition the Supreme Court of the United States as a foreign state. The Court thus decided it lacked the jurisdiction to hear the Cherokee Nation's challenge to Georgia's state legislation in the form of action the Cherokee had used. The matter did not rest there. Various missionaries were working among the Cherokee with the consent of the Cherokee Nation and under authorization from the President of the United States. In 1831, a group of these missionaries, including a Mr. Worcester, were indicted as having contravened the laws of Georgia by remaining on Cherokee land without the required licence from the governor of Georgia. The missionaries were found guilty, and Mr. Worcester was sentenced to four years hard labour. He appealed his conviction to the Supreme Court of the United States by challenging the constitutionality of the state law under which he had been convicted.

In *Worcester* v. *Georgia*, Chief Justice Marshall expanded on his findings in *Johnson* v. *M'Intosh*. He confirmed that discovery gave title in the discovered lands to the European power making the discovery, but he noted that this title was against other European powers. Although this title by discovery impaired the rights of the original inhabitants—because it forbade them from entreating with other European powers—it did not cancel their rights:

> It [the principle that discovery gives title] regulated the right given by discovery among the European discoverers; but could not affect the rights of those already in possession, either as aboriginal occupants, or as occupants by virtue of a discovery made before the memory of man. *It gave the exclusive right to purchase, but did not found that right on a denial of the right of the possessor to sell.*[15] [Emphasis added]

Chief Justice Marshall added that Aboriginal nations were self-governing nations that had never relinquished their rights to govern themselves. However, since title by discovery restricted these self-governing nations by obliging them to treat exclusively with the European power claiming discovery, their self-governing powers were impaired. Reiterating his findings in *Cherokee Nation* v. *Georgia,* Chief Justice Marshall found that this impairment transformed the Aboriginal nations into "domestic" and "dependent" nations, which nevertheless remained self-governing in other respects and entitled to the preservation of their rights as occupants of their traditional lands. He stated: "This relationship was that of a nation claiming and receiving the protection of one more powerful: not that of individuals abandoning their national character, and submitting as subjects to the laws of a master."[16]

In the British colonies, the power to entertain this relationship with the

Aboriginal nations was vested exclusively in the Crown, and over time, various treaties between the Aboriginal nations and the Crown had given substance to this relationship. Chief Justice Marshall found that the powers of the Crown in regard to the relationship with Aboriginal nations had been assumed by the United States at independence. In consequence, Chief Justice Marshall found that the state of Georgia was powerless to legislate in regard to the relationship and consequently could not impair the rights and interests of the Cherokee without their consent or without the authorization of the United States. He explained:

> The Cheerokee nation, then, is a distinct community, occupying its own territory, with boundaries accurately described, in which the laws of Georgia can have no force, and which the citizens of Georgia have no right to enter, but with the assent of the Cherokees themselves, or in conformity with treaties, and with the acts of Congress. The whole intercourse between the United States and this nation, is, by our Constitution and laws, vested in the government of the United States.
>
> The act of the state of Georgia, under which the plaintiff in error was prosecuted, is consequently void, and the judgment a nullity.[17]

These three decisions of the Marshall Court have been very influential in defining and giving content to the normative order that resulted from the contact between Aboriginal nations and the Crown.[18] The Marshall Court's decisions proposed that there existed a special and exclusive relationship between the Aboriginal nations and the sovereign European powers that claimed title to their lands. This relationship required the Aboriginal nations to treat exclusively with the sovereign power in whose sphere of influence they found themselves. Although the relationship impaired the full sovereignty of the Aboriginal nations, it did not extinguish their self-governing rights, nor did it affect their other rights as the original inhabitants of the lands they occupied. In those areas claimed by the British, this special relationship was maintained under the responsibility of the Crown to the exclusion of all other relationships, including relationships with individual citizens and non-sovereign colonial governments.

Historical Case Law

The British courts were more reluctant than their counterparts in the United States to pass judgement on the normative order that developed between the Crown and Aboriginal nations. Even today, issues of Aboriginal self-government and self-determination have not been squarely addressed by Canadian courts.[19] Issues of self-government and sovereignty were at the heart of the American Revolution, which explains why the Marshall Court approached the relationship between the United States and Aboriginal nations in the way that it did. The feudal nature of the British political and legal tradition resulted in an approach attuned to the rights of the Aboriginal populations to land rather than to their political rights as peoples. In light of the nature of the normative order that developed between the British Crown and Aboriginal nations, Canadian courts tended to avoid litigation that directly addressed the fundamental aspects of the Crown-Aboriginal relationship. Nevertheless, even though Canadian case law focussed on land rights, these rights could be properly understood only within the framework of the special and exclusive relationship between the Crown and Aboriginal nations so aptly described by the Marshall Court.

In the 1921 case of *Amodu Tijani v. Southern Nigeria (Secretary)*,[20] the Privy Council was called upon to determine the nature of the tribal interest in a tract of land that had traditionally been under the control of the Oluwa community of Nigeria. Mr. Tijani was a White Cap chief of Lagos and the head chief of the Oluwa community. The members of this community paid a small rent to him for their use of communal lands. He was also entrusted with dividing these lands among the members of the community. The lands were subsequently expropriated by the British authorities for public purposes. The nature of the interest held in the lands needed to be ascertained so that appropriate compensation could be determined. Mr. Tijani, as the representative of the community, was seeking compensation based on a full ownership right in the lands. The Privy Council was called upon to provide its opinion on the nature of Aboriginal land title.

In the opinion of Viscount Haldane, speaking for the Judicial Committee of the Privy Council, the transfer of sovereignty to the British Crown did not normally affect proprietary rights in a colony. Insofar as Aboriginal title could be considered a proprietary right, the assumption of British sovereignty did not affect that title. However, Viscount Haldane pointed out that the precise nature of this proprietary right was not uniform throughout the British Empire. The content and nature of Aboriginal title were to be understood by the British courts in the terms the concerned Aboriginal Peoples themselves understood their tenure. For Viscount Haldane, the content and nature of Aboriginal title thus varied in accordance with each population and its means of land tenure. Nevertheless, Viscount Haldane made two important generalizations about Aboriginal title.

First, in its usual form, Viscount Haldane saw Aboriginal title as a usufructuary right. A usufructuary right is the right to enjoy the use and advantage of another's property short of the destruction or waste of its substance. For Viscount Haldane, the radical or ultimate title to the land was vested in the Crown. However, this sovereign right was burdened by the usufructuary uses of the land by the Aboriginal population. The exact content of this usufructuary burden varied with the particular uses to which the land was put by its Aboriginal inhabitants. Viscount Haldane noted that, in many cases, the uses made of the land would lead the courts to conclude that Aboriginal title could be equated, for practical purposes, with a full ownership interest in the land. However, a full ownership interest would never be fully represented by Aboriginal title, in light of the underlying ultimate title of the Crown. Second, in its usual form, Viscount Haldane saw Aboriginal title as a communal title. Individuals might enjoy the benefit of the title and have parcels of the lands subject to the title apportioned to them; however, the title could not normally be relinquished without community involvement. As a result of these findings, Viscount Haldane directed that the compensation to be paid for the expropriation of the Oluwa community lands was to be determined on the basis that the Aboriginal interest in these lands was equivalent to full ownership. In light of the communal nature of the interest, he also directed that the compensation be distributed among the members of the community.

In 1887, the issue of Aboriginal title in Canada was dealt with by the Supreme Court of Canada in *St. Catharines Milling and Lumber Co. v. The Queen*.[21] In 1873, the Salteaux Tribe of Ojibway had signed a treaty with the Canadian government under which they surrendered to the Crown their Aboriginal title over some fifty thousand square miles (approximately 130,000 square kilometres) of land in exchange for various undertakings. The land was located within the "Indian Country" established under the terms of the *Royal Proclamation, 1763*. The province of Ontario claimed that part of this land had subsequently been attached to the old province of Quebec, as extended by the *Quebec Act* of 1774.[22] Since Upper Canada had been carved from the old province of Quebec, Ontario claimed that the land in question had devolved to it under the terms of the *Constitution Act, 1867*. This claim was disputed by the Government of Canada. Both governments turned to the Privy Council to resolve their dispute. In 1884, the Privy Council found that the concerned territories were indeed part of the province of Ontario.

In 1883, subsequent to the 1873 treaty but before the 1884 report of the Privy Council, the St. Catharines Milling and Lumber Company secured a licence from the Government of Canada to harvest lumber on the land. The province of Ontario took offence and sued the lumber company for declaratory relief, an injunction, and damages.[23] The province argued that under section 109 of the *Constitution Act, 1867*,[24] all Crown lands in the province were the property of the provincial Crown. The pertinent section of the act reads as follows:

All Lands, Mines, Minerals, and Royalties belonging to the several provinces of Canada, Nova Scotia, and New Brunswick at the Union, and all Sums

then due or payable for such Lands, Mines, Minerals, or Royalties, shall
belong to the several Provinces of Ontario, Quebec, Nova Scotia and New
Brunswick, in which the same are situate or arise, subject to any Trust existing
in respect thereof, and to any Interest other than that of the Province in the
same.

The Canadian government argued that Aboriginal title constituted an "Interest
other than that of the Province" and that this interest displaced any claims the
province had under the said section. Since the Aboriginal interest in the
concerned land had not been surrendered until 1873, Canada argued that the
land in question had not belonged to the province at Confederation in 1867.
Moreover, Canada argued that the land was reserve land and was therefore
under the exclusive legislative authority of Parliament. According to section
91(24) of the *Constitution Act, 1867,* Parliament has exclusive jurisdiction
over "Indians, and Lands reserved for the Indians," and therefore, Canada
argued, the ownership of the land to which Aboriginal title had been
surrendered enured to the Crown in right of Canada. The case was the subject
of a lengthy decision by the Supreme Court. In the decision, the ownership
rights of Ontario to the disputed land were upheld by four of the six Supreme
Court justices.[25]

Chief Justice Ritchie and Justice Fournier, two of the justices who found
for Ontario, recognized Aboriginal title as a right of occupancy, although
they did not explain how this right originated nor did they explain its content.
For neither justice did this right of occupancy displace the title of the Crown;
rather, both found that the Crown's title to the land was burdened by the
Aboriginal right of occupancy. They concluded that the Crown's title became
absolute when the Aboriginal right of occupancy was extinguished. In their
view, since Crown lands were devolved to the provinces under the *Constitution
Act, 1867,* the land was the property of the provincial Crown whether or not it
was burdened by Aboriginal title. Since the land in dispute was deemed to
fall within the boundaries of the province of Ontario, it belonged to the
province, subject to the Aboriginal title with which it was burdened. When
the Salteaux surrendered their interest in the disputed land by the treaty of
1873, the land became unencumbered and the province's title became absolute.
As a result, the licence issued by the Government of Canada to the St.
Catharines Milling and Lumber Company granted no rights to the company.
This reasoning was subsequently upheld in large part by the Privy Council.

Justices Henry and Taschereau also found for Ontario, but for different
reasons. They found that Aboriginal title was not recognized at common law.
Furthermore, they dismissed any claim based on the *Royal Proclamation,
1763,* since they concluded that no rights flowed to Aboriginal Peoples from
the terms of this proclamation. Even if rights had been conferred by the *Royal*

Proclamation, the justices considered that these rights would have been extinguished by the 1873 treaty. For Justice Taschereau, in particular, Aboriginal policy fell into the political rather than the judicial realm. Echoing the traditional reluctance of the judiciary to intrude on the historical relationship between the Crown and Aboriginal nations, he concluded that the courts were powerless to recognize traditional Aboriginal interests as legal rights, even where such interests were recognized and acted upon by the Crown.

In their dissenting opinions, Justices Strong and Gwynne found that Aboriginal rights had been confirmed by the terms of the *Royal Proclamation, 1763.* They added that the proclamation had never been repealed, either by the *Quebec Act* or by any other act.[26] Justice Gwynne went so far as to label the proclamation the "Indians' Bill of Rights."[27] He and Justice Strong further found that lands reserved to the Aboriginal nations under the terms of the *Royal Proclamation* fell under the exception of section 109 of the *Constitution Act, 1867* and therefore did not pass to the provinces at Confederation. Justice Strong added that Aboriginal rights to the land would, in any event, flow from common law, even if the *Royal Proclamation* had not been adopted, or even if it were found that the terms of the proclamation did not apply to the disputed land. He referred to the decisions of the Marshall Court, and using arguments similar to those of Chief Justice Marshall, he concluded that Aboriginal title was fully recognized at common law. Like Viscount Haldane after him, he found this title to be in the nature of a usufructuary right. Echoing Chief Justice Marshall, he found that such title could not be surrendered by the Aboriginal nations to any party except the Crown.

Thus, in *St. Catharines Milling and Lumber Co.,* a majority of four out of six Supreme Court justices found that Aboriginal rights to land existed in Canada, although two of these four justices declined to comment on the origin, nature, or extent of these rights.

In the appeal of this case, the Judicial Committee of the Privy Council confirmed the existence of Aboriginal land rights in Canada under the terms of the *Royal Proclamation, 1763.* However, the precise nature of these rights and their recognition at common law were issues largely ignored by the Privy Council.[28] Lord Watson recognized that Aboriginal land rights existed, but he ascribed their existence to the *Royal Proclamation.* He refused to discuss their recognition at common law, since this issue did not appear to him relevant to the resolution of the dispute at hand. Lord Watson did, however, state that the rights of Aboriginal Peoples in land were in any event less than fee simple. Fee simple rights give the owner of the land unqualified ownership and the power to dispose of the land as the owner sees fit. Under fee simple ownership, the owner has the right to control, use, and transfer property at will. For Lord Watson, the tenure of Aboriginal Peoples under the *Royal Proclamation* could be described as "a personal and usufructuary right" that could be surrendered only to the Crown and, since the passing of the *Constitution Act, 1867*, only to the Crown in right of Canada. In Lord Watson's reasoning, the exact nature and content of this title was immaterial to the resolution of the case:

> There was a great deal of learned discussion at the Bar with respect to the precise quality of the Indian right, but their Lordships do not consider it necessary to express any opinion upon the point. It appears to them to be sufficient for the purposes of this case that there has been all along vested in the Crown a substantial and paramount estate, underlying the Indian title, which became a plenum dominium [full ownership] whenever that title was surrendered or otherwise extinguished.[29]

On the constitutional issue presented in the case, Lord Watson decided for the province of Ontario. Although he recognized an Aboriginal interest in the lands contemplated by the *Royal Proclamation, 1763*, he found that interest to be in the nature of a personal and usufructuary right that burdened, but did not displace, the underlying estate of the Crown. Since the underlying estate to the disputed land was, at Confederation, vested in the Crown, Lord Watson found that this underlying estate enured to the province under the terms of section 109 of the *Constitution Act, 1867*. He further found that, under the terms of section 91(24) of the *Constitution Act, 1867*, only the federal government could accept the surrender of the Aboriginal interest in this land; however, once the Aboriginal interest was surrendered, the burden on the underlying estate of the Crown was lifted, and the province could thereinafter freely dispose of the land.[30]

Contemporary Case Law

The contemporary Canadian case law relating to Aboriginal rights begins with the 1973 decision of the Supreme Court of Canada in the case of *Calder v. A.G. of British Columbia*.[31] In that case, a declaration as to the existence of Aboriginal title in British Columbia was being sought on behalf of the Nisga'a Nation. The Nisga'a had never entered into any treaties.[32] They claimed that their title arose out of Aboriginal occupation of the land, and that such title was recognized at common law. They further asserted that although their title was not dependent on treaty, executive order, or legislative recognition, such recognition could be found under the terms of the *Royal Proclamation, 1763* and in other imperial instruments. Finally, they asserted that their title had never been extinguished. The Nisga'a claim set out clearly and plainly the issues of recognition and content of Aboriginal title.

Although the claims of the Nisga'a Nation were denied on narrow procedural grounds, the *Calder* decision represents one of the most important judicial statements on Aboriginal title. This decision influenced the development of Aboriginal law, not only in Canada but also throughout the Commonwealth. Six of the seven Supreme Court justices hearing the case clearly recognized that Aboriginal title existed in British Columbia and could be recognized at common law irrespective of the application of the *Royal Proclamation* to the province. Justice Judson stated:

> Although I think that it is clear that Indian title in British Columbia cannot owe its origin to the Proclamation of 1763, the fact is that when the settlers came, the Indians were there, organized in societies and occupying the land as their forefathers had done for centuries. This is what Indian title means and it does not help one in the solution of this problem to call it a "personal or usufructuary right."[33]

Justice Hall also took the position that Aboriginal title was recognized at common law, and he emphasized that it did "not depend on treaty, executive order or legislative enactment."[34] Justice Hall was, however, inclined to recognize the application in British Columbia of the terms of the *Royal Proclamation, 1763*. Neither justice deemed it appropriate to define the content of Aboriginal title at common law, an exercise that was finally completed by the Supreme Court of Canada nearly twenty-five years later in the case of *Delgamuukw v. B.C.*[35]

The justices in *Calder* disagreed over the issue of extinguishment of Aboriginal title. For Justice Judson, Aboriginal title at common law could be unilaterally extinguished by the sovereign without any obligation to provide compensation. Justice Judson added that such extinguishment need not be made by a direct statutory enactment. Adverse dominion over Aboriginal land resulting from legislative action fundamentally incompatible with the right of occupation by Aboriginal Peoples was, according to Justice Judson, sufficient to carry out an extinguishment of common law Aboriginal title. For example, if legislation was adopted to grant lands to settlers, and these lands were subject to Aboriginal title, the resulting incompatibility between the legislation and Aboriginal title would be sufficient to extinguish that title even if no Aboriginal land was actually granted to settlers. Aboriginal title at common law could thus be extinguished indirectly through adverse legislation even if such legislation did not specifically address Aboriginal title issues. In Justice Hall's view, Aboriginal title at common law could not be extinguished other than by the "clear and plain" intent of the sovereign. He added that the onus of proving such "clear and plain" intent was on those claiming extinguishment. For Justice Hall, Aboriginal title could not be extinguished except by voluntary surrender to the Crown or by specific legislation from the competent authority specifically purporting to extinguish it. Justice Hall also took the view that in the case where a "clear and plain" intent on the part of the sovereign was found to extinguish Aboriginal title, there existed at common law a right to fair compensation for the affected Aboriginal Peoples. The justices thus disagreed as to whether Aboriginal title recognized at common law had been extinguished or still existed in British Columbia. Since the other justices evenly supported both, no final determination was made on this issue.

The Supreme Court discussed Aboriginal title at common law a decade later in the case of *Guerin v. The Queen.*[36] Mr. Guerin was the chief of the Musqueam Indian Band. The members of that band were descendants of the original Aboriginal inhabitants of the area in and around the city of Vancouver. A reserve comprising some 416 acres (approximately 168 hectares) had been set up for them. As the city now surrounded this reserve, the land had acquired a very important commercial value. According to the Indian Affairs branch of the federal government, the reserve constituted "the most potentially valuable 400 acres [162 hectares] in metropolitan Vancouver today."[37]

In 1956, representatives of the Shaughnessy Heights Golf Club approached Indian Affairs in order to lease 160 acres (approximately 65 hectares) of reserve land for a golf course. Under the terms of the *Indian Act,*[38] the lease had to be secured through the federal government. Discussions took place in 1956 and 1957 between representatives of the golf club and Indian Affairs to determine the terms of the lease.

Under the *Indian Act,* the band was required to "surrender" the land to the Crown prior to any lease being entered into between the Crown and the golf club. A meeting of the band was held in October 1957 at which the land was surrendered. The band members at the meeting surrendered the land on the understanding that the lease would be fifteen years for the first term with subsequent renewal terms of ten years, and that there would be no limits on rental increases at each renewal period. The band members present at the meeting were not told that the golf club could remove any buildings or structures or other improvements at the end of the proposed lease, nor were they informed that future rent on renewal periods would be determined as if the land under lease was still in an uncleared and unimproved condition.

The lease was entered into in January 1958 on terms that differed substantially from those understood by the band members present at the surrender meeting. The term of the lease was seventy-five years, and the rent for the first fifteen years was fixed at $29,000 per year. For the four fifteen-year renewal periods, the annual rent was to be determined on the basis that the land was in an uncleared and unimproved condition and that the use of the land was limited to golf activities. Moreover, the maximum increase in rent for the second fifteen-year period was limited to a 15-percent increase over the basic $29,000 rent. Finally, the golf club was authorized to terminate the lease at any renewal period, and it could remove any buildings and other structures, as well as any course improvements and facilities, at any time during the lease and up to six months after its termination. Although this case concerned, in large part, the duties of Canada when dealing with *Indian Act* reserve land, both Justice Wilson and Justice (later Chief Justice) Dickson dealt with the issue of Aboriginal title at common law, since this was what both justices understood the nature of the Aboriginal interest in the land to be. Justice Dickson stated:

> It does not matter, in my opinion, that the present case is concerned with the interest of an Indian Band in a reserve rather than with unrecognized aboriginal title in traditional tribal lands. *The Indian interest in the land is the same in both cases:* see *Attorney General for Quebec* v. *Attorney General for Canada,* [1921] 1 A.C. 401 at pp. 410-11 (the *Star Chrome* case).[39] [Emphasis added]

As noted above, the normative order that evolved from contact between the Crown and Aboriginal nations contained an obligation on Aboriginal Peoples to treat exclusively with the Crown, particularly in regard to their interests in land. This normative order diminished the sovereignty of the Aboriginal nations by imposing on them a Crown monopoly in dealing with their interests. However, the Supreme Court now found that this normative order imposed a correlative duty on the Crown:

> The fiduciary relationship between the Crown and the Indians has its roots in the concept of aboriginal, native or Indian title. The fact that Indian Bands have a certain interest in lands does not, however, in itself give rise to a fiduciary relationship between the Indians and the Crown. The conclusion that the Crown is a fiduciary depends upon the further proposition that the Indian interest in the land is inalienable except upon surrender to the Crown.
>
> An Indian Band is prohibited from directly transferring its interest to a third party. Any sale or lease of land can only be carried out after a surrender has taken place, with the Crown then acting on the Band's behalf. The Crown first took this responsibility upon itself in the Royal Proclamation of 1763. It is still recognized in the surrender provisions of the *Indian Act*. The surrender requirement, and the responsibility it entails, are the source of a distinct fiduciary obligation owed by the Crown to the Indians.[40]

The fiduciary relationship and its attendant duties and obligations will be further reviewed in chapter three. Suffice it to say for now that, in light of the close relationship between the fiduciary duties of the Crown and Aboriginal title, Justice Dickson proceeded to explore further the concept of Aboriginal title.

Justice Dickson confirmed that Aboriginal title does not depend on any prior legislative or Crown recognition or on the terms of *Royal Proclamation, 1763*. Aboriginal title results from the use and occupation of the land by Aboriginal Peoples prior to the arrival of the Europeans. It is a title that is recognized by the courts at common law.[41] However, Justice Dickson declined to define the content and scope of Aboriginal title, referring to it as a *sui generis* interest. Literally, *sui generis* means unique, and a *sui generis* interest is a special interest that cannot be defined in usual terms. Justice Dickson summarized his view of the Aboriginal *sui generis* interest in land as follows:

> Indians have a legal right to occupy and possess certain lands, the ultimate title to which is in the Crown. While their interest does not, strictly speaking, amount to beneficial ownership, neither is its nature completely exhausted by the concept of a personal right. It is true that the *sui generis* interest which the Indians have in the land is personal in the sense that it cannot be transferred to a grantee, but it is also true, as will presently appear, that the interest gives rise upon surrender to a distinctive fiduciary obligation on the part of the Crown to deal with the land for the benefit of the surrendering Indians. These two aspects of Indian title go together, since the Crown's original purpose in declaring the Indians' interest to be inalienable otherwise than to the Crown was to facilitate the Crown's ability to represent the Indians in dealings with third parties. The nature of the Indians' interest is therefore best characterized by its general inalienability, coupled with the fact that the Crown is under an obligation to deal with the land on the Indians' behalf when the interest is surrendered. Any description of Indian title which goes beyond these two features is both unnecessary and potentially misleading.[42]

The *Constitution Act, 1982*

The coming into force of the *Constitution Act, 1982* considerably affected the position of Aboriginal rights. In particular, section 35(1), with its explicit recognition and affirmation of the Aboriginal and treaty rights, elevated these rights to a constitutional plane:

> 35.(1) The existing aboriginal and treaty rights of the aboriginal peoples of Canada are hereby recognized and affirmed.
> (2) In this Act, "aboriginal peoples of Canada" includes the Indian, Inuit and Métis peoples of Canada.
> (3) For greater certainty, in subsection (1) "treaty rights" includes rights that now exist by way of land claims agreements or may be so acquired.
> (4) Notwithstanding any other provision of this Act, the aboriginal and treaty rights referred to in subsection (1) are guaranteed equally to male and female persons.

Despite these provisions, it is important to remember that Aboriginal rights existed prior to the 1982 constitutional amendments. It is clear from the case law developed prior to and independently of these constitutional provisions that section 35 of the *Constitution Act, 1982* should not be regarded as the legal origin or basis of Aboriginal rights. It must always be kept clearly in mind that Aboriginal rights are fully recognized at common law irrespective of any constitutional provision that may pertain to them. Thus, Aboriginal rights existed prior to the 1982 constitutional amendments and exist as legal rights irrespective of these constitutional provisions.

In the 1996 case of *R. v. Van der Peet*,[43] in which the Supreme Court of Canada considered Aboriginal rights within the context of section 35 of the *Constitution Act, 1982*, Chief Justice Lamer clearly pointed out that the common law recognizes Aboriginal rights as legal and enforceable rights. His position was fully supported by Justice L'Heureux-Dubé and Justice McLachlin in their separate opinions in that case.[44] Thus, the doctrine of Aboriginal rights is essentially a *common law doctrine,* which, through section 35 of the *Constitution Act, 1982,* among other instruments, has been provided with constitutional status.[45] Having acquired constitutional status, Aboriginal rights at common law are protected from unilateral extinguishment and can be regulated only in accordance with the rules set out by the Supreme Court of Canada in application of section 35 of the *Constitution Act, 1982*. However, Aboriginal rights existed as enforceable and compensable rights at common law prior to 1982.

Since the adoption of the *Constitution Act, 1982,* the courts have had a greater opportunity to discuss the nature and content of these common law rights. Of particular interest to our discussion are the cases of *R. v. Van der Peet*,[46] *R. v. Adams*,[47] and *Delgamuukw v. B.C.*[48]

It flows from the decisions in *R. v. Van der Peet* and *R. v. Adams* that common law Aboriginal rights lie on a spectrum. At one end of the spectrum are those rights that relate to the traditional practices and customs of Aboriginal Peoples. These rights may have nothing or little to do with land. At the other end of the spectrum there is Aboriginal title in its full form, which is a quasi–full ownership interest in the land itself. As Chief Justice Lamer stated in *Delgamuukw:*

> The picture which emerges from *Adams* is that the aboriginal rights which are recognized and affirmed by s. 35(1) fall along a spectrum with respect to their degree of connection with the land. At the one end, there are those aboriginal rights which are practices, customs and traditions that are integral to the distinctive aboriginal culture of the group claiming the right. However, the *"occupation and use of the land"* where the activity is taking place is not *"sufficient to support a claim of title to the land"*. (at para. 26) (Emphasis in

original) Nevertheless, those activities receive constitutional protection. In the middle, there are activities which, out of necessity, take place on land and indeed, might be intimately related to a particular piece of land. Although an aboriginal group may not be able to demonstrate title to the land, it may nevertheless have a site-specific right to engage in a particular activity. . . .

At the other end of the spectrum, there is aboriginal title itself. As *Adams* makes clear, aboriginal title confers more than the right to engage in site-specific activities which are aspects of the practices, customs and traditions of distinctive aboriginal cultures. Site-specific rights can be made out even if title cannot. What aboriginal title confers is the right to the land itself.[49]

The Identification and Content of Aboriginal Rights

The general method for identifying and defining common law Aboriginal rights was first discussed by the Supreme Court of Canada in the 1996 case of *R. v. Van der Peet* and in its companion cases of *R. v. N.T.C. Smokehouse Ltd.*[50] and *R. v. Gladstone.*[51]

Dorothy Van der Peet was a member of the Sto:lo Nation, whose members have fished for salmon from time immemorial. Ms. Van der Peet sold for $50 ten salmon that had been caught by her common-law spouse. She was charged under the *Fisheries Act*[52] with selling fish caught under the authority of an Indian food-fishing licence contrary to the provisions of the *British Columbia Fishery (General) Regulations.*[53] At the time Ms. Van der Peet was charged, these regulations prohibited the sale or barter of any fish caught under the authority of such a licence. Ms. Van der Peet stated in her defence that the sales restrictions found in the regulations infringed on an Aboriginal right and were therefore invalid under the terms of section 35 of the *Constitution Act, 1982.*

The case worked its way up to the Supreme Court of Canada. The main issue was to determine if the sale of fish constituted for Ms. Van der Peet an Aboriginal right affirmed and recognized under the terms of section 35. This required the Supreme Court to define and identify those common law Aboriginal rights contemplated by section 35 of the *Constitution Act, 1982.* The majority opinion was rendered by then Chief Justice Lamer. Two forceful dissenting opinions were rendered by Justice L'Heureux-Dubé and Justice (now Chief Justice) McLachlin.

Chief Justice Lamer found that because Aboriginal rights are held by only one segment of the Canadian population, they cannot be defined within the philosophical precepts of liberalism as enshrined in the *Canadian Charter of Rights and Freedoms.* The liberal values enshrined in the *Charter* are thus of little assistance in determining the nature and content of Aboriginal rights. In order to identify which rights are to be recognized and affirmed under section 35, it is necessary to first identify the purpose of this section. In taking this purposive approach, a generous and liberal interpretation must be given to the section. As we shall discuss further in subsequent chapters, this interpretative principle flows from the fiduciary nature of the relationship between the Crown and Aboriginal Peoples.

Chief Justice Lamer noted that when identifying the basis for the recognition and affirmation of Aboriginal rights, it is important to remember that Aboriginal rights existed and were recognized at common law.[54] The common law doctrine of Aboriginal rights arose because when Europeans arrived in North America, Aboriginal Peoples were already there. To reconcile the assertion of sovereignty over these lands by the Crown with the prior presence of Aboriginal Peoples, a normative order developed, which came to be called the doctrine of Aboriginal rights. By asserting sovereignty, the Crown impaired the fundamental rights of Aboriginal Peoples. This impairment resulted in the Crown assuming a fiduciary relationship towards the Aboriginal Peoples whose fundamental rights it had thus impaired. Chief Justice Lamer argued that the substantive rights of Aboriginal Peoples protected through the common law, and now through the Constitution, must be understood within this context.[55]

Thus, for Chief Justice Lamer, section 35 of the *Constitution Act, 1982* provided a constitutional framework through which the fact of prior Aboriginal occupation of the Americas was acknowledged and reconciled with the sovereignty of the Crown. In order to fulfil the purpose underlying section 35, the test for identifying those Aboriginal rights recognized and affirmed by that section must highlight the crucial elements of those pre-existing, distinct Aboriginal societies. It must "aim at identifying the practices, traditions and customs *central* to the aboriginal societies that existed in North America *prior to contact with the Europeans*" [emphasis added].[56]

The test offered by Chief Justice Lamer in *R. v. Van der Peet* involves two steps. The first step is to determine the precise nature of the claim being made. In making this determination, account must be made of such factors as the nature of the action taken pursuant to the claimed Aboriginal right; the government regulation argued to infringe on the right; and the tradition, custom, or practice relied upon to establish the right. The second step is to determine whether the practice or custom claimed to be an Aboriginal right was, prior to contact with Europeans, an integral part of the distinctive Aboriginal society of the Aboriginal People in question. In other words, was the practice or custom of central significance to the concerned Aboriginal society? Was it one of the things that truly made the society what it was prior to European contact? Chief Justice Lamer argued that when assessing such a claim, equal weight should be given to the perspective of the concerned Aboriginal Peoples and to the perspective of the common law.[57]

The approach taken by the majority of Supreme Court justices in the *Van der Peet* case implies that Aboriginal rights are not general and universal to all Aboriginal communities. Aboriginal rights are thus to be determined on a case-by-case basis and are specific to each community. In addition, for such rights to be recognized under section 35 of the *Constitution Act, 1982*, there must be some continuity between the practice, custom, or tradition prior to contact with Europeans and modern times. Thus, the claimed practice must still be integral to the distinctive culture of the concerned Aboriginal Peoples today. The evolution of the practice, custom, or tradition to modern forms will not impede its protection as an Aboriginal right recognized and affirmed under section 35; however, where the practice, custom, or tradition arose solely in response to European influences, then that practice, custom, or tradition will not meet the standard for recognition as an Aboriginal right under the terms of section 35 of the *Constitution Act, 1982*. This requirement seems to deny constitutional recognition to those practices, customs, and traditions that emerged from Aboriginal contact with Europeans. The exclusion of post-contact practices, customs, and traditions sharply divided the Court and was the subject of strong dissenting opinions by Justice L'Heureux-Dubé and Justice McLachlin.[58]

The position of Chief Justice Lamer and of the majority of the Supreme Court on the method of identification and definition of those Aboriginal rights recognized and affirmed under section 35 of the *Constitution Act, 1982* restricts the scope and extent of such rights. By confining Aboriginal rights to those practices, customs, and traditions that existed prior to contact with Europeans, the majority of the Court has, to some extent, ignored the dynamic nature of Aboriginal societies since first contact.[59] This position overlooks, to some extent, the impact contact between Europeans and Aboriginal Peoples has had in shaping both Aboriginal and mainstream Canadian societies and cultures.[60] Furthermore, the approach based on Aboriginal "practices, traditions and customs" considers only part of Aboriginal culture. It calls for a separation between particular elements of a culture and the general cultural and social context in which these elements are rooted. This approach makes it difficult to take a holistic approach to Aboriginal rights based on an analysis of the concerned Aboriginal culture and society as a dynamic whole interrelating with strong external factors such as European society. It can be argued that the approach taken by the majority of the Supreme Court is somewhat culturally static. Nevertheless, this approach is the one applicable in Canada for identifying and defining those common law Aboriginal rights that are recognized and affirmed under section 35 of the *Constitution Act, 1982*.

It is appropriate to note here that the method used by the majority of the Supreme Court in *Van der Peet* to identify Aboriginal rights was developed in the context of section 35 of the *Constitution Act, 1982* and the infringement and justification tests contained therein. Pursuant to section 35, the courts have a major role to play in controlling the administrative and legislative actions of governments that infringe on Aboriginal rights. This power of review and control over administrative and legislative actions did not exist at common law. However, it can be argued that certain rights of Aboriginal Peoples may exist at common law irrespective of their recognition under the terms of section 35. The method for identifying and defining Aboriginal rights stated in the *Van der Peet* decision and its companion cases may recognize fewer rights as constitutionally protected Aboriginal rights than may be recognized by the common law. Thus, a wider range of rights may be recognized at common law for Aboriginal Peoples than are recognized and affirmed under section 35.

This distinction helps to reconcile, to a certain extent, the different approaches to the identification and definition of Aboriginal rights found in the reasons of Chief Justice Lamer and of Justices L'Heureux-Dubé and McLachlin in *R. v. Van der Peet*. These latter two would arguably be dealing, in their dissenting opinions, with rights of Aboriginal Peoples recognized at common law generally. The opinion of Chief Justice Lamer and of the majority of the Court would arguably deal with that subset of those common law rights that have been afforded constitutional protection and that warrant judicial supervision and control over government actions that affect them. It may thus be possible to distinguish those Aboriginal rights that, to some extent, require conciliation with the sovereignty of the Crown, from those other rights of Aboriginal Peoples that are compatible with the assertion of sovereignty and that may, in fact, have developed as a consequence of the assertion of sovereignty by the Crown. The first set of rights would be afforded the protection of section 35, while the second set would simply be recognized at common law.

Section 25 of the *Constitution Act, 1982* may be referring to rights extending beyond those set out in section 35 when it refers to the "aboriginal, treaty *or other rights* or freedoms that pertain to the Aboriginal peoples of Canada" [emphasis added].[61] Moreover, the recognition of an Aboriginal right at common law is not in itself a prerequisite for recognition under section 35 of the *Constitution Act, 1982*. Aboriginal rights may receive constitutional protection irrespective of their recognition at common law.[62] Conversely, it may be argued that certain common law rights of Aboriginal Peoples may exist irrespective of their recognition as constitutionally protected rights. However, no case has dealt specifically with this issue. Since this distinction has not been explicitly recognized by the Supreme Court of Canada, this book discusses the issue of the identification and definition of the common law rights of Aboriginal Peoples as if these were limited to those common law rights contemplated by section 35 of the *Constitution Act, 1982* and identified through the methodology developed by the majority opinion in *Van der Peet*.

In *Van der Peet,* Chief Justice Lamer found that although the Sto:lo had traded fish extensively with the Hudson's Bay Company, this practice had arisen as a result of contact with the Europeans. In light of the finding that the Sto:lo society prior to European contact had not developed a fishing trade, the practice of trading in fish could not have been an integral component of its culture at the time of European contact. In consequence, the claim of Ms. Van der Peet to an Aboriginal right to sell fish was denied, and her conviction was upheld.

Using the same analysis, in *R. v. Gladstone,*[63] Chief Justice Lamer concluded that the exchange and trade of herring spawn was an integral part of the distinctive culture of the Heiltsuk. In that case, Donald and William Gladstone, who were members of the Heiltsuk, had been charged with offering to sell herring spawn on kelp contrary to provisions of the *Fisheries Act* and of certain of the regulations adopted under that act. The accused raised in defence their Aboriginal right to trade in herring spawn. The evidence showed that the Heiltsuk had engaged in extensive inter-tribal trading and barter of herring spawn on kelp prior to contact with Europeans. It was further shown that this trade had been a central and significant feature of Heiltsuk society. Using the analysis he had developed in *Van der Peet,* Chief Justice Lamer concluded that an Aboriginal right to trade in herring spawn on kelp existed for the Heiltsuk.

In the third case in the *Van der Peet* trilogy, *N.T.C. Smokehouse Ltd.,*[64] the Chief Justice did not recognize an Aboriginal right to exchange fish for money or other goods. In that case, N.T.C. Smokehouse Ltd. owned and operated a food-processing plant near Port Alberni, British Columbia. The company was charged with selling and purchasing fish not caught under the authority of a commercial fishing licence or caught under the authority of an Indian food-fishing licence contrary to the *Fisheries Act* and some of its regulations. The charges resulted from purchases of large quantities of Chinook salmon caught by members of the Sheshalt and Opetchesaht Bands. The company argued that the provisions under which it was charged violated the Aboriginal rights of those from whom it had purchased the salmon. The evidence in this case did not show that the concerned bands were sellers or barterers of fish prior to European contact. At best it showed that the selling or bartering of fish was incidental to the pre-contact cultures of the Sheshalt and Opetchesaht. An Aboriginal right to exchange fish for money or other goods was thus found not to exist.

Although the Supreme Court of Canada has discussed methods for identifying Aboriginal rights at length, it has not afforded the same attention to the content of such rights. This can be explained by the Court's preference for a case-by-case review of these rights, which does not allow for gener-alizations. Certain general features of Aboriginal rights have nevertheless been determined by the Court. These rights have been characterized as *sui generis* and as possessing attributes similar to those of Aboriginal title, including the inalienability of the rights, the particular origin of the rights rooted in prior occupation of the land, and the collective nature of the rights.[65]

Content of Aboriginal Title

The Supreme Court of Canada has, however, proceeded with an extensive discussion of the content of Aboriginal title in the seminal case of *Delgamuukw v. B.C.*[66]

The *Delgamuukw* case resulted from the claims of Gitksan and Wet'suwet'en hereditary chiefs to 58,000 square kilometres in British Columbia over which they asserted ownership and jurisdiction. These claims lead to a marathon trial comprising 374 days of evidence and arguments and a four-hundred-page decision from the trial judge, Justice McEachern.[67] At trial, the plaintiffs asserted that their rights to their traditional lands were equivalent, at the very least, to a common law, fee simple ownership, coupled with sweeping quasi-sovereign jurisdiction. The judge rejected these claims because he found them incompatible with the nature of Aboriginal title as he understood it and incompatible with the ultimate sovereignty of the Canadian state. He recognized that the Gitksan and Wet'suwet'en had an interest in certain parts of the claimed land at the time when the British Crown assumed sovereignty over British Columbia; however, he held that this Aboriginal interest had been extinguished prior to the admission of the colony of British Columbia into Canada.

The *Delgamuukw* case specifically addressed the nature and extent of Aboriginal land rights in Canada. On appeal, in addition to their claims to full ownership and jurisdiction, the plaintiffs decided to assert claims to communal Aboriginal title and to self-government. The British Columbia Court of Appeal overturned the trial judge on the issue of pre-Confederation extinguishment of Aboriginal title in British Columbia.[68] The Court of Appeal also decided that Aboriginal title was a collective right of the Aboriginal community that held it. The Court of Appeal was, however, sharply divided on the precise nature of this Aboriginal title.

In *Delgamuukw,* the Supreme Court of Canada was thus faced with the arduous task of determining the nature and content of Aboriginal title. In its decision, the Court directly addressed the nature of Aboriginal title, the proof required to establish such a title, the circumstances under which Aboriginal title may be infringed, and the justification test applicable in such circumstances, as well as the manner and circumstances by which Aboriginal title might have been extinguished prior to the *Constitution Act, 1982.* The Court reiterated that Aboriginal title is but one particular manifestation of Aboriginal rights generally. Like all other Aboriginal rights, it is recognized at common law as a legal right enforceable by the courts. In addition, common law Aboriginal title is recognized and affirmed under section 35 of the *Constitution Act, 1982*. Aboriginal title is a *sui generis* interest in land distinguishable from a fee simple interest.[69] This interest cannot be entirely explained in terms of traditional common law property. The principal characteristics of Aboriginal title at common law are its inalienability except to the Crown in right of Canada; its origin, which flows from the prior occupation of Canada by the Aboriginal Peoples; and its collective nature, in that it is held collectively by all the members of the concerned Aboriginal nation. Aboriginal title differs from most other Aboriginal rights in that it involves a right to the land itself.

In order to take into account the specificity of Aboriginal title, the Supreme Court of Canada adapted the test set out in *R. v. Van der Peet*.[70] Thus, whereas an Aboriginal right generally requires establishing that a practice existed *prior to European contact,* in the case of Aboriginal title, it must rather be established that the concerned Aboriginal Peoples occupied the land *prior to the assertion of sovereignty by the Crown.*

The content of Aboriginal title is quite broad. In *Delgamuukw* v. *B.C.,* Chief Justice Lamer summarized this content under the common law as follows:

> I have arrived at the conclusion that the content of aboriginal title can be summarized by two propositions: first, that aboriginal title encompasses the right to exclusive use and occupation of the land held pursuant to that title for a variety of purposes, which need not be aspects of those aboriginal practices, customs and traditions which are integral to distinctive aboriginal cultures; and second, that those protected uses must not be irreconcilable with the nature of the group's attachment to that land.[71]

It is clear from this quote that Aboriginal title is not equivalent to a common law, fee simple interest in the land. However, Aboriginal title allows for the exclusive use of the land for broad purposes that are not limited to traditional Aboriginal uses of the land. Although Aboriginal title flows from the use and occupation of the land for traditional Aboriginal activities, once this title has been established, the concerned Aboriginal Peoples may use the land, on an exclusive basis, for all kinds of purposes, including commercial purposes unrelated to Aboriginal practices. Aboriginal title also extends to the natural resources on or in the land.[72]

There are, however, some inherent limitations to common law Aboriginal title. First, it cannot be sold or otherwise alienated except by surrender to the Crown. Second, the land cannot be used by the Aboriginal Peoples for purposes that are completely at odds and totally incompatible with their traditional activities on the land. This means that Aboriginal title cannot justify uses of the land by the Aboriginal Peoples that would sever their special relationship with the land. This last limitation has been compared to the land-use restriction found at common law under the concept of equitable waste, under which a person who holds a life estate cannot commit wanton and extravagant acts of destruction.[73] Barring such rare, incompatible uses, Aboriginal title provides to the concerned Aboriginal Peoples the undisturbed and exclusive use of the land for a large variety of purposes that need not be tied to traditional Aboriginal activities.

Conclusion

Aboriginal rights are *sui generis,* common law rights that flow from the prior occupation of Canada by Aboriginal Peoples. These rights are collective in nature, and they are inalienable except to the Crown. The rights that benefit from the protection of section 35 of the *Constitution Act, 1982* are those practices, traditions, and customs that were, prior to contact with Europeans, an integral part of the distinctive Aboriginal society of the Aboriginal People claiming the rights.

Aboriginal rights lie on a spectrum with respect to their connection with land. At one end are the practices, customs, and traditions integral to the distinctive culture of the concerned Aboriginal group, the exercise of which does not support a claim of title to the land where they are carried out. In the middle, there are those activities that of necessity take place on land and that may be intimately related to a particular piece of land. At the other end of the spectrum, there is Aboriginal title. Aboriginal title is but one manifestation of Aboriginal rights generally. This title is a right to the land itself and it flows from the occupation of the land by Aboriginal Peoples prior to the assertion of sovereignty by the Crown. Aboriginal title includes the right to use the land for all purposes that are not fundamentally irreconcilable with the nature of the Aboriginal group's attachment to the land.

Chapter 2

Treaty Rights

Introduction

The normative order that developed from the contact between European powers and the Aboriginal nations of the Americas, which we now call the doctrine of Aboriginal rights, required the Aboriginal nations to treat exclusively with the sovereign of the European power claiming discovery. In many cases, the method by which the Crown and the Aboriginal nations interacted within this normative order often took the form of what we now call Aboriginal treaties. The exclusiveness of the relationship, as well as the nature of the issues dealt with within the framework of the relationship, ensured that the understandings reached between the Crown and Aboriginal nations in the treaties were solemn and sacred. Some of these understandings concerned matters of war and peace;[1] others concerned the use of the lands subject to Aboriginal title for the purposes of European settlement;[2] many concerned multiple aspects of the relationship between the Crown and the concerned Aboriginal nations.[3]

These understandings often concerned fundamental aspects of the relationship between the Crown and Aboriginal nations. They served to shape and to give new normative content to this relationship. Treaties are thus fundamental components of the Crown's relationship with Aboriginal nations. Whereas Aboriginal rights are inherent and exist irrespective of formal Crown recognition, treaty rights are closely tied to the relationship between the Crown and Aboriginal Peoples and cannot exist outside this relationship. Treaty rights flow from the agreements made between Aboriginal Peoples and the representatives of the Crown.[4]

Treaties were often used to carry out a complete or partial surrender of Aboriginal title, but the scope of the treaties is certainly not restricted to land transactions. Treaty rights can concern issues directly related to Aboriginal rights and to any other issues of interest to the concerned Aboriginal Peoples and the Crown. As was stated by Justice (later Chief Justice) Lamer in the case of *R*. v. *Sioui:* "There is no reason why an agreement concerning something other than a territory, such as an agreement about political or social rights, cannot be a treaty within the meaning of s. 88 of the Indian Act."[5]

Although treaty rights are inherently different in origin from Aboriginal rights, they often serve to confirm or to regulate pre-existing Aboriginal rights.[6] Thus, Aboriginal hunting and fishing rights may be confirmed in a treaty, or treaty reserve land may be carved out of lands subject to Aboriginal title. When, as they often do, treaties confirm to the Aboriginal signatories the continuation of their hunting and fishing activities, the scope and extent of such activities may often be found in the underlying Aboriginal right recognized at common law. Likewise, the nature of the rights of Aboriginal Peoples in traditional land reserved to them by treaty must also be found in common law Aboriginal title.[7] A treaty may modify these inherent common law rights; however, absent clear language to the contrary in the treaty, the common law applicable in such matters will be presumed to have been maintained and confirmed by the treaty. Thus, treaties often provide superadded protection to underlying surviving common law Aboriginal rights.[8] In particular, the incorporation of an Aboriginal right within the terms of a treaty releases the Aboriginal beneficiaries of the treaty from the requirement of proving the right under the rules laid out in *Van der Peet* or *Delgamuukw*.[9]

Although treaties can be characterized as contracts, they are very special contracts of a *sui generis* nature and they are governed by public law rules.[10] Treaties are *sui generis* in that they often purport to be binding in perpetuity; they are often binding not only on the Aboriginal signatories, but also on whole Aboriginal Peoples as well as their descendants; and they often create various forms of *sui generis* rights. Treaties are governed by public law rules in that they clearly bind the Crown; they purport to regulate the relationship of the Crown with entire populations, often over vast territories; and they are regulated by a corpus of public common law rules regarding, among other things, the capacity of the parties to enter into a treaty, the formalities related thereto, and the rules governing treaty interpretation.[11] Many cases have dealt with these common law rules.[12] In particular, treaties allow Aboriginal Peoples and the Crown to create new rights unknown or unrecognized at common law, and to extinguish or regulate underlying common law Aboriginal rights.

It can be surmised from the case law that treaties with Aboriginal Peoples represent an exchange of solemn promises between the Crown and the concerned Aboriginal Peoples. This exchange of promises takes the form of an agreement whose nature is said to be sacred, and which places upon the Crown a high responsibility for the fulfilment of all the undertakings made in the context of the agreement. The integrity and honour of the Crown are always at stake in the implementation of treaties with Aboriginal Peoples. Thus, no sharp dealings with Aboriginal Peoples will be sanctioned, nor will the courts provide a restrictive interpretation of the commitments of the Crown in the treaties it has signed. Consequently, restrictions to common law Aboriginal rights, as well as extinguishments of such rights carried out by a treaty, will be narrowly construed in favour of the Aboriginal party. Moreover, it will be incumbent upon the party relying on the restriction or extinguishment to prove that such a restriction or extinguishment was indeed carried out by the treaty. Strict evidence of a clear and plain intent to effect such a restriction or to carry out such an extinguishment is required.[13]

Treaty rights are provided with statutory protection from interference by the provincial legislatures through the terms of section 88 of the *Indian Act*.[14] Although this protection may have existed in any event under the principles of the constitutional division of powers discussed in chapter four, the terms of the *Indian Act* clearly indicate the importance of treaty rights and the priority such rights are to be afforded.

Like common law Aboriginal rights, treaty rights have also been constitutionally recognized and affirmed through, among other instruments, the terms of section 35 of the *Constitution Act, 1982*. The wording of section 35 has been held to support a common approach to infringements of Aboriginal rights and of treaty rights.[15] The similarities between these rights are not limited to the infringement and justification principles implicit in section 35, but extend to the common law principles of compensation applicable in cases of infringement or extinguishment.

As noted above, treaties flow from those aspects of the doctrine of Aboriginal rights that oblige the Aboriginal nations to treat exclusively with the Crown. In light of the "domestic dependent" status of Aboriginal nations, Aboriginal treaties are not recognized as instruments of international law. Nevertheless, in many ways they are analogous to international law treaties.[16] In particular, like international law treaties, Aboriginal treaties are prerogative instruments. As instruments of the royal prerogative, treaties bind the Crown, but prior to the *Constitution Act, 1982,* they did not have the force of legislation unless confirmed by Parliament. Moreover, Aboriginal treaties are not simple contracts between the Crown and some of its subjects. They are far-reaching and important documents, since it is through such treaties that the territories now forming Canada were gathered together.[17]

Form of Treaties and the Capacity to Enter into Treaties

In the 1964 case of *R. v. White and Bob,*[18] two members of the Saalequun Tribe on Vancouver Island had been charged with possessing game during a closed season without a valid permit, which was contrary to the provincial game legislation. Various defences were raised based on Aboriginal rights, on the *Royal Proclamation, 1763,* and on treaty rights. The British Columbia Court of Appeal upheld the dismissal of the charges based on a treaty right to hunt. The majority of the Court did not address issues relating to Aboriginal rights or to the *Royal Proclamation,* although Justice Norris did make some interesting comments on these matters, in which he was supported by Justice Sullivan.

The treaty at issue in *White and Bob* was entered into between the Saalequun Tribe and Governor Douglas in 1854. It principally concerned the sale of land on Vancouver Island to the Hudson's Bay Company. The document included a provision by which the Aboriginal signatories were "at liberty to hunt over the unoccupied lands, and to carry on our fisheries as formally."

The Crown submitted that the document was not a treaty under section 87 (now section 88) of the *Indian Act,* because it did not have the formalities of a treaty attached to it and it was signed by representatives of the Hudson's Bay Company rather than by representatives of the Crown. The majority in the British Columbia Court of Appeal found these arguments hollow. The majority argued that when considering whether a document is an Aboriginal treaty, the history of the occupation and settlement of the country in which the document was made and the context in which the document was signed must be taken into consideration. After reviewing the history of the European occupation of Vancouver Island and the role played by the Hudson's Bay Company as an instrument of imperial policy, the majority of the Court had no difficulty finding that a treaty had been made by Governor Douglas with the Saalequun Tribe. In an often-quoted statement of the law, Justice Norris defined an Aboriginal treaty as the "word of the white man":

> In the section "Treaty" is not a word of art and in my respectful opinion, it embraces all such engagements made by persons in authority as may be brought within the term "the word of the white man" the sanctity of which was, at the time of British exploration and settlement, the most important means of obtaining the goodwill and co-operation of the native tribes and ensuring that the colonists would be protected from death and destruction. On such assurance the Indians relied.[19]

In the 1985 case of *Simon v. R.,*[20] a member of the Shubenacadie Indian Brook Band (No. 2) of the Mi'kmaq people had been charged with illegal possession of a rifle during a closed hunting season pursuant to the terms of legislation adopted by the province of Nova Scotia. Mr. Simon set up as a defence that he was exercising a right to hunt under the terms of a treaty of peace and friendship executed in 1752 between the then-governor of Nova Scotia, P.T. Hobson, and various Mi'kmaq chiefs. Under the terms of the treaty, it was agreed that the Mi'kmaq "shall not be hindered from, but have free liberty of Hunting & Fishing as usual." Mr. Simon claimed that, in light of section 88 of the *Indian Act,* which makes the application of provincial laws to "Indians" subject to the terms of any treaty,[21] he was exempted from the provincial law under which he was charged.

The capacity of the parties to enter into this treaty was questioned. It was argued that Governor Hobson had no power to enter into international treaties for the British Crown as he had not been specifically authorized to do so. It was further argued that the Aboriginal signatories to the treaty had no standing in international law and thus no legal capacity to enter into a treaty.

In the *Simon* decision, the Supreme Court of Canada found that Aboriginal treaties are not governed by the norms and rules that govern international treaties. Though analogies may be made between an Aboriginal treaty and an international treaty, the instruments are distinct one from another. Aboriginal treaties are *sui generis* instruments governed by their own set of legal rules. These rules flow not from European international law but rather from the normative order that resulted from contact between Europeans and Aboriginal nations. The norms and rules that govern Aboriginal treaties are distinct and special, and are to be found in the history of the relationship between the Crown and Aboriginal Peoples. Thus, the issue of the capacity of both Governor Hobson and the Mi'kmaq chiefs to enter into the treaty of 1752 was to be determined within the historical context of that treaty.

At the time the treaty was concluded, Aboriginal nations were important military allies of the French and English in northeastern America. Both European powers considered the Mi'kmaq to be particularly important allies, and neither had any difficulty recognizing the national character of the Mi'kmaq and entering into treaties with them. Treaty-making with Aboriginal nations was common and was a preferred means of seeking an alliance with or the neutrality of Aboriginal Peoples. Put in such a historical context, there was no doubt as to the capacity of the Mi'kmaq chiefs to enter into the treaty of 1752. Indeed, the normative order resulting from contact between Aboriginal Peoples and the British Crown required Aboriginal nations to treat with the Crown through the quasi-international law instruments that are known as Aboriginal treaties.

Likewise, in the historical context, there was no doubt that colonial governors appointed by the Crown had the capacity to enter into Aboriginal treaties for the Crown. As treaty-making was common, it was to be expected that the governor of Nova Scotia would attempt to secure treaties with the Mi'kmaq. From the perspective of the Mi'kmaq, there was no doubt that Governor Hobson represented the Crown and had the capacity to enter into the treaty of 1752 for and in the name of the Crown. The normative order resulting from contact required the Crown to treat with Aboriginal nations through a variety of representatives. Insofar as the Aboriginal Peoples had reasonable cause to believe that these representatives could act for the Crown by entering into a treaty, there was no ground to argue decades later that such representatives were incompetent to bind the Crown. The historical relationship between the Crown and Aboriginal Peoples, and the normative order resulting from this relationship, required the courts to recognize both the legally binding nature of Aboriginal treaties and the capacity of those who entered into these instruments. These issues were to be understood as those who entered into a treaty would have understood them at the time the treaty was made.

Having found that the treaty had been validly executed, the Supreme Court of Canada next considered whether the treaty had ever been terminated. The prosecution argued that the treaty was terminated when the Mi'kmaq and the Crown resumed hostilities soon after its conclusion. The prosecution also argued that any treaty right to hunt was extinguished when Europeans occupied the land pursuant to Crown land grants or leases.

Under international law, a treaty between two powers may be terminated through hostilities. The Supreme Court of Canada refused to state whether this standard applied to Aboriginal treaties. Instead, the Court reiterated that standards of international law do not automatically apply to Aboriginal treaties; the rules governing Aboriginal treaties must be found in the historical relationship between the Crown and Aboriginal nations. Since in the *Simon* case there was insufficient evidence as to the nature of the military relationship between the parties after the conclusion of the treaty, the Court left open the question of whether the treaty had been terminated through hostilities. Likewise, the Court found it unnecessary to answer the question of termination through adverse land use, in light of the fact that the land on which Mr. Simon had hunted was adjacent to a reserve and was not adversely occupied.

The Court once again referred to the normative order resulting from contact as the backdrop against which Aboriginal treaties must be understood. The Court also understood the scope of Aboriginal treaties to include transactions unrelated to land cessions. Chief Justice Dickson stated:

> In my view, Parliament intended to include within the operation of s. 88 [of the *Indian Act*] all agreements concluded by the Crown with the Indians that would otherwise be enforceable treaties, whether land was ceded or not.[22]

The Nature of Treaty Rights

In the 1990 case of *R. v. Sioui*,[23] the Supreme Court of Canada once again examined the nature of Aboriginal treaties and the capacities of parties to enter into them. In *Sioui,* a group of Hurons had been charged with cutting trees, camping, and making fires in a provincial park, contrary to regulations of the province of Quebec. The accused Hurons relied for their defence on the terms of a short document dated September 5, 1760, and signed by Brigadier General James Murray. This document certified that the Hurons had submitted to the British and made peace. This document also stated that the Hurons were to be "allowed the free Exercise of their Religion, their Customs, and Liberty of trading with the English."[24] The defendants claimed that this document constituted a treaty. They further claimed that in light of section 88 of the *Indian Act,* the rights provided in the document shielded them from the provincial legislation under which they had been charged.

On the general capacity of the Crown to enter into treaties with Aboriginal nations, the Supreme Court reiterated its findings in *Simon.*[25] Once again, it grounded this capacity within the normative order resulting from the historical relationship between Aboriginal Peoples and the Crown. The issue was particularly pressing in *Sioui,* because the British Crown had not fully taken control of Canada at the time the document was signed. Moreover, the Hurons had been allies of the French. As noted in our discussion above,[26] the doctrine of Aboriginal rights requires that Aboriginal nations treat exclusively with the European power claiming discovery. In this case, that European power was clearly France. Thus, the question was whether the Hurons and the British Crown could validly transact a treaty under the meaning of this doctrine in circumstances where territorial claims between European powers were subject to dispute, war, and ongoing conquest. The Supreme Court of Canada resolved this question by once again looking at the issue from a historical and contextual perspective, and by placing great emphasis on the perspective of the Hurons:

> Both *Simon* and *White and Bob* make it clear that the question of capacity must be seen from the point of view of the Indians at that time, and the Court must ask whether it was reasonable for them to have assumed that the other party they were dealing with had the authority to enter into a valid treaty with them. I conclude without any hesitation that the Hurons could reasonably have believed that the British Crown had the power to enter into a treaty with them that would be in effect as long as the British controlled Canada.[27]

On the more specific issue of the capacity of General Murray to represent the Crown in an Aboriginal treaty, the Court again took a historical and contextual approach, taking into account the Aboriginal perspective. Even though General Murray was at the time subordinate to his commander-in-chief, General Amherst, he nevertheless remained one of the senior British actors in the conquest of Canada. The Court found that in light of the historical role played by General Murray, it was reasonable for the Hurons to assume that he was capable of "giving the word of the white man." Given the relationship between the Crown and Aboriginal nations and the normative order resulting from this relationship, the capacity of the Crown's representatives to bind the Crown through treaty must rest on a historical and contextual analysis in which the Aboriginal perspective is given very important weight.

The Court also took a historical and contextual approach to determine if a particular document constituted an Aboriginal treaty. Referring back to the decision of the Ontario Court of Appeal in *R. v. Taylor and Williams*,[28] Justice Lamer identified five basic, but not exclusive, factors to consider when determining whether the parties intended to conclude an Aboriginal treaty:

1. whether the right has been continuously exercised in the past and at present;
2. the reasons the Crown made a commitment;
3. the situation prevailing at the time the document was signed;
4. the evidence of relations of mutual respect and esteem at the time the document was signed; and
5. the subsequent conduct of the parties.[29]

All five factors are important when determining whether a given document is an Aboriginal treaty; however, it appears that the fundamental question is whether or not the document falls under the doctrine of Aboriginal rights. As already noted, this doctrine restricts Aboriginal nations by requiring them to treat exclusively with the Crown in regard to their rights. Insofar as the document is one that the Aboriginal Peoples could make with the Crown under the doctrine of Aboriginal rights, it follows that the document constitutes an Aboriginal treaty. It is this more than any other factor that leads to the conclusion that a document is a treaty. Thus, in *Sioui*, the document signed by General Murray was a treaty, because only the Crown could receive the Hurons under its protection, and only the Crown could provide the Hurons with formal undertakings in regard to the unimpeded exercise of their customs. The Court thus found that the document constituted a valid and binding treaty between the Crown and the Hurons.

The Court then reviewed the scope of the treaty. Once again, the Court resorted to the historical context to determine the nature of the rights protected under the treaty and their territorial application. In the absence of any express mention in the treaty as to its territorial scope, the Court concluded from the historical context that the parties intended to reconcile the Hurons' need to protect their customs with the desire of the British to expand their empire. This reconciliation could be achieved by protecting the exercise of these customs in all parts of the territory frequented by the Hurons where this exercise was not incompatible with the Crown's occupancy of the concerned territory.[30] The Court thus found that the Hurons' right to exercise their customs in the provincial park was protected by the treaty. The Court consequently found that the provincial regulations that did not allow the Hurons to exercise their customs in this way were inapplicable to the accused through the operation of section 88 of the *Indian Act*.

The nature of treaty rights was further considered by the Supreme Court of Canada in the case of *R. v. Sundown*.[31] Mr. John Sundown was a Cree Indian and a member of the Joseph Bighead First Nation located in the province of Saskatchewan. While he was out hunting, Mr. Sundown entered a provincial park and cut down some trees, which he used to build a log cabin. The provincial regulations prohibited the cutting of trees and the construction of dwellings in the park without permission. Mr. Sundown was charged under the provincial regulatory scheme applicable to the park.

In his defence, Mr. Sundown raised his treaty rights to hunt under Treaty 6. This treaty is one of eleven numbered treaties concluded between the Crown and various First Nations between 1871 and 1923. These numbered treaties were negotiated in order to facilitate European settlement of western Canada. Treaty 6 was signed in 1876. The area ceded under the treaty covered much of central Alberta and Saskatchewan. In exchange for the land, the Crown promised to provide reserves, schools, annuities, farm equipment, ammunition, and assistance in times of famine or pestilence. The treaty also secured the Aboriginal Peoples' right to hunt, fish, and trap. At Mr. Sundown's trial, it was placed into evidence that the guarantee of these hunting, fishing, and trapping rights was an essential consideration for the Aboriginal nations in their acceptance of the treaty.

In 1930, Treaty 6 was modified by the terms of the *Natural Resources Transfer Agreement* entered into between the province of Saskatchewan and the Government of Canada. This agreement transferred the ownership of natural resources in Saskatchewan from the federal government to the province. The agreement was given constitutional status by the *Constitution Act, 1930*.[32] The *Natural Resources Transfer Agreement* extinguished the treaty right to hunt commercially, but it expanded the geographical area in which the treaty right to hunt for food might be exercised.[33]

The issue in *Sundown* was to determine whether the treaty right to hunt for food included the right to cut down trees to build a log cabin and the right to build a cabin. The Court applied the principle set out by Chief Justice Dickson in *Simon v. R.*, which provided that "[t]he right to hunt to be effective must embody those activities reasonably incidental to the act of hunting itself."[34] On the evidence presented, the Court found that the members of the Joseph Bighead First Nation had traditionally hunted in expeditions lasting weeks at a time, and that it was customary for hunters to set out in different directions from a base camp. In these circumstances, a hunter's cabin was found to be reasonably incidental to the right to hunt of the members of that First Nation. In consequence, the provincial regulations under which Mr.

Sundown was charged were found to be inapplicable to him. In the course of its reasons in *Sundown,* the Court took the opportunity to discuss the nature of treaty rights, emphasizing the *sui generis* and collective aspects of such rights:

> Treaty rights, like aboriginal rights, must not be interpreted as if they were common law property rights. Chief Justice Dickson and La Forest J. made this point in *Sparrow* [*R.* v. *Sparrow,* [1990] 1 S.C.R. 1075] at pp. 1111-12:
>
>> Our earlier observations regarding the scope of the aboriginal right to fish are relevant here. Fishing rights are not traditional property rights. They are rights held by a collective and are in keeping with the culture and existence of that group. *Courts must be careful, then, to avoid the application of traditional common law concepts of property as they develop their understanding of what the reasons for judgment in Guerin, [[1984] 2 S.C.R. 335], at p. 382, referred to as the "sui generis" nature of aboriginal rights.* [Emphasis added]
>
> Aboriginal and treaty rights cannot be defined in a manner which would accord with common law concepts of title to land or the right to use another's land. Rather, they are the right of aboriginal people in common with other aboriginal people to participate in certain practices traditionally engaged in by particular aboriginal nations in particular territories.
>
> Any interest in the hunting cabin is a collective right that is derived from the treaty and the traditional expeditionary method of hunting. It belongs to the Band as a whole and not to Mr. Sundown or any individual member of the Joseph Bighead First Nation. It would not be possible, for example, for Mr. Sundown to exclude other members of this First Nation who have the same treaty right to hunt in Meadow Lake Provincial Park.[35]

The Interpretation of Treaties

Aboriginal treaties constitute a unique type of agreement and attract special principles of interpretation.[36]

In *R.* v. *Taylor and Williams,*[37] charges had been laid in relation to the taking of bullfrogs during a closed season contrary to legislation of the province of Ontario. The accused set up as their defence their rights under a treaty of 1818 that had been entered into by six chiefs of the Chippewa Nation and the then–deputy superintendent general of Indian Affairs on behalf of the Crown. Under the terms of the treaty, the Chippewa had surrendered a tract of land to the Crown in exchange for money. The question raised by the proceedings was whether the Chippewa had preserved their Aboriginal hunting and fishing rights in that tract of land notwithstanding the surrender provisions of the treaty. These rights were claimed to have been preserved through the oral undertakings that were made to the Chippewa at the time the treaty was negotiated and signed.

The Ontario Court of Appeal found that the Chippewa's Aboriginal hunting and fishing rights had been preserved notwithstanding the surrender provisions of the treaty. The Court of Appeal stated that cases involving treaties can never be determined in a vacuum. Thus, in determining the effect of the treaty, the Court had to consider not only the formal text of the treaty and of its surrender provisions, but also the history and oral traditions of the Chippewa and the surrounding circumstances at the time of the treaty.

It had been placed into evidence that the oral traditions of the Chippewa confirmed that their hunting and fishing rights had been recognized and preserved at the time the treaty was made. These oral traditions corresponded to some degree with notes of the negotiations leading to the treaty taken by officials of the Crown. Moreover, the Chippewa had continued to hunt and fish on the land subsequent to the signature of the treaty, and they had not been prevented from carrying out such activities.

In order to decide how treaties should be interpreted, the Ontario Court of Appeal placed great emphasis on the historical relationship between the Crown and Aboriginal nations and on the normative order resulting from this relationship. As Aboriginal nations have no choice but to treat exclusively with the Crown, when interpreting treaties, great emphasis must be placed on the nature of the transaction as understood by the Aboriginal party. Moreover, the Crown is to be held to a high standard in its treaty dealings. Justice MacKinnon stated these principles as follows:

> In approaching the terms of a treaty quite apart from the other considerations already noted, the honour of the Crown is always involved and no appearance of "sharp dealing" should be sanctioned. . . . Further, if there is any ambiguity in the words or phrases used, not only should the words be interpreted as against the framers or drafters of such treaties, but such language should not be interpreted or construed to the prejudice of the Indians if another construction is possible. . . . Finally, if there is evidence by conduct or otherwise as to how the parties understood the terms of the treaty, then such understanding and practice is of assistance in giving content to the term or terms.[38]

The interpretation of Aboriginal treaties must thus be carried out within the special context in which such instruments were made. Under the doctrine of Aboriginal rights, the Aboriginal nations are restricted to dealing with the Crown. The Aboriginal nations thus have no choice but to transact with the

Crown in regard to their Aboriginal rights. This renders the relationship fiduciary in nature and gives rise to fiduciary duties. The nature of the relationship requires that the terms of the treaties, as well as the terms of any other documents in which this special relationship is articulated, be interpreted liberally and generously in favour of the Aboriginal party. This principle was reiterated in forceful terms by the Justice Sopinka in *R.* v. *Badger:*[39]

> The key interpretative principles which apply to treaties are first, that any ambiguity in the treaty will be resolved in favour of the Indians and, second, that treaties should be interpreted in a manner that maintains the integrity of the Crown, particularly the Crown's fiduciary obligation toward aboriginal peoples. These principles apply equally to the rights protected by the [Natural Resources Transfer Agreement]; the principles arise out of the nature of the relationship between the Crown and aboriginal peoples with the result that, whatever the document in which that relationship has been articulated, the principles should apply to the interpretation of that document.[40]

R. v. *Marshall*[41] provides an example of the application of these rules of treaty interpretation. In that case, a Mi'kmaq from Nova Scotia had been charged with fishing without a licence and with a prohibited net during closed seasons. Mr. Marshall and a companion had fished for eels in Pomquet Harbour in Antigonish County, Nova Scotia. They had landed 463 pounds (210 kilograms) of eels, which were then sold for $787. Mr. Marshall had caught and sold the eels to support himself and his family. He raised in his defence various treaty rights to fish and to trade in fish.

Mr. Marshall first raised the rights set out in the 1752 peace and friendship treaty that had been successfully used as a defence in *Simon* v. *R.*[42] This treaty specifically guaranteed the "free liberty of Hunting and Fishing as usual." In *Simon,* the Supreme Court had left open the question of the termination of this treaty through the resumption of hostilities between the Mi'kmaq and the British. In the case against Mr. Marshall, substantial evidence was produced to show that hostilities had followed the 1752 treaty, and Mr. Marshall abandoned reliance on this treaty. The Supreme Court of Canada was thus not called upon to consider the 1752 treaty.

Mr. Marshall then turned to a treaty of peace and friendship that had been concluded in 1760. Its provisions included the following statement: "And I do further engage that we will not traffick, barter or Exchange any Commodities in any manner but with such persons or the managers of such Truck houses as shall be appointed or Established by His Majesty's Governor at Lunenbourg or Elsewhere in Nova Scotia or Accadia."[43] Justice Binnie, speaking for the majority of the Court and referring extensively to the historical context in which the treaty was made, found this provision to include a treaty right to trade in fish. Moreover, although not specified by the terms of the treaty, this right to trade was found to include an implicit right to fish. Referring back to *Sioui,* Justice Binnie found that the courts must recognize the necessity of supplying the deficiencies of Aboriginal treaties when the circumstances warrant:

> The law has long recognized that parties make assumptions when they enter into agreements about certain things that give their arrangements efficacy. Courts will imply a contractual term on the basis of presumed intentions of the parties where it is necessary to assure the efficacy of the contract, e.g., where it meets the "officious bystander test": *M.J.B. Enterprises Ltd. v. Defence Construction (1951) Ltd.,* [1999] 1 S.C.R. 619, at para. 30. (See also: *The "Moorcock"* (1889), 14 P.D. 64; *Canadian Pacific Hotels Ltd. v. Bank of Montreal,* [1987] 1 S.C.R. 711; and see generally: Waddams, [S.M., *The Law of Contracts,* 3rd ed. Toronto: Canada Law Book, 1993,] at para. 490; Treitel, [G.H., *The Law of Contract,* 9th ed. London: Sweet and Maxwell, 1995,] at pp. 190-194.) Here, if the ubiquitous officious bystander had said, "This talk about truckhouses is all very well, but if the Mi'kmaq are to make these promises, will they have the right to hunt and fish to catch something to trade at the truckhouses?," the answer would have to be, having regard to the honour of the Crown, "of course." If the law is prepared to supply the deficiencies of written contracts prepared by sophisticated parties and their legal advisors in order to produce a sensible result that accords with the intent of both parties, though unexpressed, the law cannot ask less of the honour and dignity of the Crown in its dealings with First Nations. The honour of the Crown was, in fact, specifically invoked by courts in the early 17th century to ensure that a Crown grant was effective to accomplish its intended purpose: *The Case of the Churchwardens of St. Saviour in Southwark* (1613), 10 Co. Rep. 66b, 77 E.R. 1025, at p. 67b and p. 1026, and *Roger Earl of Rutland's Case* (1608), 8 Co. Rep. 55a, 77 E.R. 555, at p. 56b and pp. 557-58.[44]

Justice Binnie found that neither the terms of the treaty nor the circumstances in which the treaty was made supported contentions of exclusivity, and that therefore these treaty rights to fish and to trade in fish did not preclude others from fishing and trading in fish. However, even if these rights were enjoyed with others, the fact that they were incorporated in a treaty offered the Mi'kmaq a degree of protection in the exercise of those rights that was not enjoyed by others fishing and trading in fish in Nova Scotia. Indeed, as treaty rights, the right to fish and to trade in fish, even if enjoyed with others, offered special protections through, among other instruments, the operation of section 91(24) of the *Constitution Act, 1867;* section 88 of the *Indian Act;* and section 35 of the *Constitution Act, 1982.*

Justice Binnie found, however, that these treaty rights had their own internal limitations, which were reflected in the records of discussions contemporary with the treaty. The rights were limited to what was needed in order to supply the Mi'kmaq with "necessaries," which, in a modern perspective, can be viewed as what is required to sustain a moderate livelihood:

> The recorded note of February 11, 1760 was that "there might be a Truckhouse established, for the furnishing them with *necessaries*" (emphasis added). What is contemplated therefore is not a right to trade generally for economic gain, but rather a right to trade for necessaries. The treaty right is a regulated right and can be contained by regulation within its proper limits.
>
> The concept of "necessaries" is today equivalent to the concept of what Lambert J.A., in *R. v. Van der Peet* (1993), 80 B.C.L.R. (2d) 75, at p. 126, described as a "moderate livelihood." Bare subsistence has thankfully receded over the last couple of centuries as an appropriate standard of life for aboriginals and non-aboriginals alike. A moderate livelihood includes such basics as "food, clothing and housing, supplemented by a few amenities," but not the accumulation of wealth (*Gladstone,* [[1996] 2 S.C.R. 723,] at para. 165). It addresses day-to-day needs. This was the common intention in 1760. It is fair that it be given this interpretation today.[45]

Justice Binnie thus found that the imposition of a closed season, of a discretionary licensing system, and of a ban on sales of fish infringed upon Mr. Marshall's treaty right to trade fish for sustenance purposes. In the absence of justification for these regulatory prohibitions, Mr. Marshall was entitled to an acquittal.

In her dissenting opinion, Justice (now Chief Justice) McLachlin took a different view. She started by setting out some basic principles of Aboriginal treaty interpretation as developed over the years in the case law.[46] She then pointed out that the *Marshall* proceedings raised two major issues concerning Aboriginal treaty interpretation.

First was the question whether it was proper to divide treaties into different categories for the purpose of applying rules of interpretation. Specifically, would the rules of interpretation be more restrictive for peace and friendship treaties than they would be for treaties in which Aboriginal title is surrendered? This issue was raised in *Marshall* since the Court of Appeal for Nova Scotia in that case had suggested that peace treaties were in a different category from land cession treaties for purposes of interpretation. Specifically, the Court of Appeal had found that there was no presumption that rights were granted to Aboriginal Peoples when entering a peace treaty. Justice McLachlin found that Aboriginal treaties should not be divided into separate categories for purposes of interpretation. Her conclusion is consistent with the premise that the rules for interpreting Aboriginal treaties flow from the nature of the relationship between the Crown and Aboriginal nations as set out under the doctrine of Aboriginal rights. Since it is the nature of the relationship that leads to the special interpretative principles, it follows that these principles should be the same for all Aboriginal treaties.

Second was the question of using extrinsic evidence in the interpretation of Aboriginal treaties. Here Justice McLachlin, confirming prior case law, stated clearly that extrinsic evidence of the historical and cultural context of a treaty may be received, and she added that such evidence may be received even in the absence of ambiguity in the terms of the treaty.[47]

Justice McLachlin then developed a two-step approach to Aboriginal treaty interpretation:

> The fact that both the words of the treaty and its historic and cultural context must be considered suggests that it may be useful to approach the interpretation of a treaty in two steps. First, the words of the treaty clause at issue should be examined to determine their facial meaning, in so far as this can be ascertained, noting any patent ambiguities and misunderstandings that may have arisen from linguistic and cultural differences. This exercise will lead to one or more possible interpretations of the clause. As noted in *Badger*, [[1996] 1 S.C.R. 771,] at para. 76, "the scope of treaty rights will be determined by their wording." The objective at this stage is to develop a preliminary, but not necessarily determinative, framework for the historical context inquiry, taking into account the need to avoid an unduly restrictive interpretation and the need to give effect to the principles of interpretation.
>
> At the second step, the meaning or different meanings which have arisen from the wording of the treaty right must be considered against the treaty's historical and cultural backdrop. A consideration of the historical background may suggest latent ambiguities or alternative interpretations not detected at first reading. Faced with a possible range of interpretations, courts must rely on the historical context to determine which comes closest to reflecting the parties' common intention. This determination requires choosing "from among the various possible interpretations of the common intention the one which best reconciles" the parties' interests: *Sioui*, [[1990] 1 S.C.R. 1025,] at p. 1069. Finally, if the court identifies a particular right which was intended to pass from generation to generation, the historical context may assist the court in determining the modern counterpart of that right: *Simon*, [[1985] 2 S.C.R. 387,] at pp. 402-403; *Sundown*, [[1999] 1 S.C.R. 393,] at paras. 30 and 33.[48]

Using this two-step approach, Justice McLachlin concluded that neither the wording nor the historical and cultural backdrop of the 1760 treaty relied upon by Mr. Marshall supported a general treaty right to trade. Rather, she found that the treaty sought to restrict Mi'kmaq trade to certain British trading posts. If any right could be said to have been conferred to the Mi'kmaq, it was a limited right to bring trade goods to these trade houses. She further found that by the 1780s, the trade restrictions on the Mi'kmaq had fallen, and with them the trading regime established under the treaty. She thus deeply diverged from Justice Binnie on the nature and scope of the treaty rights at hand:

> The treaty reference to the right to bring goods to truckhouses was required by and incidental to the obligation of the Mi'kmaq to trade with the British, and cannot be stretched to embrace a general treaty right to trade surviving the exclusive trade and truckhouse regime. To do so is to transform a specific right agreed to by both parties into an unintended right of broad and undefined scope.[49]

The essential differences between the reasons of Justice Binnie and of Justice McLachlin in *Marshall* rest on the extent to which the honour of the Crown requires the courts to give contemporary meaning to treaty undertakings. For Justice Binnie, the honour of the Crown requires that the courts avoid making "an empty shell of a treaty promise."[50] For Justice McLachlin, treaty rights cannot be stretched beyond the terms commonly understood by the parties at the time the treaty was made. Both apply the same basic rules of Aboriginal treaty interpretation. They reach divergent conclusions because they perceive quite differently the means by which the honour of the Crown is to be preserved in the specific circumstances of the case.

We can conclude this review of the case law in regard to Aboriginal treaty interpretation by restating some of the applicable principles.

1. An Aboriginal treaty is an undertaking that is said to be sacred. It is an exchange of solemn promises between the Crown and an Aboriginal nation. These promises must be held in high regard by the courts.[51]
2. Treaties, and all other instruments witnessing the special relationship between the Crown and Aboriginal nations, must be interpreted in a manner that is consistent with preserving the honour of the Crown.[52]
3. The oral undertakings made at the time the treaty was concluded form part of the treaty. The oral traditions of the Aboriginal signatories are to be given weight in ascertaining these oral undertakings.[53]
4. Treaties should be liberally construed and ambiguities or doubtful expressions in the wording of a treaty are to be resolved in favour of the Aboriginal party.[54]
5. The historical and cultural contexts in which the treaty was concluded

are important in ascertaining the meaning of the undertakings found in the treaty. In this regard, extrinsic evidence may be received, whether or not the terms of the treaty are ambiguous.[55]

6. In interpreting an Aboriginal treaty, the court is to choose from among the various possible interpretations of common intent the one that best reconciles the interests of both parties. The natural sense of the wording of an Aboriginal treaty as realistically held by the parties at the time it was entered into must be considered.[56] In this regard, the implied terms of the treaty should be given weight.[57]

7. A static approach to treaty rights is to be avoided. These rights may be exercised in accordance with contemporary usages.[58]

8. Restrictions to and extinguishments of the rights of Aboriginal Peoples under a treaty must be narrowly construed.[59]

9. The onus of proving that a treaty or a treaty right has been restricted or extinguished is on the party relying on such restriction or extinguishment. There must be strict proof of the fact of restriction or extinguishment, as well as evidence of a clear and plain intent to carry out such restriction or extinguishment.[60]

10. The principles related to the interpretation of treaties are to be applied to all treaties alike, and categorizations of treaties for this purpose are to be avoided.[61]

The Effect of Treaties

Treaties are entered into by the Crown as instruments of the royal prerogative. An Aboriginal treaty does not normally require parliamentary legislation in order to come into effect, unless the provisions of the treaty so provide. Treaties bind the Crown, and if the Crown does not execute the promises it made in the treaty, redress can be sought against the Crown irrespective of any parliamentary approval. Treaties thus "create enforceable obligations based on the mutual consent of the parties."[62]

The case of *Dreaver* v. *R.*[63] serves as an example. Under a treaty of 1876, the Plains and Woods Cree surrendered their Aboriginal title in exchange for various undertakings, including reserve lands and a "medicine chest." The Mistawasis Band was a beneficiary of this treaty. At various subsequent dates, the Mistawasis Band surrendered substantial portions of its treaty reserve lands to the Government of Canada in exchange for money. Under the terms of the surrender documents, part of the money could be used to provide certain services to band members. The government officials used the money for a number of different purposes, including the acquisition of medical supplies. The chief of the band sued for recovery of the money, which the chief claimed had been used contrary to the terms of the surrender documents and of the treaty. In particular, the chief claimed that using money generated from the surrender of reserve lands to acquire medical supplies violated the "medicine chest" provision of the treaty.

The Exchequer Court found that the "medicine chest" provision of the treaty entitled the beneficiaries of the treaty to be provided with all the medicines, drugs, or medical supplies they might need entirely free of charge. The use of band money resulting from the surrender transactions to acquire medical supplies was thus found to be in violation of the treaty provision. The chief's claim was upheld, and the Crown was ordered to pay into the funds of the Mistawasis Band the amounts it had used from the surrender money to acquire medical supplies.[64] The treaty was thus enforced even though it had not received any parliamentary approval.

However, because treaties are prerogative instruments, prior to the *Constitution Act, 1982,* they could not displace federal legislation without the consent of Parliament, nor were their terms protected against subsequent adverse legislation by Parliament.[65] This principle was forcefully expressed in *Sikyea* v. *R.*[66] Mr. Sikyea, a member of a band party to Treaty 11, was convicted of killing a duck near Yellowknife contrary to regulations adopted under the *Migratory Birds Convention Act.*[67] Under the terms of Treaty 11, the Crown had agreed to preserve to those Aboriginal Peoples subject to the treaty "their usual vocations of hunting, trapping, and fishing." However, the *Migratory Birds Convention* entered into by Great Britain (acting for Canada) and the United States in 1916 had established closed seasons on the hunting of migratory birds. In 1917, under the *Migratory Birds Convention Act,*[68] Parliament sanctioned and ratified the convention and granted to the governor-in-council various regulatory powers to implement its terms. The regulations adopted pursuant to this act were found to take away the rights to hunt migratory birds that had been incorporated in Treaty 11 and other Aboriginal treaties.

The Northwest Territories Court of Appeal, later confirmed by the Supreme Court of Canada, found that the regulatory scheme adopted under the *Migratory Birds Convention Act* prevailed over the rights set out under the Aboriginal treaties:

> It is always to be kept in mind that the Indians surrendered their rights in the territory in exchange for these promises. This "promise and agreement," like any other, can, of course, be breached, and there is no law of which I am aware that would prevent Parliament by legislation, properly within s. 91 of the *B.N.A. Act* from doing so.[69]

As of 1982, this reasoning is no longer valid. The *Constitution Act, 1982* substantially curtailed the powers of Parliament to interfere with the terms of an Aboriginal treaty. Under the provisions of section 35, treaty rights are now constitutionally affirmed and recognized. As we shall further discuss in chapter five, legislative schemes affecting treaty rights are now subject to review by the courts, and infringements of such rights must now be strictly justified.[70]

In regard to provincial legislation that would affect treaty rights, the protection of section 35 of the *Constitution Act, 1982* also applies. In addition, the framework of the constitutional division of powers ensures that treaty rights normally fall under the core concept of "Indianness" and are protected from adverse provincial legislation under section 91(24) of the *Constitution Act, 1867*. Moreover, Parliament has adopted general legislation that protects treaty rights from adverse provincial legislation under the terms of section 88 of the *Indian Act*. This section renders provincial laws of general application applicable to "Indians" subject to the terms of Aboriginal treaties. These issues will be further reviewed in chapter four.

Conclusion

Treaty rights flow from the agreements between the Crown and Aboriginal Peoples. Like Aboriginal rights, treaty rights are *sui generis*. Though treaty rights often serve to provide superadded protection to underlying Aboriginal rights, they are not limited in scope and can extend to political, social, and economic rights and to any other rights the parties to the treaty deem appropriate. Treaties can thus create new rights unknown or unrecognized at common law, and they may extinguish or regulate underlying Aboriginal rights.

Treaties represent an exchange of solemn promises between the Crown and Aboriginal Peoples. These promises are deemed sacred, and they place upon the Crown a high responsibility to ensure that they are fulfilled.

Treaties are governed by special rules and constitute a unique type of agreement. They attract special principles of interpretation.

Treaties bind the Crown and the fulfilment of the Crown's undertakings therein may be sought irrespective of any parliamentary approval. However, prior to 1982 treaties could not displace federal legislation without the consent of Parliament, nor were their terms protected against adverse legislation from Parliament. Treaties were, however, shielded from adverse provincial legislation under, among other instruments, section 91(24) of the *Constitution Act, 1867* and under the terms of section 88 of the *Indian Act*. Since 1982, treaty rights are, moreover, affirmed and recognized pursuant to section 35 of the *Constitution Act, 1982*.

Chapter 3

The Fiduciary Relationship Between Aboriginal Peoples and the Crown

Introduction

Contact between Europeans and Aboriginal Peoples resulted in the doctrine of Aboriginal rights. This doctrine limits, to a certain extent, the sovereignty of Aboriginal nations, putting them, in certain circumstances, at the mercy of the discretion of the Crown. It is these limits to Aboriginal sovereignty and the resulting discretions afforded to the Crown that lead to the characterization of the relationship between the Crown and Aboriginal Peoples as fiduciary in nature. This fiduciary relationship must be taken into account by the courts in most circumstances where the rights or interests of Aboriginal Peoples are affected, including circumstances where Aboriginal or treaty rights are at issue.

The fiduciary nature of the relationship also triggers fiduciary duties and obligations when the Crown exercises its discretion in dealing with Aboriginal Peoples, such as when it seeks the surrender of lands or when it concludes a treaty. The Crown is under no obligation to seek the surrender of title or to enter into treaty or to otherwise transact with Aboriginal nations; however, when it seeks to do so, it leaves the Aboriginal nations little choice but to transact with it. The political, economic, and military might of the Crown is such as to have historically provided it with a disproportionately large advantage in its dealings with Aboriginal nations.

The fiduciary relationship implies political obligations and duties for government in its dealings with Aboriginal Peoples; however, the fiduciary relationship is not limited to the political arena. It also finds judicial expression and recognition as the courts are bound to consider and take into account this relationship when reviewing government actions affecting Aboriginal Peoples. The Supreme Court of Canada has recognized that a *sui generis* fiduciary

relationship binds the Crown and Aboriginal Peoples and colours all government actions relating to Aboriginal matters.[1] This relationship colours the
interpretation of legislation, treaties, and other documents relating to Aboriginal
Peoples.[2] This relationship also finds expression in section 35 of the
Constitution Act, 1982 and must be taken into account by the courts when
applying this constitutional provision. As the Supreme Court of Canada stated
in *R. v. Sparrow:*

> In our opinion, *Guerin,* [[1984] 2 S.C.R. 335,] together with *R. v. Taylor and
> Williams* (1981), 34 O.R. (2d) 360, ground a general guiding principle for s.
> 35(1). That is, the Government has the responsibility to act in a fiduciary
> capacity with respect to aboriginal peoples. The relationship between the
> Government and aboriginals is trust-like, rather than adversarial, and
> contemporary recognition and affirmation of aboriginal rights must be defined
> in light of this historic relationship.[3]

Judicially Enforceable Duties and Obligations

In addition to serving as a guiding principle for courts reviewing legal issues
involving Aboriginal Peoples, the fiduciary relationship can also lead to
judicially enforceable fiduciary duties on the Crown, particularly when the
Crown assumes or exercises a discretionary power over the rights or interests
of Aboriginal Peoples. Professor Slattery broadly outlined this judicially
enforceable fiduciary duty in his seminal 1987 article "Understanding
Aboriginal Rights," in which he stated: "The Crown has a general fiduciary
duty towards native people to protect them in the enjoyment of their aboriginal
rights and in particular in the possession and use of their lands."[4]

For example, in *Guerin v. The Queen,*[5] the Supreme Court of Canada
confirmed a lower court award of $10 million against Canada for mishandling
land transactions involving the lease of lands reserved to the Musqueam Indian
Band. In this case, the Supreme Court set aside the "political trust" theories
of the British courts discussed in *Kinlock v. Secretary of State for India in
Council*[6] and in *Tito v. Waddell (No. 2),*[7] and found instead that the Crown
was subject to a judicially enforceable fiduciary duty towards Aboriginal
Peoples in cases involving Aboriginal land transactions. The Court found the
origin of this judicially enforceable fiduciary duty in the historical relationship
between the Crown and Aboriginal Peoples, coupled with the nature of
Aboriginal title and, in particular, with the proposition that the Aboriginal
interest in land is inalienable except upon surrender to the Crown. Because of
the nature of Aboriginal title and of the surrender restrictions relating thereto,
these judicially enforceable fiduciary duties are always present in cases
involving the surrender or management of Aboriginal land; however, the

judicially enforceable fiduciary duties of the Crown are not limited to transactions involving Aboriginal land. They exist each time "where by statute, agreement, or perhaps by unilateral undertaking, one party has an obligation to act for the benefit of another, and that obligation carries with it a discretionary power."[8]

The courts have acted upon the fiduciary duties of the Crown in varied circumstances,[9] although the full range of circumstances in which such duties apply remains uncertain.[10] A judicially enforceable fiduciary duty does not arise in every facet of the relationship between the Crown and Aboriginal Peoples, nevertheless the fiduciary relationship is clearly the cornerstone of Aboriginal law. It is thus incontestable that the Crown-Aboriginal relationship is governed by fiduciary principles.

In *Blueberry River Indian Band* v. *Canada* (also known as *Apsassin*),[11] a treaty had been entered into in 1916 by which the band surrendered Aboriginal title in exchange for, among other considerations, reserve land in northeastern British Columbia. The band never resided permanently on this reserve, and in 1940, the band surrendered the reserve's mineral rights to the Crown so the Crown could lease them out. In 1945, the band surrendered the whole reserve for $70,000. The Crown used this money to acquire new reserve land for the band. The surrender of the original reserve was sought in order to facilitate the settlement of war veterans. Between 1948 and 1956, these veterans were allocated the surrendered reserve land through various sales transactions with the Crown. In 1976, an important oil find was made in the land, resulting in some $300 million of economic value for the veterans who had acquired it. In 1977, the Blueberry River Indian Band sued the Crown for various fiduciary breaches in the transactions under which it had previously surrendered the land.

The Supreme Court of Canada rejected the band's arguments related to breaches of pre-surrender fiduciary obligations of the Crown. The Court found that the scheme of the *Indian Act* imposed on the Crown a duty to prevent exploitive bargains in regard to reserve land surrender transactions, but that the circumstances of the case showed neither an exploitive bargain nor misinformation to the band by the Crown officials about the nature and consequences of the surrender.

The Court did find, however, that the terms of the surrender imposed on the Crown post-surrender fiduciary duties in regard to the manner in which it dealt with the surrendered land. As was noted by Justice Gonthier:

> The terms of the 1945 surrender transferred I.R. 172 to the Crown "in trust to sell or lease the same to such person or persons, and upon such terms as the Government of the Dominion of Canada may deem most conducive to our Welfare and that of our people." By taking on the obligations of a trustee in

relation to I.R. 172, the DIA [Department of Indian Affairs] was under a fiduciary duty to deal with the land in the best interests of the members of the Beaver Band. This duty extended to both the surface rights and the mineral rights.[12]

Justice Gonthier, speaking for the majority of the Court, was of the opinion that by failing to reserve the subsurface rights when selling the land to the veterans, the Crown had breached its fiduciary duty to the band. He noted that the mineral rights had been conveyed, even though it was the policy of the Department of Indian Affairs to avoid the transfer of such rights when surrendered reserve lands were sold. The case was thus remitted to the Federal Court Trial Division for an assessment of damages.

Although the *Blueberry River Indian Band* case turns largely on its own facts, Justice (now Chief Justice) McLachlin did outline the Crown's fiduciary duties prior to the surrender transaction. In her opinion, the scheme of the *Indian Act* did not prevent the band from making its own decisions about the surrender transaction. The act imposed on the Crown a duty to avoid exploitive bargains, but it did not impose on the Crown a duty to ensure the best surrender arrangement for the band. The courts will not interfere in a surrender transaction if it is not exploitive and if its terms are clearly and fairly explained to the concerned Aboriginal Peoples by the representatives of the Crown. When, however, the Crown assumes a discretion in the management of the surrendered lands, or when the terms of the surrender transaction are misrepresented by the Crown, or when the transaction is an exploitive bargain, the courts may intercede and hold the Crown to its fiduciary duties and obligations.

The extent of the Crown's fiduciary duties in avoiding exploitive bargains in reserve land transactions was further reviewed by the Federal Court of Appeal in *Semiahmoo Indian Band* v. *Canada*.[13] In 1889, the Crown had designated approximately some 382 acres (155 hectares) of land in British Columbia as reserve land for the use and benefit of the band. The reserve land was adjacent to the border between Canada and the United States. In 1951, the Crown sought and obtained from the band the surrender of a little more than 22 acres (9 hectares) to allow the Department of Public Works to expand customs facilities; however, no such expansion of the customs facilities was ever carried out. Over the years, the band requested the return of the surrendered land, but its requests were refused by government officials. The band finally sought judicial redress.

A unanimous Federal Court of Appeal found that, under the principles set out in *Blueberry River Indian Band,* the Crown owed the band a judicially enforceable fiduciary duty to avoid exploitive bargains in surrender transactions. The 1951 surrender was found to be exploitive because the band would not have surrendered the land in the normal course of events and felt powerless before the Crown in this transaction. Chief Justice Isaac stated the Crown's duty as follows:

> I should emphasize that the Crown's fiduciary obligation is to *withhold its own consent* to surrender where the transaction is exploitative. In order to fulfil this obligation, the Crown itself is obliged to scrutinize the proposed transaction to ensure that it is not an exploitative bargain. As a fiduciary, the Crown must be held to a strict standard of conduct. Even if the land at issue is required for a public purpose, the Crown cannot discharge its fiduciary obligation simply by convincing the Band to accept the surrender, and then using this consent to relieve itself of the responsibility to scrutinize the transaction. The Trial Judge's findings of fact, however, suggest that this is precisely what the respondent did. I note, for example, the first sentence of her reasons for judgment reads: "The issue in this case is whether the defendant breached its fiduciary duty to the plaintiffs *when it encouraged (required)* the surrender of part of the plaintiffs' reserve." (Emphasis added.) In failing to alleviate the Band's sense of powerlessness in the decision-making process, the respondent failed to protect, to the requisite degree, the interests of the Band.[14] [Emphasis in original]

The band had relied on Crown representations that the surrender was required for a public purpose in order to expand customs facilities. The land was obviously not needed for this public purpose. In these circumstances, the Court found that the Crown had a clear duty to protect the band by refusing to consent to an absolute surrender of reserve land for which there was no foreseeable public need. This pre-surrender fiduciary duty was also found to extend post-surrender, since the Crown was under a further fiduciary duty to restore the surrendered land to the band. Again referring to the *Blueberry River Indian Band*, the Chief Justice of the Federal Court explained the fiduciary duties of the Crown subsequent to the surrender:

> In *Apsassin* [the Blueberry River Indian Band case], the Crown's mistake in the original surrender was in failing to reserve the mineral rights for the benefit of the Indian band contrary to a long-standing government policy to do so. In my view, the Crown made a similar mistake in this case as to the quality or scope of the surrender that was required. The Crown obtained an absolute surrender from the Band when, having regard to the uncertainty of the public need for the land, a conditional or qualified surrender would have sufficed. In both cases, the result was that the original surrender did not impair as little as possible the interests of the affected Indian band. Therefore, I am of the view that in this case, as in *Apsassin,* the Crown was under a

post-surrender fiduciary duty to correct the error that it made in the original surrender for as long as it remained in control of the land.[15]

The Court ordered the return of the surrendered lands through a constructive trust to the benefit of the band. The Court also decided that the band could be provided with equitable damages for lost opportunities and for injurious affection to the remainder of its reserve lands consequential to the deprivation of the surrendered lands for such a long period of time. The issue of equitable compensation was referred to the Federal Court Trial Division.

Treaties and the Fiduciary Relationship

The fiduciary relationship of the Crown extends to treaties with Aboriginal Peoples. In interpreting and applying the terms of a treaty, the courts will always consider the underlying fiduciary relationship. Moreover, in most treaties, the Crown assumes certain obligations. In executing these obligations, the Crown will normally be held by the courts to the standards of execution required under a fiduciary relationship.

This is exemplified in the decision of the Supreme Court of the United States in the case of *Seminole Nation* v. *United States*.[16] In that decision, the Supreme Court of the United States reviewed a damage award from the U.S. Court of Claims in which the Seminole Nation had sued the United States for failing to make various treaty payments. It had been established that the Seminole tribal government was utterly corrupt during the years 1870 to 1874, yet the United States continued treaty payments to this tribal government, knowing that the money would be diverted from tribal uses. The Supreme Court decided that a judicially enforceable duty of care in the nature of a fiduciary duty was incumbent upon the government in discharging its treaty obligations, and it asked the Court of Claims to review the case based on a breach of the United States' fiduciary duty in discharging its treaty undertakings. For the Supreme Court, the conduct of government in discharging treaty undertakings must be judged "by the most exacting fiduciary standards."[17]

This is also the position held in Canada. In *Ontario (A.G.)* v. *Bear Island Foundation*,[18] the Supreme Court of Canada rejected the Aboriginal rights claims of the Teme-Augawa Anishnabay and the Temagami on the basis that the rights they claimed had been surrendered by arrangements under which their ancestors had adhered to the Robinson-Huron Treaty in exchange for treaty annuities and a reserve. It was, however, recognized in that case that the Crown had failed to discharge its undertakings as provided for under the terms of the treaty. The Supreme Court found that by failing to comply with the terms of the treaty, the Crown had breached its fiduciary duty towards the

Teme-Augawa Anishnabay and the Temagami.[19]

The concept of the Crown's fiduciary obligations in discharging treaty undertakings had been expressed in Canada as early as 1895, in the dissenting opinion of Justice Gwynne in *Ontario v. Dominion of Canada and Quebec: In Re Indian Claims:*

> [W]hat is contended for and must not be lost sight of, is that the British sovereigns, ever since the acquisition of Canada, have been pleased to adopt the rule or practice of entering into agreements with the Indian nations or tribes in their province of Canada, for the cession or surrender by them of what such sovereigns have been pleased to designate the Indian title, by instruments similar to these now under consideration to which they have been pleased to give the designation of "treaties" with the Indians in possession of and claiming title to the lands expressed to be surrendered by the instruments, and further that the terms and conditions expressed in those instruments as to be performed by or on behalf of the Crown, *have always been regarded as involving a trust graciously assumed by the Crown to the fulfilment of which with the Indians the faith and honour of the Crown is pledged,* and which trust has always been most faithfully fulfilled as a treaty obligation of the Crown.[20] [Emphasis added]

This very quote has been approved as a correct statement of the law by the majority decision in *R. v. Marshall.*[21]

The Fiduciary Relationship and the Provincial Crown

In addition, the fiduciary relationship and its attending fiduciary duties extend in certain circumstances to the provincial Crown, particularly when the provinces affect Aboriginal lands, rights, property, or interests, or assume discretionary powers over Aboriginal Peoples or their lands, rights, property, or interests. Clearly the courts have found this fiduciary relationship to extend to the provincial Crown when section 35 of the *Constitution Act, 1982* comes into play.[22]

Under the terms of the *Constitution Act, 1867,* the fiduciary relationship and its attending duties and obligations fall primarily on the federal Crown. This does not mean that the provincial Crown is exempt from this relationship and its attending duties and obligations. Rather, for the provincial Crown, the application of the fiduciary relationship will not automatically be assumed. The relationship will be deemed fiduciary when the province places itself within the traditional Crown-Aboriginal bond, such as when the provincial Crown assumes undertakings in a treaty or attempts to infringe on Aboriginal or treaty rights.

Thus, insofar as the provincial Crown assumes powers or responsibilities over Aboriginal Peoples or their interests within the traditional Crown-Aboriginal relationship, there appears to be no cogent reason why it would not also assume the duty and obligation to discharge these powers and responsibilities in accordance with fiduciary standards. In particular, should a provincial government assume obligations through treaty undertakings with Aboriginal Peoples,[23] it seems that in so doing, the provincial Crown assumes a superadded duty to discharge these treaty undertakings following fiduciary standards.[24]

These standards probably extend to all cases in which a provincial Crown has a discretionary power to affect the rights of Aboriginal Peoples.[25] Professor Slattery put it this way:

> The Crown's general fiduciary duty binds both the federal Crown and the various provincial Crowns within the limits of their respective jurisdictions. The federal Crown has primary responsibility toward native peoples under section 91(24) of the Constitution Act, 1867, and thus bears the main burden of the fiduciary trust. But insofar as provincial Crowns have the power to affect native peoples, they also share in the trust.[26]

Conclusion

The relationship between the Crown and Aboriginal Peoples is fiduciary in nature, and the fiduciary nature of the relationship colours all aspects of Aboriginal law. When the Crown exercises discretionary powers over Aboriginal Peoples or in the management of Aboriginal lands, rights, property, or interests, it assumes duties or obligations to discharge these powers in accordance with fiduciary standards that are subject to review and enforcement by the courts. In implementing treaty undertakings, the Crown will be held to the standards of a fiduciary. The courts will review Crown action in this regard in light of both the general fiduciary relationship and the specific duty to discharge treaty undertakings with due regard to the most exacting fiduciary standards.

Chapter 4

Federal Common Law
and Aboriginal and Treaty Rights

Introduction

The law pertaining to Aboriginal rights, to treaty rights, and to matters of Aboriginal law generally is governed by a corpus of rules that can be termed the federal common law of Aboriginal rights, otherwise known as the doctrine of Aboriginal rights. These rules are in large part *sui generis*. They include elements of international law and of imperial policy, as well as various rules and principles found in or derived from the common law relating to Aboriginal and treaty rights, Aboriginal treaties, the *Royal Proclamation, 1763,* the provisions of sections 91(24) and 109 of the *Constitution Act, 1867,* and the provisions of sections 25 and 35 of the *Constitution Act, 1982.* The main purpose of these *sui generis* rules is to govern the relationship resulting from contact between Aboriginal and European societies.

In Canada, the *sui generis* rules that govern this relationship, and that are incorporated within the doctrine of Aboriginal rights, belong to a branch of constitutional law that developed out of British imperial policy. Because of the geopolitical and historical importance of Aboriginal nations to imperial designs in North America, the policy issues relating to Aboriginal matters were closely guarded by the imperial authorities. British control of North America—including control through the Hudson's Bay Company[1]—depended to a large extent on ensuring the support of the Aboriginal nations as allies of the Crown or at least on ensuring their neutrality. The relationship between Aboriginal nations and the imperial Crown often involved issues of war and peace, and of jurisdiction and control over large territories. Consequently, Aboriginal policy—and by extension legal matters relating to Aboriginal Peoples—held a special position in the British imperial, political, legal, and constitutional system. Aboriginal rights form part of the unwritten principles underlying the Constitution of Canada,[2] and the protection of these rights reflects important underlying constitutional values.[3]

At Confederation, the imperial authority in relation to Aboriginal affairs was devolved to the Crown in right of Canada. Section 91(24) of the *Constitution Act, 1867* specifically assigns exclusively to Parliament all matters relating to "Indians, and Lands reserved for the Indians." The doctrine of Aboriginal rights was thus placed within the federal sphere of constitutional authority. As a result, Aboriginal law is now a branch of federal law. As the fundamental rules that govern the relationship between Aboriginal Peoples and mainstream Canadian society are within the federal sphere of constitutional authority, they cannot be substantially affected or modified by provincial legislation. When the *Constitution Act, 1982* came into force, many aspects of the doctrine of Aboriginal rights were given constitutional protection, and the *sui generis* rules that governed the relationship between the Crown and Aboriginal Peoples that had, in the past, been largely beyond the reach of the provincial legislatures, were now also largely beyond the reach of Parliament.

It is important not to confuse the doctrine of Aboriginal rights with the common law in a private-law sense or with the civil law of a province. The doctrine of Aboriginal rights is an autonomous branch of the law that operates within the federal sphere of constitutional authority and thus operates uniformly across Canada. It is also, to a large extent, a body of federal public law.

Federal Common Law

The leading case in regard to the doctrine of Aboriginal rights as part of the federal common law is the decision of the Supreme Court of Canada in *Roberts* v. *Canada*.[4] The case revolved around the jurisdiction of the Federal Court of Canada to adjudicate a trespass action brought by one *Indian Act* band against another. In *Roberts,* the Supreme Court found that federal common law formed part of the laws of Canada under the meaning of section 101 of the *Constitution Act, 1867*. The Court then went on to add that federal common law includes the common law of Aboriginal title, as well as the rules governing the fiduciary relationship between the federal Crown and Aboriginal Peoples. As a result, the common law rules relating to Aboriginal title and to the fiduciary relationship and duties of the federal Crown apply uniformly across Canada within the federal sphere of authority. As Professors Evans and Slattery commented when discussing this case:

> In this manner, the common law of aboriginal title—and indeed the common law governing aboriginal and treaty rights generally—became federal common law. To put the point precisely, it became a body of basic public law

operating uniformly across the country within the federal sphere of competence.[5]

The idea that the common law of Aboriginal title—and by extension the common law of Aboriginal and treaty rights generally—applies uniformly across Canada in the guise of federal common law was reiterated in the companion cases of *R. v. Côté*[6] and *R. v. Adams*.[7]

In *R. v. Adams*,[8] a Mohawk had been charged with fishing without a licence contrary to the federal regulatory scheme governing fishing within the province of Quebec. Mr. Adams was fishing for food in Lake St. Francis, a part of the St. Lawrence River, at a location some fifteen kilometres from the Mohawk community of Akwesasne. He challenged the charge by stating that he was exercising an Aboriginal right to fish recognized and affirmed by section 35(1) of the *Constitution Act, 1982*. The fundamental question to be answered in the case was whether a claim to an Aboriginal right must rest in a claim to Aboriginal title. The Supreme Court of Canada found that an Aboriginal right to fish could exist independently and irrespective of Aboriginal title. Thus, in the circumstances of this case, Mr. Adams could invoke his Aboriginal right to fish to challenge the charge, whether or not the Mohawk Nation held Aboriginal title to the area where Mr. Adams was fishing.

In *R. v. Côté*,[9] five members of the Desert River Band who were residents of the Maniwaki Reserve had entered a Controlled Harvest Zone in the Outaouais region of Quebec in order to teach traditional hunting and fishing practices. On entering the Controlled Harvest Zone, they refused to pay the motor-vehicle access fee levied under a provincial regulatory scheme. Then, Mr. Côté proceeded to fish without a licence to demonstrate traditional Algonquin fishing practices. All five were charged under the provincial regulatory scheme relating to the vehicle access fee, and Mr. Côté was further charged under the federal regulatory scheme governing fishing in the province of Quebec. They all defended the charges on the basis of their Aboriginal and treaty rights.

In *Côté*, the Supreme Court of Canada confirmed its findings in *Adams* that an Aboriginal right may exist independently of Aboriginal title. Since the Algonquins had established an Aboriginal right to fish, which included by implication the right to teach fishing practices, the Court proceeded to apply the infringement and justification tests it had developed under *Sparrow*.[10] These tests and their application in both *Adams* and *Côté* will be further reviewed in the next chapter.

Both *Adams* and *Côté* raised the issue of the recognition of Aboriginal land rights in the province of Quebec. The province argued that the French had never recognized Aboriginal title in New France and that British common law relating to Aboriginal title had not been received in Quebec. In rejecting these arguments, Chief Justice Lamer cast doubt on the contention that the French had failed to recognize Aboriginal land rights in their colonial empire in North America. Equally, if not more importantly, he found that section 35 of the *Constitution Act, 1982* ensured the affirmation and recognition of Aboriginal rights irrespective of the colonial legal regime in force prior to the assertion of sovereignty by the British Crown and irrespective of whether the common law of Aboriginal title had been received in a particular province or territory. He reiterated that the doctrine of Aboriginal rights is a component of federal common law and applies uniformly across Canada.

Chief Justice Lamer added that the doctrine of Aboriginal rights was a necessary incident of British sovereignty, which displaced any prevailing foreign colonial law on the subject. He reiterated the findings in *Roberts* v. *Canada*[11] that the doctrine of Aboriginal rights represented a distinct species of federal common law and was not a simple subset of the common, civil, or property law operating within a province. He added that the doctrine of Aboriginal rights was part of a body of fundamental constitutional law:

> The doctrine of aboriginal rights, like other doctrines of colonial law, applied automatically to a new colony when the colony was acquired. In the same way that colonial law determined whether a colony was deemed to be "settled" or "conquered," and whether English law was automatically introduced or local laws retained, it also supplied the presumptive legal structure governing the position of native peoples. The doctrine of aboriginal rights applied, then, to every British colony that now forms part of Canada, from Newfoundland to British Columbia. Although the doctrine was a species of unwritten British law, it was not part of English common law in the narrow sense, and its application to a colony did not depend on whether or not English common law was introduced there. Rather the doctrine was part of a body of fundamental constitutional law that was logically prior to the introduction of English common law and governed its application in the colony.
>
> Indeed, this Court has held that the law of aboriginal title represents a distinct species of federal common law rather than a simple subset of the common or civil law or property law operating within the province: *Roberts* v. *Canada*, [1989] 1 S.C.R. 322, at p. 340. See the views of the Royal Commission on Aboriginal Peoples on the status of aboriginal rights as federal common law in *Partners in Confederation: Aboriginal Peoples, Self-Government, and the Constitution* (1993), at p. 20.[12]

Constitutional Division of Powers

Chief Justice Lamer reviewed the implications of including the doctrine of Aboriginal rights within the federal sphere of constitutional authority in the case of *Delgamuukw* v. *B.C.* Though *Delgamuukw* deals in large part with Aboriginal title, as the Chief Justice himself notes,[13] the constitutional concepts discussed within the context of Aboriginal title extend to Aboriginal rights generally. The comments of the Supreme Court in this regard can be extended to treaty rights as well.[14]

A proper discussion of these constitutional considerations must begin with a brief analysis of section 109 of the *Constitution Act, 1867*. This provision states that the ownership of the land and natural resources located in a province at Confederation belongs to the Crown in right of that province. Provincial propriety interest under section 109 may, however, be burdened by Aboriginal title. Aboriginal title is an underlying burden on provincial lands and, by extension, on the natural resources of the provinces.

In *St. Catherine's Milling & Lumber Company* v. *The Queen*,[15] the Privy Council recognized that this burden fell under the notion of "Lands reserved for the Indians" under section 91(24) of the *Constitution Act, 1867*.[16] Consequently, the exclusive power to pass legislation concerning the Aboriginal title burdening these lands is vested with Parliament. The Privy Council decision confirms that the federal authorities have the exclusive power to receive a surrender of Aboriginal title. However, if this surrender concerns land that is subject to section 109 of the *Constitution Act, 1867,* then the beneficiary of the surrender of the Aboriginal title is the province, which sees the Aboriginal burden on its proprietary interest lifted.[17] The provinces are, however, powerless to lift the Aboriginal title or to otherwise deal with matters of Aboriginal title, even if this title affects land or natural resources contemplated by section 109 of the *Constitution Act, 1867.*

In *Delgamuukw* v. *B.C.,*[18] the Supreme Court of Canada considered the proposition that the province of British Columbia had extinguished Aboriginal title and other Aboriginal land rights through legislation adopted by the provincial legislature after British Columbia joined Canada. Chief Justice Lamer rejected this contention as constitutionally inaccurate, since only Parliament is constitutionally empowered to legislate in relation to Aboriginal title, and, prior to 1982, under the terms of the *Constitution Act, 1867,* only Parliament could validly extinguish Aboriginal title. In consequence, provincial legislation adopted pursuant to the terms of the *Constitution Act, 1867* could not extinguish Aboriginal title.[19]

In order to properly understand this proposition, a brief review of the case law pertaining to the application of provincial laws to "Indians" is in order.[20] The exclusive federal authority under section 91(24) of the *Constitution Act, 1867* contains two branches. One branch concerns "Indians," and much case law exists as regards its impact on provincial laws.[21] The other branch concerns the "Lands reserved for the Indians," and the case law regarding its impact on provincial laws is still in a state of flux.[22]

Section 91(24) clearly precludes the provinces from legislating directly in relation to "Indians."[23] What is less clear is the impact this branch of federal power has on provincial laws of *general* application. As a general constitutional principle, otherwise valid provincial laws that are general in their application and that do not single out "Indians" are deemed to apply to "Indians."[24] These provincial laws of general application are said to apply *ex proprio vigore* (on their own force) and thus do not require any enabling federal legislation to ensure their application in regard to "Indians." The example of provincial traffic regulations is usually given to illustrate this principle. When the province sets speed limits for travel on provincial roads, these limits apply to Aboriginal people, even though Parliament is entrusted with the exclusive power to legislate in regard to "Indians." Despite this principle, there are serious constitutional limits on the extent to which such provincial laws of general application actually apply to "Indians."

It has been held that section 91(24) of the *Constitution Act, 1867* protects a core of "Indianness" from provincial legislation of general application.[25] In consequence, provincial laws of general application cannot affect this core of "Indianness" *ex proprio vigore* and without the assistance of enabling federal legislation. The extent of this core remains largely undefined. However, as then Chief Justice Lamer stated in *Delgamuukw,* Aboriginal rights fall squarely within it:

> The core of Indianness at the heart of s. 91(24) has been defined in both negative and positive terms. Negatively, it has been held to not include labour relations (*Four B*) [[1980] 1 S.C.R. 1031] and the driving of motor vehicles (*Francis*) [[1988] 1 S.C.R. 1025]. The only positive formulation of Indianness was offered in *Dick* [[1985] 2 S.C.R. 309]. Speaking for the Court, Beetz J. assumed, but did not decide, that a provincial hunting law did not apply *proprio vigore* to the members of an Indian band to hunt and [fish] because those activities were "at the centre of what they do and what they are" (at p. 320). But in *Van der Peet* [[1996] 2 S.C.R. 507], I described and defined the aboriginal rights that are recognized and affirmed by s. 35(1) in a similar fashion, as protecting the occupation of land and the activities which are integral to the distinctive aboriginal culture of the group claiming the right. *It follows that aboriginal rights are part of the core of Indianness at the heart of s. 91(24).* Prior to 1982, as a result, they could not be extinguished by provincial laws of general application.[26] [Emphasis added]

According to the constitutional framework that separates the powers of provincial legislatures and Parliament, Aboriginal rights fall within the exclusive jurisdiction of Parliament. This means that these rights cannot be regulated detrimentally by the provinces alone through laws of general application. For example, the regulation of "Indian" hunting rights would normally fall under federal rather than provincial jurisdiction.[27]

These constitutional principles extend to the treaty rights of Aboriginal Peoples.[28] Only federal authorities can validly accept the surrender of Aboriginal title, and this surrender is often made through a treaty. As we have already stated, treaties are not limited to transactions in which Aboriginal title is surrendered. They cover a wide range of transactions involving Aboriginal interests. The crucial role treaties play in defining the relationship between Aboriginal Peoples and mainstream Canadian society militates strongly in favour of including treaty rights within the core of "Indianness" protected under section 91(24) of the *Constitution Act, 1867.*

The fact that Parliament has shielded treaty rights from provincial legislation under the terms of section 88 of the *Indian Act* strongly supports this view. This view is further reinforced by the inclusion of treaty rights within sections 25 and 35 of the *Constitution Act, 1982,* which demonstrates the central or core importance of treaties in the relationship between the Crown and Aboriginal Peoples. Aboriginal and treaty rights thus fall under the core of "Indianness" protected by section 91(24) of the *Constitution Act, 1867.* Therefore, they cannot be directly or incidentally regulated by the provinces acting on their own force alone (*ex proprio vigore*), nor can provincial laws of general application detrimentally affect them on their own force alone. Since 1982, they have also been protected from detrimental federal legislative and regulatory activities through the terms of the *Constitution Act, 1982.*

The second branch of federal jurisdiction under section 91(24) of the *Constitution Act, 1867,* namely that branch relating to the "Lands reserved for the Indians," involves similar constitutional considerations. Though the case law is much less developed, it can nevertheless be safely concluded that the constitutional rules governing the application of provincial laws to "Indians" also apply to the second branch of federal powers relating to "Lands reserved for the Indians."

In *Derrickson* v. *Derrickson,*[29] two members of the Westbank Indian Band were involved in divorce proceedings. The wife was requesting the division of family assets pursuant to the legislation of the province of British Columbia. The family assets included lands allotted to the spouses by the band for which they held certificates of possession issued pursuant to the *Indian Act.* The principal issue in this case was to determine whether the provincial legislation providing for the division of assets could extend to reserve lands. A unanimous Supreme Court of Canada had no difficulty finding that provincial legislation of general application could not regulate the right of possession of Indian reserve lands.[30] Thus, although provincial laws of general application may, under certain circumstances, apply to territories subject to Aboriginal title, these laws can neither regulate that title nor limit the enjoyment by the

"Indians" of the land subject to that title. In particular, provincial laws of general application cannot regulate the means and conditions under which Aboriginal title or Aboriginal treaty land rights may be surrendered or detrimentally affected,[31] nor may they—by implication—regulate the principles governing compensation in such circumstances.

It is important to note that although provincial laws of general application may not detrimentally affect or regulate Aboriginal and treaty rights when they are applied directly, provincial laws of general application may be made to regulate such rights when they are incorporated into federal law. This incorporation may be achieved through direct parliamentary legislation, through the terms of constitutional documents, or through the terms of treaties with Aboriginal Peoples. This application of provincial legislation through federal law is subject, of course, to certain legal and constitutional limits, including those limits set out in the *Constitution Act, 1982*. It is thus open for Parliament to adopt laws incorporating provincial legislation or rendering such provincial legislation applicable to "Indians" or to "Lands reserved for the Indians." In fact Parliament has, to a limited extent, rendered provincial laws of general application applicable to "Indians" through the operation of section 88 of the *Indian Act,* which reads as follows:

> 88. Subject to the terms of any treaty and any other Act of Parliament, all laws of general application from time to time in force in any province are applicable to and in respect of Indians in the province, except to the extent that those laws are inconsistent with this Act or any order, rule, regulation or by-law made thereunder, and except to the extent that those laws make provision for any matter for which provision is made by or under this Act.[32]

Section 88 confirms the primary federal jurisdiction over treaties. It also confirms that the terms of treaties with Aboriginal Peoples cannot normally be regulated or affected by provincial legislation, including provincial legislation of general application. Section 88 appears to confirm that provincial legislation cannot detrimentally affect treaty rights.[33] Moreover, section 88 also confirms the overriding power of Parliament to legislate in relation to Aboriginal affairs generally, including incorporating provincial legislation into federal law. By making provincial laws of general application subject to the terms of any act of Parliament, including the *Indian Act,* Parliament is simply affirming its overriding and exclusive jurisdiction to deal with Aboriginal and treaty rights.[34] This federal jurisdiction is now, however, fettered by section 35 of the *Constitution Act, 1982*.

Through section 88, provincial laws of general application are made to apply to the first branch of federal powers under section 91(24) of the *Constitution Act, 1867,* namely that branch relating to "Indians." Section 88 does not appear to extend provincial laws of general application to the second branch of federal powers relating to "Lands reserved for the Indians," though this question is not definitely settled. Thus, it is generally understood that provincial laws of general application may not normally regulate the Aboriginal interest in "Lands reserved for the Indians" under the meaning of section 91(24) of the *Constitution Act, 1867*.[35] However, the extent to which provincial legislation of general application may incidentally regulate Aboriginal lands remains somewhat unsettled.[36] Nevertheless, it can be safely stated that such provincial laws cannot affect the core Aboriginal interests in such lands. Furthermore, these provincial laws may be displaced by federal Aboriginal land legislation, such as those provisions found in the *Indian Act* relating to the regulation of "reserves" under the meaning of that act.

Section 88 contemplates only those provincial laws that would not otherwise be constitutionally applicable and that regulate or affect "Indians" indirectly or incidentally. The section does not allow the provinces to legislate directly in regard to "Indians"—and by extension in regard to Aboriginal rights—and its terms do not validate provincial laws that destroy or detrimentally affect the core of federal jurisdiction under section 91(24) of the *Constitution Act, 1867*. All section 88 does is to provide for the application to "Indians" of provincial laws of general application that would not otherwise be constitutionally applicable on their own force (*ex proprio vigore*) and that *incidentally affect* the core of "Indianness."[37] For example, provincial hunting laws of general application that incidentally affect Aboriginal hunting activities may be made to apply to Aboriginal Peoples through the operation of section 88 of the *Indian Act,* even though the hunting or fishing activities may be carried out pursuant to an Aboriginal right.[38] Section 88 thus makes provincial laws of general application applicable to "Indians" in certain circumstances and subject to certain legal and constitutional constraints.[39]

In the absence of section 88, provincial laws, including those of general application, could not operate—even incidentally—to infringe on or restrict Aboriginal rights. This results from the exclusive federal jurisdiction provided under section 91(24) of the *Constitution Act, 1867* and from the concept of the core of "Indianness" that section 91(24) is intended to encompass. This core includes Aboriginal rights. With section 88 of the *Indian Act,* it is thus possible for provincial legislation of general application referentially incorporated through that piece of federal legislation to incidentally affect this core of "Indianness." In so incidentally affecting Aboriginal rights, this federally incorporated provincial legislation is subject to certain constraints that flow from the doctrine of Aboriginal rights.[40] These constraints are the same as those that apply at common law and under the Constitution to any federal legislation affecting Aboriginal rights.[41]

Conclusion

Aboriginal and treaty rights are governed by a corpus of rules that are part of federal common law and that consequently apply uniformly across Canada. These common law rules fall within the exclusive jurisdiction of Parliament. They cannot be changed or detrimentally affected by provincial legislatures acting directly or through laws of general application.

This federal common law has a strong public law component and comprises *sui generis* rules that are exorbitant of and, to a large degree, unrelated to common law property principles and private-law rules.[42] The doctrine of Aboriginal rights that is embodied within this federal common law is itself part of a larger body of fundamental constitutional law.[43]

Chapter 5

Legal Principles
Governing the Infringement
of Aboriginal and Treaty Rights

Introduction

The nature of Aboriginal and treaty rights described in the first and second
chapters, the fiduciary relationship between Aboriginal Peoples and the Crown
described in the third chapter, and the *sui generis* rules of the applicable federal
common law described in the fourth chapter, all allow us to conclude that
significant remedies are available when Aboriginal or treaty rights are
infringed. These remedies are analogous to those available when a fiduciary
duty or obligation is breached. New remedies have been added through section
35 of the *Constitution Act, 1982.* These constitutional remedies were superadded to those remedies already available under the doctrine of Aboriginal
rights. This chapter considers the remedies available under both the doctrine
of Aboriginal rights and the Constitution.

Extinguishment of Aboriginal and Treaty Rights

Aboriginal rights are not absolute. Under the doctrine of Aboriginal rights,
such rights may be extinguished unilaterally by appropriate legislation in
extraordinary circumstances. In *Calder* v. *A.G. of British Columbia,* Justice
Hall clearly stated that common law Aboriginal title may be extinguished not
only by an appropriate surrender to the Crown, but also without the consent
of the concerned Aboriginal Peoples through specific legislation carried out
by the competent legislative authority.[1] The legislative intent to carry out such
extinguishment must, however, be clear and plain, and the onus of proving
either express or implicit extinguishment is on the Crown.[2]

Since 1867, the power to unilaterally extinguish common law Aboriginal rights, including Aboriginal title, has rested exclusively with Parliament. Chief Justice Lamer noted this in *Delgamuukw:*

> Since 1871, the exclusive power to legislate in relation to "Indians, and Lands reserved for the Indians" has been vested with the federal government by virtue of s. 91(24) of the *Constitution Act, 1867*. That head of jurisdiction, in my opinion, encompasses within it the exclusive power to extinguish aboriginal rights, including aboriginal title.[3]

For the period prior to 1867, it has been argued that the *Royal Proclamation, 1763* imposed constitutional limitations on Canadian legislatures and consequently that unilateral extinguishments of Aboriginal title could be carried out only through imperial action.[4] This issue is somewhat theoretical. Most cases concerning the unilateral extinguishment of Aboriginal rights prior to 1867 revolve around the required clear and plain intent by the local Canadian legislatures to carry out such a unilateral extinguishment.[5] Few decisions have examined the pre-Confederation limitations on extinguishment since it has rarely been found that a unilateral extinguishment has been carried out. Thus, there does not appear to be much, if any, pre-1867 "clear and plain" colonial legislation or imperial action purporting to unilaterally extinguish Aboriginal title or other Aboriginal rights in Canada. Moreover, there are very few pieces of federal legislation subsequent to 1867 that purport to achieve such an extinguishment without the consent of the concerned Aboriginal Peoples.[6]

When it comes to extinguishment, treaty rights are in much the same position as Aboriginal rights. Some distinctions are nevertheless in order. Prior to 1982, treaty rights could be infringed by the competent legislative authority if a clear and plain intent for this purpose was expressed.[7] However, it has been argued that, prior to 1982, treaty rights could not be unilaterally extinguished even though they could be substantially infringed.[8] Unlike Aboriginal rights, treaty rights arise from the clear commitments of the Crown. As these commitments are deemed to be sacred, it can be argued that, barring extraordinary action by the signatories (such as war) justifying the repudiation of the treaty, treaty rights could not be unilaterally extinguished prior to 1982. Moreover, treaties often involve large transfers of land and of jurisdictions; thus, many treaties have been seen as quasi-constitutional instruments.[9] In *R. v. Sioui,* Justice (subsequently Chief Justice) Lamer stated that the definition of a treaty "makes it impossible to avoid the conclusion that a treaty cannot be extinguished without the consent of the Indians concerned."[10] However, this approach seems to have been discarded in *Marshall*, where Justice Binnie clearly stated that until the enactment of the *Constitution Act, 1982,* "the treaty rights of aboriginal peoples could be overridden by competent legislation as easily as could the rights and liberties of other inhabitants."[11]

In summary, prior to 1982 Aboriginal rights could be unilaterally extinguished by the competent legislative authority through clear and plain legislation for this purpose. Since 1867, this legislative authority has been exclusively vested in Parliament.[12] However, very few laws purporting to unilaterally extinguish Aboriginal rights have been adopted. Treaty rights appear to be in a similar position to Aboriginal rights. Since 1982, the power to unilaterally extinguish Aboriginal or treaty rights has been severely curtailed by the terms of section 35 of the *Constitution Act, 1982*.[13]

Infringement of Aboriginal and Treaty Rights

The principal unilateral restrictions to Aboriginal and treaty rights are not to be found in purported extinguishments of these rights. Unilateral extinguishments of Aboriginal or treaty rights are rare. It is the right to unilaterally *regulate* and *infringe* on common law Aboriginal rights and on treaty rights that has had a substantial impact on these rights and not the rare cases of unilateral extinguishment.

Aboriginal and treaty rights can be regulated by the competent legislative authorities. As with extinguishment, since 1867, the constitutional authority to regulate these rights has belonged to Parliament under the terms of section 91(24) of the *Constitution Act, 1867*. In this regard, reference may be made to the discussion in the preceding chapter. Thus, Parliament may adopt legislation to regulate Aboriginal and treaty rights. Prior to 1982, such legislation was not normally subject to review and control by the courts.

Although the provinces are usually powerless to regulate Aboriginal and treaty rights directly, much provincial legislation of general application has been made to apply and indeed effectively regulates certain Aboriginal rights. As discussed in the previous chapter, this has been carried out, in large part, through section 88 of the *Indian Act*. In the case of treaty rights, the terms of the treaties themselves often render provincial legislation applicable for the purposes of regulating certain of the rights they contain, particularly as they pertain to hunting and fishing.

The power to regulate Aboriginal and treaty rights has important implications for our discussion of compensation in cases of infringements of such rights. Indeed, it is not obvious that compensation would be available in all cases where Aboriginal and treaty rights are regulated. Regulating the exercise of a common law right—including a property right—through otherwise constitutionally valid legislation does not necessarily entail an ensuing common law right to compensation.[14] If this were otherwise, governments would be constantly called upon to provide compensation to their constituents when adopting laws, since the very purpose of much legislation is to regulate the exercise of common law rights. For example, reasonable restrictions on the use of motor vehicles through traffic regulations do not normally entail a common law right to compensation for those affected. It is thus difficult to sustain the argument that a common law right to compensation exists each time an Aboriginal or treaty right is otherwise validly regulated.[15]

However, there are situations where the outright extinguishment of an Aboriginal or treaty right may not be achieved, but where the regulation negates or considerably restricts the exercise of the right. Such a situation exists where the right is not extinguished unequivocally but is affected to such an extent as to render the exercise of that right difficult or meaningless. There is, therefore, a distinction to be made at common law between the regulation of an Aboriginal and treaty right and the impairment or infringement of such a right. In the case of the regulation of an Aboriginal or treaty right that does not impair the right, compensation would not normally be available under the doctrine of Aboriginal rights. For example, regulations restricting the use of certain firearms, such as automatic weapons, in hunting activities for purposes of public safety would not normally impair an Aboriginal right to hunt. Though such regulations may affect an Aboriginal or treaty hunting right, they do not necessarily impair or infringe the exercise of such a right and thus do not necessarily lead to compensation under the doctrine of Aboriginal rights. Conversely, if lands used by Aboriginal Peoples are granted for agricultural purposes or if authorizations are granted to use such lands for incompatible activities, such as hydroelectric operations, this might lead to an impairment of the affected Aboriginal right to such a degree as to render the exercise of the right on the affected lands difficult or meaningless.[16] Thus, even if regulations do not fully extinguish Aboriginal or treaty rights, they may impair them to such a degree that compensation is justified.

In consequence, in certain circumstances, legislation may infringe on or impair an Aboriginal right or the exercise of that right. This may lead to compensation under the doctrine of Aboriginal rights.[17]

Infringement and Justification Tests

These common law principles have, to a large extent, been incorporated in section 35 of the *Constitution Act, 1982*. This section incorporates within its terms the doctrine of Aboriginal rights and, by extension, the basic common law rules relating to Aboriginal and treaty rights generally. Thus, the doctrine of Aboriginal rights is, in large part, encompassed within section 35, including the right to just and adequate compensation in cases of extinguishment or impairment of such rights. What section 35 has achieved is the constitutionalization of these rights and the underlying common law principles that sustain them.[18]

When Aboriginal or treaty rights are infringed, the courts may grant the common law remedies that flow from the recognition at common law of Aboriginal and treaty rights. With the coming into force of section 35 of the *Constitution Act, 1982,* they may also grant new constitutional remedies.[19] In particular, the courts may now set aside by judicial fiat federal and provincial legislative or regulatory schemes that infringe on an Aboriginal or treaty right and that cannot be constitutionally justified. This supervisory role of the courts over federal and provincial legislative and regulatory activities was not available at common law. As was stated in *R.* v. *Sparrow:*

> The constitutional recognition afforded by the provision [s. 35(1)] therefore gives a measure of control over government conduct and a strong check on legislative power. While it does not promise immunity from government regulation in a society that, in the twentieth century, is increasingly more complex, interdependent and sophisticated, and where exhaustible resources need protection and management, it does hold the Crown to a substantive promise. The government is required to bear the burden of justifying any legislation that has some negative effect on any aboriginal right protected under s. 35(1).[20]

The 1990 case of *R.* v. *Sparrow,*[21] was the first decision of the Supreme Court of Canada that determined the scope of section 35(1) of the *Constitution Act, 1982.* Mr. Sparrow, a member of the Musqueam Indian Band in British Columbia, had been charged under the federal *Fisheries Act* with the offence of fishing with a drift net longer than permitted by the Indian food-fishing licence issued to his band. Mr. Sparrow had fished in a portion of the Fraser River located some sixteen kilometres from his reserve. The drift net he used was substantially longer than what was allowed under the band's licence. Mr. Sparrow set up a defence based on an Aboriginal right to fish. He claimed that the net-length restriction in the band's licence was contrary to section 35(1) of the *Constitution Act, 1982.* The evidence showed that the Musqueam had lived in the area as an organized society long before the arrival of Europeans, and that the taking of salmon had always been and still was at the time of trial an integral part of their lives. The Supreme Court of Canada did not make a final determination in *Sparrow,* but ordered a re-trial to allow findings of fact in accordance with the tests it first set out in that case.

The Court's decision in *Sparrow* was unanimous, and the reasons were jointly drafted by then Chief Justice Dickson and Justice La Forest. First, the Court addressed the meaning of the word "existing" in section 35(1). It found that the rights to which that constitutional provision applied had to be in existence at the time the provision came into force. Those rights that had been extinguished under the doctrine of Aboriginal rights prior to the coming into force of the *Constitution Act, 1982* were not revived by section 35(1). The Court, however, rejected the contention that the specific manner in which Aboriginal rights were regulated at the time the *Constitution Act, 1982* came into force were incorporated within the term "existing." This meant the Crown could not claim that the manner in which it had regulated such rights in the past was incorporated in the terms of section 35(1). Rather, Aboriginal rights must be given a meaning consistent with the fundamental nature of the rights rather than with their prior regulation.

The Crown contended that any Aboriginal right to fish that the Musqueam might have had in the past had been extinguished through the prior regulation of fisheries in British Columbia. The Crown claimed that these regulations constituted a complete code that was inconsistent with the continued existence of an Aboriginal right to fish. The Court dismissed this argument by distinguishing between the extinguishment of a right and its regulation. Though the Aboriginal fisheries had been considerably regulated prior to the *Constitution Act, 1982,* such regulation could not have extinguished the Musqueam's Aboriginal right to fish unless a clear and plain intent to extinguish the right could be demonstrated. The Court found no such clear and plain intent in the *Fisheries Act:*

> There is nothing in the *Fisheries Act* or its detailed regulations that demonstrates a clear and plain intention to extinguish the Indian aboriginal right to fish. The fact that express provision permitting the Indians to fish for food may have applied to all Indians and that for an extended period permits were discretionary and issued on an individual rather than a communal basis in no way shows a clear intention to extinguish. These permits were simply a manner of controlling the fisheries, not defining underlying rights.[22]

The Court further found that Crown policy cannot determine the content or scope of an Aboriginal right. Aboriginal rights are to be defined on their own terms.

The *Sparrow* case raised issues about the commercial aspects of the Musqueam's right to fish; however, since the case had not been presented in the lower courts as concerning an Aboriginal right to fish for commercial purposes, the Supreme Court of Canada confined its reasons to the meaning of a constitutional recognition and affirmation of an Aboriginal right to fish for food and for social and ceremonial purposes. Furthermore, the precise manner in which an Aboriginal right was to be identified was left open; the Court finally addressed this matter a few years later in *R. v. Van der Peet*.[23]

The Court in *Sparrow* then reviewed the impact of section 35(1) of the *Constitution Act, 1982* on the regulatory powers of Parliament. The Supreme Court found that the provisions of this section incorporate the fiduciary relationship between Aboriginal Peoples and the Crown and therefore restrain the exercise of sovereign power. Section 35 imposes a strong check on legislation affecting Aboriginal rights by requiring that government action in regard to such rights be subject to judicial review and that any infringement of such rights be justified.[24] The scope of this judicial review was found to be very broad:

> By giving aboriginal rights constitutional status and priority, Parliament and the provinces have sanctioned challenges to social and economic policy objectives embodied in legislation to the extent that aboriginal rights are affected. Implicit in this constitutional scheme is the obligation of the legislature to satisfy the test of justification. The way in which a legislative objective is to be attained must uphold the honour of the Crown and must be in keeping with the unique contemporary relationship, grounded in history and policy, between the Crown and Canada's aboriginal peoples. The extent of legislative or regulatory impact on an existing aboriginal right may be scrutinized so as to ensure recognition and affirmation.[25]

In *Sparrow,* the Supreme Court of Canada set out a two-step process for reviewing infringements of Aboriginal rights. First, there is a test to establish a *prima facie*[26] infringement of a right recognized and affirmed under section 35. Second, there is a test for the justification of such an infringement. The Court later found, in *R. v. Badger,* that the *Sparrow* tests applied to infringements of treaty rights as well.[27]

The first question to be asked in cases involving infringements of Aboriginal and treaty rights is whether the legislation interferes with a right contemplated by section 35 of the *Constitution Act, 1982.* If it does, it represents a *prima facie* infringement of section 35. The inquiry begins by examining the characteristics or incidents of the right at stake.[28] Speaking for a unanimous Supreme Court, Chief Justice Dickson and Justice La Forest stated:

> To determine whether the fishing rights have been interfered with such as to constitute a *prima facie* infringement of s. 35(1), certain questions must be asked. First, is the limitation unreasonable? Second, does the regulation impose undue hardship? Third, does the regulation deny to the holders of the right their preferred means of exercising that right? The onus of proving a *prima facie* infringement lies on the individual or group challenging the legislation.[29]

The *Sparrow* test for infringement was further reviewed in *R. v. Gladstone,* where the Court noted that the original formulation of the infringement test suggested an internal inconsistency, as it equated an analysis of *prima facie* infringement with an analysis of whether the infringement was unreasonable or undue.[30] The Court further explained the test by specifying, first, that the three factors identified in *Sparrow* are not exhaustive and other factors can be taken into account; and second, that there is no need to answer all three *Sparrow* factors in order to conclude a *prima facie* infringement.[31] Thus, the test to determine whether an infringement has occurred should not be too onerous on those claiming infringement.

The Supreme Court of Canada also subsequently found that infringements of Aboriginal or treaty rights are to be presumed in cases where statutory or regulatory instruments confer an administrative discretion that might be exercised in a manner that encroaches on a right recognized and affirmed under section 35 of the *Constitution Act, 1982*. This approach is significantly different from the approach taken by the Supreme Court in regards to *Charter* rights. As stated by Chief Justice Lamer in *R. v. Adams:*

> In a normal setting under the *Canadian Charter of Rights and Freedoms,* where a statute confers a broad, unstructured administrative discretion which may be exercised in a manner which encroaches upon a constitutional right, the court should not find that the delegated discretion infringes the *Charter* and then proceed to a consideration of the potential justifications of the infringement under s. 1. Rather, the proper judicial course is to find that the discretion *must* subsequently be exercised in a manner which accommodates the guarantees of the *Charter.* . . .
>
> I am of the view that the same approach should not be adopted in identifying infringements under s. 35(1) of the *Constitution Act, 1982*. In light of the Crown's unique fiduciary obligations towards aboriginal peoples, Parliament may not simply adopt an unstructured discretionary administrative regime which risks infringing aboriginal rights in a substantial number of applications in the absence of some explicit guidance. If a statute confers an administrative discretion which may carry significant consequences for the exercise of an aboriginal right, the statute or its delegate regulations must outline specific criteria for the granting or refusal of that discretion which seek to accommodate the existence of aboriginal rights. In the absence of such specific guidance, the statute will fail to provide representatives of the Crown with sufficient directives to fulfil their fiduciary duties, and the statute will be found to represent an infringement of aboriginal rights under the *Sparrow* test.[32] [Emphasis in original]

The second step set out in *Sparrow* comes into play when a *prima facie* interference to an Aboriginal or treaty right has been found. The analysis then moves to the issue of justification. This second step addresses the question of what constitutes a legitimate regulation of an Aboriginal or treaty right. The concept of reasonableness forms an integral part of the test for justification and colours all the aspects of the test.[33] In addition, the onus of proving the justification of an infringement is on the government.[34]

The first stage of the justification test is to find a valid and compelling legislative objective. This objective must be something more than the public interest, since such an objective is so vague as to provide no meaningful guidance. The courts must be satisfied that the legislative objective is compelling and substantial.[35] Legislative objectives that are compelling and substantial can be very broad. For example, in the context of an Aboriginal right to fish for subsistence, conservation and resource management answer the test.[36] Within the context of commercial fisheries, additional objectives such as the pursuit of economic and regional fairness and the recognition of historical reliance on and participation in the fishery by other groups may also constitute compelling and substantial objectives.[37] Within the context of Aboriginal title, objectives such as the "development of agriculture, forestry, mining, and hydroelectric power, the general economic development of the interior of British Columbia, protection of the environment or endangered species, the building of infrastructure and the settlement of foreign populations to support those aims" are all, in principle, sufficiently compelling and substantial to justify the infringement of such title.[38] If a valid legislative objective is found, the analysis proceeds to the second stage of the justification test. Courts determining whether a legislative or regulatory scheme is a legitimate interference with a right contemplated by section 35 of the *Constitution Act, 1982* must take into account the special fiduciary relationship between governments and Aboriginal Peoples. In essence, the courts must ensure not only that the legislative objective is compelling and substantial, but also that the government has fully discharged its fiduciary responsibilities and that the affected Aboriginal Peoples have been treated fairly and in a manner consistent with the preservation of the honour of the Crown.

The standards of the justification test are set very high. This is to ensure that Aboriginal and treaty rights are taken seriously.[39] The courts cannot supply their own justifications; it is up to those who claim that the infringement is justified to demonstrate that the standards set out in the justification test have been met.[40] In *Sparrow,* the Supreme Court of Canada found that the constitutional nature of the Musqueam food-fishing right, coupled with the fiduciary nature of the Crown's duties towards Aboriginal Peoples, mandated that, after conservation measures for the fisheries had been implemented, top priority must be given to the Aboriginal right to fish for food.[41]

The Supreme Court of Canada refined the justification test in *R. v. Gladstone.*[42] In that case, two members of the Heiltsuk Band, Donald and William Gladstone, had been charged with offering to sell and attempting to sell herring spawn on kelp contrary to the federal regulatory scheme relating to fisheries in British Columbia. They had transported some 4,200 pounds (1,900 kilograms) of herring spawn to a suburb of Vancouver and had tried, unsuccessfully, to sell the herring spawn to the representative of a fish store. A defence based on section 35(1) was raised.

Using the test set out in *R. v. Van der Peet*,[43] the majority of the Court found that, prior to contact with Europeans, the Heiltsuk had pursued the exchange of herring spawn on kelp on a scale characterized as commercial, and that this activity was an integral part of their distinctive culture. The majority of the Court further found that this commercial Aboriginal right had not been extinguished through adverse regulatory schemes relating to fisheries, since a plain and clear intent to proceed to such an extinguishment had not been established.[44]

Having established that an Aboriginal right of a commercial nature existed in *Gladstone,* the Supreme Court had to decide how to apply the infringement and justification tests set out in *Sparrow*. In regard to infringement, the simple fact that the regulatory scheme limited the amount of herring spawn on kelp that could be harvested by the Heiltsuk was found sufficient to constitute an infringement of the Aboriginal right. In regard to justification, the majority of the Court made substantial adaptations to the *Sparrow* test to take into account the commercial nature of the Aboriginal right at hand. A distinction was found between those Aboriginal rights that are internally limited—such as an Aboriginal right to fish for food, which is limited by the fact that those exercising it cannot fish in excess of what is required to feed themselves—and those Aboriginal rights that are not internally limited—such as the commercial fishing right set out in *Gladstone*. As was stated by Chief Justice Lamer in the majority opinion:

> Where the aboriginal right is one that has no internal limitation then the doctrine of priority does not require that, after conservation goals have been met, the government allocate the fishery so that those holding an aboriginal right to exploit that fishery on a commercial basis are given an exclusive right to do so. Instead, the doctrine of priority requires that the government demonstrate that, in allocating the resource, it has taken account of the existence of aboriginal rights and allocated the resource in a manner respectful of the fact that those rights have priority over the exploitation of the fishery by other users. This right is at once both procedural and substantive; at the stage of justification the government must demonstrate both that the process by which it allocated the resource and the actual allocation of the resource which results from that process reflect the prior interest of aboriginal rights holders in the fishery.[45]

Chief Justice Lamer added that with regards to the distribution of the fisheries resource, after conservation preoccupations have been satisfied, objectives such as the pursuit of economic and regional fairness, and the recognition of the historical reliance upon and participation in the fishery by non-Aboriginal groups can satisfy the justification test. The justification test, in the context of Aboriginal rights that are not internally limited, must thus be seen as an exercise in the reconciliation of Aboriginal societies with the rest of Canadian society. In the specific circumstances of *Gladstone,* the case was sent back to trial in order to allow a determination of fact in regard to the justification issue in accordance with the guidelines established by the Court in that case.

Principal Factors in the Justification Test

The Supreme Court of Canada has identified three main but not exhaustive factors that must be taken into account by the courts when determining whether the burden of justification has been properly discharged.[46] First, there must be as little infringement as possible of the concerned right. Second, the affected Aboriginal Peoples must be consulted. Third, the issue of compensation must be addressed.

The first requirement is for as little infringement as possible to the concerned right. It is important for the courts to determine whether all appropriate measures were taken to ensure that the Aboriginal or treaty right would be impacted as little as possible. For example, in a case where land subject to Aboriginal title is required for a compelling and substantial legislative purpose, only that part of the land or of its resources that is absolutely required for that purpose may be infringed. If reasonable alternatives not requiring the use of Aboriginal land or resources are available, the infringement will not be justified. Moreover, if more Aboriginal land than absolutely necessary is affected, the burden of justification will not have been discharged. Similar principles of minimal impairment will be applied when other types of Aboriginal and treaty rights are infringed. The courts will determine the standards of minimal impairment on a case-by-case basis, depending on the type of Aboriginal or treaty right affected and the alternatives reasonably available.

The second requirement is for consultation with the concerned Aboriginal group.[47] The absence of such consultation or its inadequacy will, in many circumstances, lead to the conclusion that the burden of justification has not been discharged. The scope of the duty to consult varies with the nature of the Aboriginal right affected and the extent of the impacts of the proposed infringement on that right.[48]

The requirement for consultation contains an implied duty to fully and adequately inform the concerned Aboriginal Peoples or their representatives of all pertinent aspects of the proposed legislation, regulation, action, or decision that may infringe on their Aboriginal or treaty rights.[49] In particular, the impacts on the concerned rights and the reasonable alternatives to avoid such impacts should be explained in sufficient detail in order for a reasonable person to make informed decisions on the matter. The consultation should also include sufficient details of all proposals for remedies or compensation so that a reasonable person may make informed decisions about their adequacy. The extent of the information required will be assessed in each case, taking into account all the circumstances. The courts would certainly be displeased if fundamental aspects of the proposal were not revealed or if misleading information about the proposal was willfully provided.

Since Aboriginal rights and most treaty rights are collective rights, the required information should usually be channelled through the representatives of the Aboriginal group holding the right. Again, the content of such information and its method of distribution will vary according to the circumstances. A reasonable approach that takes into account the reasonable wishes and preoccupations of the leadership of the concerned Aboriginal group should be favoured.[50]

The consultation process should take place in a timely manner and in such a way that the results of the consultation may be fully taken into account before final or irremediable decisions or actions are taken. In particular, alternatives to eliminate or reduce the proposed infringement, including remedial measures and compensation packages, should be discussed with the concerned Aboriginal group or its representatives. These matters should be discussed at the earliest stage of the proposal and, in any event, prior to final decisions being made.

In short, the consultation must be in good faith and with the intention of substantially addressing the concerns of the affected Aboriginal community as expressed by its representative leadership. Plays on dissensions within Aboriginal groups or attempts to avoid or circumvent Aboriginal leadership—particularly elected Aboriginal leadership—will not be looked on favourably by the courts.

The requirement for consultation may include an additional requirement for Aboriginal consent, including, in appropriate circumstances, the consent of the affected Aboriginal community as a whole. Full consent is normally required when Aboriginal title, Aboriginal rights, or treaty rights are surrendered. In *Delgamuukw* v. *B.C.,* Chief Justice Lamer added that the full consent of the affected Aboriginal community may be required in other circumstances, such as when provinces adopt hunting and fishing regulations that affect Aboriginal lands.[51] These other circumstances remain for the most part to be determined. As a general rule, any proposal that substantially affects Aboriginal lands or any other substantive Aboriginal or treaty rights—including hunting and fishing rights—should normally be subject to the consent of the affected Aboriginal community. Usually, when such consent is sought but not obtained, the proposed action should be abandoned. However, the proposed action could still be pursued absent Aboriginal consent if it can be shown (a) that the legislative objective underlying the action is so compelling and substantial as to justify the infringement, notwithstanding the absence of consent, and (b) that the refusal to consent is patently unreasonable, taking into account all the circumstances. In these cases, the requirements of minimum impairment described above and of just and adequate compensation discussed below take on added importance.

It is appropriate to note that the consent of the affected Aboriginal community may be required in most cases of infringements of treaty rights resulting from provincial legislative schemes. This results in part from the terms of section 88 of the *Indian Act* and from the special constitutional position of treaties. It is not yet clear whether an implied justification requirement exists in section 88. As Chief Justice Lamer stated in *R.* v. *Côté:*

> Section 88 accords a special statutory protection to Aboriginal treaty rights from contrary provincial law through the operation of the doctrine of federal paramountcy. . . . This second purpose, of course, has become of diminished importance as a result of the constitutional entrenchment of treaty rights in 1982. But I note that, on the face of s. 88, treaty rights appear to enjoy a broader protection from contrary provincial law under the *Indian Act* than under the *Constitution Act, 1982.* Once it has been demonstrated that a provincial law infringes "the terms of [a] treaty," the treaty would arguably prevail under s. 88 even in the presence of a well-grounded justification. The statutory provision does not *expressly* incorporate a justification requirement analogous to the justification stage included in the *Sparrow* framework. But the precise boundaries of the protection of s. 88 remains a topic for future consideration. I know of no case which has authoritatively discounted the potential existence of an *implicit* justification stage under s. 88.[52] [Emphasis in original]

The third requirement is adequate compensation. In cases of extinguishment or impairment of Aboriginal title or of other Aboriginal or treaty rights, compensation may be owed under the doctrine of Aboriginal rights.[53] The issue of compensation takes on an added importance within the context of section 35(1) of the *Constitution Act.*[54] Considering the importance of compensation in regard to both the doctrine of Aboriginal rights and the context of section 35(1), it is to the method of determining such compensation that we now turn our attention.

Conclusion

Prior to 1982, Aboriginal rights could be unilaterally extinguished by appropriate legislation if a clear and plain legislative intent could be found for this purpose. Treaty rights could also be so extinguished prior to 1982, although some controversy still exists in this regard. Since 1867, the legislative authority to extinguish such rights has been vested in Parliament. Since 1982, the power to unilaterally extinguish Aboriginal or treaty rights has been severely curtailed by the terms of section 35 of the *Constitution Act, 1982.*

Aboriginal and treaty rights may be regulated by the competent legislative authorities. Since 1867, the constitutional authority to regulate such rights has belonged to Parliament. When Aboriginal or treaty rights are impaired or infringed, this may lead to compensation under the doctrine of Aboriginal rights.

Section 35 of the *Constitution Act, 1982* incorporates within its terms the doctrine of Aboriginal rights and also provides for new constitutional remedies in cases of infringements of Aboriginal or treaty rights. In particular, the courts may now set aside legislative or regulatory schemes that infringe on an Aboriginal or treaty right and that cannot be constitutionally justified.

In application of section 35 of the *Constitution Act,* the Supreme Court of Canada has set out tests to establish a *prima facie* infringement of an Aboriginal or treaty right recognized and affirmed under that section and to justify such an infringement.

The Court has stressed that in order to justify such an infringement, there must exist a compelling and substantial legislative objective, and it must be shown that the government has fully discharged its fiduciary responsibilities. The affected Aboriginal Peoples must be treated fairly and in a manner consistent with the preservation of the honour of the Crown.

Some of the factors to take into account when determining whether the burden of justification has been properly discharged are whether there has been as little infringement as possible of the concerned right, whether the affected Aboriginal Peoples have been properly consulted, and whether adequate compensation has been provided.

Part II
Principles of Compensation

Chapter 6

A Review of Compensation in Cases of Expropriation Unrelated to Aboriginal and Treaty Rights

Introduction

This chapter briefly reviews the basic principles of compensation in cases of property expropriation unrelated to Aboriginal or treaty rights. The right to fair and adequate compensation in cases of expropriation is one of the fundamental pillars of Canadian law, and statutes are usually read as requiring just compensation in cases of expropriation unless a legislative intention to deny compensation has been clearly expressed.[1]

The principal question to answer when assessing compensation in cases of expropriation is to determine what constitutes "just compensation" in each case. To understand what is meant by this expression, we need to review the basic principles of compensation developed in cases of expropriation. Since most cases of expropriation concern land and buildings, the courts have developed principles for compensation based on such issues as market value, potential value and special adaptability, intrinsic value and equivalent reinstatement, consequential impacts, and injurious affection. Although the principles of compensation discussed in this chapter deal almost exclusively with buildings and land, we can use them as a starting point for our examination of adequate compensation in cases of infringement of Aboriginal and treaty rights.

Market Value

In general, where land is at issue, the courts have attempted to assess compensation based on the notion of the market value of the land at the time of taking. The courts assess market value by estimating the price at which an owner who is willing but not obliged to sell would sell the land to a person who is willing but not obliged to buy.[2] As Lord Romer stated in *Vyricherla* v. *Revenue Divisional Office:*

> The compensation must be determined, therefore, by reference to the price which a willing vendor might reasonably expect to obtain from a willing purchaser. The disinclination of the vendor to part with his land and the urgent necessity of the purchaser to buy must alike be disregarded. Neither must be considered as acting under compulsion. This is implied in the common saying that the value of the land is not to be estimated at its value to the purchaser. But this does not mean that the fact that some particular purchaser might desire the land more than others is to be disregarded.[3]

Regardless of how the land was used at the time of expropriation, the court's assessment of its market value may take into account the highest and most profitable uses to which the land could be put.[4] Again, as stated by Lord Romer:

> For it has been established by numerous authorities that the land is not to be valued merely by reference to the use to which it is being put at the time at which its value has to be determined, . . . but also by reference to the uses to which it is reasonably capable of being put in the future. No authority indeed is required for this proposition. It is a self-evident one. No one can suppose in the case of land which is certain, or even likely, to be used in the immediate or reasonably near future for building purposes, but which at the valuation date is waste land or is being used for agricultural purposes, that the owner, however willing a vendor, will be content to sell the land for its value as waste or agricultural land as the case may be. It is plain that, in ascertaining its value, the possibility of its being used for building purposes would have to be taken into account.[5]

Potential Value and Special Adaptability

One of the major difficulties in assessing market value is the added value the land may have as a result of the expropriation scheme. For example, agricultural land expropriated for hydroelectric purposes may have more value to the hydroelectric company than it has to the farmer. The extent to which this added value is to be taken into account when determining just compensation is problematic.

As a general rule, the courts have been hesitant to provide expropriated owners with windfalls resulting from schemes that were unforeseeable prior to the expropriation. Owners are not usually compensated for increases in value to the land that are entirely attributable to the scheme underlying the expropriation.[6] However, if the land is particularly suited for a special purpose, including the special purpose for which it has been expropriated, its adaptability for this purpose is to be considered when determining the appropriate level of compensation if this adaptability was sufficiently foreseeable by market forces prior to the expropriation.[7]

In *Cedar Rapids Manufacturing and Power Company* v. *Lacoste,* two islands and certain reserved rights over a point of land in the St. Lawrence River were expropriated. In that case, the principal value lay not in the land itself but in its location. The islands were so situated as to be necessary for the construction of a hydroelectric development. Lord Dunedin stated:

> Where, therefore, the element of value over and above the bare value of the ground itself . . . consists in adaptability for a certain undertaking . . . the value is not a proportional part of the assumed value of the whole undertaking, but is merely the price, enhanced above the bare value of the ground which possible intended undertakers would give. That price must be tested in the imaginary market which would have ruled had the land been exposed for sale before any undertakers had secured the powers, or acquired the other subjects which made the undertaking as a whole a realized possibility.[8]

Thus, the special value of the land for a particular scheme is to be considered, but not to the extent of granting compensation that provides a share of the full value of the proposed development that has crystallized at the time of expropriation. The value of the land to the owner consists in the present value of all advantages of the land and of all special future uses for which it is suited, without regard to the particular scheme for which the land is being expropriated. This special added value is to be determined by the imaginary market that would have ruled immediately prior to the expropriation. This rule ensures that the prospective or potential value and the special adaptability of the concerned land are adequately considered when the market value is assessed.[9]

Thus, in cases of expropriation, the courts usually take into account the special value of the land related to its fitness for a particular use, which may not be its current use. So long as the potentiality of the future uses or special adaptability of the land are reasonably foreseeable, it follows that the owner would take into account this potential future added value of the land when determining the price at which he or she would part with it. Likewise, a purchaser would factor this potential value into the transaction, and a court would take this into account when determining appropriate levels of compensation. This valuation of the land by its unusual features, special adaptability, or potentiality applies even where there is only one possible purchaser who is acquiring under powers enabling compulsory acquisition.[10]

Intrinsic Value and Equivalent Reinstatement

The level of compensation to be provided in cases of expropriation is not necessarily limited to the market value of the property. The owner is always entitled to the market value, including the added market value for the unusual features, special adaptability, or potentiality of the land as discussed above. However, the land may have a value to the owner that goes beyond simple market considerations. In such circumstances, the intrinsic value to the owner must be taken into account in order to fairly compensate the owner for the true but unmarketable value of the property. As was stated in *St. Michael's College* v. *City of Toronto:* "Fair compensation would include payment of the value of the land taken, not necessarily limited to the market value but the value to the college in view of the purposes for which the land was used and to which it had been dedicated."[11]

In *R.* v. *Sisters of Charity of Rockingham,*[12] the Crown had expropriated property in order to build a railway yard. The lower courts had assessed compensation for the property taken, but had refused to allow compensation for the injurious affection to that part of the property not taken. (Injurious affection is discussed in the next section of this chapter.) The Judicial Committee of the Privy Council reversed the lower courts and remitted the case to the Exchequer Court for an assessment of the damages for injurious affection to the remaining property, which was used for educational purposes. In assessing the issue of compensation for injurious affection to the educational facility, Justice Audette commented:

> It is impossible, in a case like the present one, to ascertain the actual market value of such a property by the usual tests which presuppose a willing buyer; the conditions upon which such values are based are not present. In a case of this character, market value is not the measure of compensation. Therefore some other measure must be sought. In the absence of market value, the intrinsic value or value to the owners is the real value to ascertain for measuring the compensation.[13]

The law of expropriation in France developed notions of *"valeur de convenance,"* being that ascertainable but unmarketable value that the property affords a particular owner, and of *"valeur d'affection,"* which aims to address the more subjective value that a particular property may have for its owner.[14]

These notions have found some support in cases of expropriation within Quebec.[15] However, without entirely disregarding such notions, in circumstances where no market exists for a property, expropriation law prefers to deal with these situations through the concept of equivalent reinstatement. Under this concept, in appropriate circumstances, the owner is provided with sufficient funds in order to be reinstated in an equivalent facility of comparable utility and commodity. This principle of equivalent reinstatement was developed at common law to provide adequate compensation in cases where concepts such as market value could not capture the true value of a property in regard to the particular purpose for which the property was being used, such as cases involving churches, schools, or hospitals.[16]

The concept of equivalent reinstatement is not intended to deprive an owner of the existing or potential economic value of the land. Indeed, one can imagine a situation where land on which a church is located would take on a new added value, for example, if a gold deposit was found to exist within the land. In such circumstances, it is the true market value of the land, including the value in excess of the cost of reinstatement, that would constitute appropriate compensation.

Consequential Impacts and Injurious Affection

In addition to dealing with property values, just compensation must extend to the consequential impacts of expropriation (also referred to as "disturbance damages") and to the injurious affection caused to the adjacent land and property.

The expropriation of property is often accompanied by a series of consequential impacts. These consequential impacts are unrelated to the value of the property, but the owner would never have incurred them had it not been for the act of expropriation. Consequential impacts include the costs of relocating; legal fees and appraisal costs involved in obtaining advice and in negotiating or otherwise setting appropriate levels of compensation; business losses resulting from relocation; and the general overall disturbance, stress, and aggravation almost invariably associated with expropriation. All these impacts are subject to compensation in the appropriate circumstances.[17]

Injurious affection can also have an impact on levels of compensation. The rules relating to injurious affection in cases of expropriation generally vary depending on whether the injury is against land remaining in the hands of the owner after expropriation or whether the injury is incurred where no land of the injured party has been expropriated.

Where the land remaining after an expropriation is injuriously affected by the expropriation itself, or by the activities for which the land was expropriated, compensation will be owed irrespective of whether the injury would be actionable at common law, as a nuisance or under some other cause of action. As stated by Justice Anglin in *Canadian Pacific Railway Company* v. *Albin:*

> While . . . no clear principle can be deduced from the English authorities why the measure of compensation should be more liberal in the case of a taking of land than in that of mere injurious affection, the distinction is too well established in England to admit of further discussion here.[18]

The general rules in cases of injurious affection to the remaining land may be summarized as follows. First, the land affected must be held by the same owner as the land taken. The pieces of land need not be contiguous, but they must be related in some way. Second, the injury must result either from the expropriation itself—such as in cases where the land is severed—or from the activities for which the expropriation was made. The injury includes not only impediments to the activities carried out on the remaining land, but also the reduction in value that the remaining land suffers as a consequence of the uses resulting from the expropriation or reasonably anticipated as resulting therefrom. Finally, the injury must not be too remote from the expropriation or the activities or uses resulting therefrom. When all three conditions are present, the scope of compensation for injurious affection to the remaining land will generally extend to all consequential damages resulting from the expropriation itself, from construction on the expropriated property, or from the operations carried out as a result of the expropriation.

Where no land is taken, the rules related to injurious affection are more restrictive. Someone who is affected by constructions or operations resulting from the expropriation of land held by a third party may recover damages from the expropriating party; however, damages are available only insofar as they are already accessible at common law, irrespective of the expropriation. In such circumstances, in common law jurisdictions, the aggrieved party does not find itself in a more favourable situation than if the expropriation had not occurred. In common law jurisdictions, the issues raised in such cases usually revolve around tort law and nuisance concepts. However, in cases of injurious affection resulting from third-party expropriation, the defence of acting upon statutory authority is generally deemed unavailable, and it is the bar to such a defence that makes injurious affection claims easier to sustain in circumstances of expropriation.

The classic conditions that must be fulfilled to justify a claim for injurious affection if no land is taken have been set forth as follows by the Ontario Law Reform Commission:

The remedy is not available on the same condition as where lands have been taken. Here, the conditions are considerably more restrictive. Four have been laid down:

1. the damage must result from an act rendered lawful by the statutory powers of the authority;
2. the damage must be such as would have been actionable at common law, but for the statutory powers;
3. the damage must be an injury to the land itself and not a personal injury or an injury to business or trade; and
4. the damage must be occasioned by the construction of the public work, not by its user.[19]

Finally, compensation available in cases of expropriation need not be determinable or determined with mathematical accuracy. Thus, the courts generally apply the principles for compensation in a flexible manner and may award compensation as a global amount. Indeed, the granting of a global amount reached by applying the above-mentioned principles appears to be an appropriate way of allocating compensation. In this regard, a reasonable degree of discretion is afforded the courts in determining what constitutes fair compensation in the circumstances of a particular case.[20]

Conclusion

The principles of compensation in cases of expropriation provide a useful but incomplete starting point for discussing compensation in cases of infringements of Aboriginal and treaty rights. The concepts of market value, consequential or disturbance damages, and injurious affection all find some application in Aboriginal cases. However, the concept of market value fails to capture many important considerations that need to be taken into account when dealing with Aboriginal issues. In many circumstances, the concept is simply irrelevant, given the location and nature of many Aboriginal lands. The concept of market value appeals to a commercial perspective, but it fails to take into account the special relationship and bond between Aboriginal Peoples and their traditional lands and activities, and it ignores the cultural, spiritual, and social aspects of Aboriginal and treaty rights. Aboriginal cultures are often rooted in a relationship with particular territories. The use of such territories for activities unrelated to or incompatible with traditional Aboriginal activities can result in the disruption of Aboriginal societies—a damaging effect that can never be captured in the concept of market value. Moreover, one of the fundamental aspects of the doctrine of Aboriginal rights is to place the Crown between Aboriginal Peoples and the general market. Surely this indicates that pure market valuations are generally at odds with Aboriginal and treaty rights. From this perspective, it seems that the notions of intrinsic value to the owner and of equivalent reinstatement may be more helpful when discussing methods of just compensation in Aboriginal cases.

Notwithstanding these reservations, the principles guiding appropriate compensation in cases of expropriation constitute a comparative base from which a discussion of compensation in cases of infringements of Aboriginal and treaty rights can proceed.

Chapter 7

The Experience in the United States

Introduction

Before we pursue our discussion of compensation in Canada, a brief review
of the experience in the United States will be helpful. As we shall see in this
chapter, the American experience cannot be fully transposed to Canada;
however, it provides a useful benchmark from which to view the Canadian
situation.

If, paraphrasing the Supreme Court of Canada in *Sparrow,* we cannot
recount with much pride the treatment of Aboriginal Peoples in Canada,[1] it
can be argued that the historical treatment of Aboriginal Peoples by the United
States has also been questionable. The history of the relations between
Aboriginal Peoples and the United States will not be retold here. Suffice it to
say that the role of the judicial system of the United States in this troubled
relationship has often been questioned.[2] As was recently stated by the United
States Court of Appeals for the District of Columbia: "Since the founding of
this nation, the United States' relationship with the Indian tribes has been
contentious and tragic."[3]

Recognized Aboriginal Interests

One of the leading characteristics of the legal status afforded Aboriginal rights
in the United States is the refusal to extend to Aboriginal Peoples many of the
fundamental rights provided for in the Constitution of the United States. This
refusal has greatly influenced the issue of compensation in cases of the taking
of Aboriginal lands. Of particular interest is the refusal to extend to Aboriginal
Peoples the full protection of the Fifth Amendment, which provides for the
right to just compensation in cases of property taken for public use.[4]

In the case of *Tee-Hit-Ton Indians* v. *United States,*[5] the dispute revolved around a claim by a small Aboriginal community from Alaska that was seeking Fifth Amendment compensation following the sale of lumber rights by the United States in the Tongass National Forest. This timber sale had been authorized pursuant to an act of the United States Congress notwithstanding any claims by Alaskan natives. Although this case could have been treated as a form of unilateral extinguishment without compensation for the Aboriginal rights in and to the timber, the Supreme Court of the United States went further.

In light of the limited sovereignty afforded Aboriginal nations within the concept of "domestic dependent nation,"[6] Aboriginal nations are deemed to stand somewhat outside the Constitution of the United States. Consequently, in *Tee-Hit-Ton Indians* v. *United States,* the United States Supreme Court confirmed that Aboriginal title is not afforded the full protection of the Fifth Amendment. Only the taking of land "recognized" by Congress as subject to some form of Aboriginal interest can give rise to compensation claims cognizable by the judiciary. In essence, the *Tee-Hit-Ton Indians* case stands for the proposition that compensation will be owed for the taking of Aboriginal lands only insofar as the United States Congress agrees. This case essentially justifies the dispossession of Aboriginal Peoples as a necessary expedient for the progress of the United States, and it precludes the judiciary from interfering in this process of dispossession unless specifically mandated to do so by Congress:

> In the light of the history of Indian relations in this Nation, no other course would meet the problem of the growth of the United States except to make congressional contributions for Indian lands rather than to subject the Government to an obligation to pay the value when taken with interest to the date of payment. Our conclusion does not uphold harshness as against tenderness toward the Indians, but it leaves with Congress, where it belongs, the policy of Indian gratuities for the termination of Indian occupancy of Government-owned land rather than making compensation for its value a rigid constitutional principle.[7]

Nor are Aboriginal Peoples extended the full protection of the due process and equality provisions found in the Fourteenth Amendment, which could ensure them just compensation in cases of taking of land through due process or equality considerations.[8] Thus, in regards to the taking of their traditional lands, Aboriginal Peoples are to some extent denizens whose rights to compensation are largely dependent on the goodwill of a Congress in which they have little or no voice.

This approach is fundamentally incompatible with the Canadian doctrine of Aboriginal rights.[9] It is also at odds with the treatment afforded Aboriginal rights throughout the Commonwealth and in countries that closely follow the British tradition.[10] Despite these fundamental incompatibilities, the methods of compensation used when recognized Aboriginal lands are expropriated in the United States constitute a groundwork from which to examine the issue in Canada.

The Plenary Power of Congress

Under the legal system of the United States, compensation for taking of land subject to an Aboriginal interest is not an issue that can be addressed by the courts unless the Aboriginal interest in the land has been somehow recognized by treaty, agreement, legislation, or otherwise. Even when such interest is recognized, the involvement of the courts in the determination of compensation is curtailed by the plenary power of Congress.

The concept of the plenary power of Congress in cases where Aboriginal land has been taken was exemplified at its worst in the 1903 case of *Lone Wolf* v. *Hitchcock.*[11] The dispute revolved around a breach of a treaty. Lands reserved under the treaty were ceded without following the procedure provided for in the treaty. The treaty specifically provided that any land cession was subject to the consent of "at least three fourths of all adult male Indians occupying" the reserved lands. The United States Congress had enacted legislation to sell the land, even though the procedural requirements under the treaty had not been fulfilled.

The principal findings of the Supreme Court of the United States in that case were that the Congress could unilaterally abrogate treaties with Aboriginal nations, and that the courts would review neither congressional legislation in this regard nor the adequacy of the compensation provided by the Congress to the aggrieved Aboriginal Peoples. The Court expressed the following opinion:

Indeed, the controversy which this case presents is concluded by the decision in *Cherokee Nation v. Hitchcock,* 187 U.S. 294, decided at this term, where it was held that full administrative power was possessed by Congress over Indian tribal property. In effect, the action of Congress now complained of was but an exercise of such power, a mere change in the form of investment of Indian tribal property, the property of those who, as we have held, were in substantial effect the wards of the government. We must presume that Congress acted in perfect good faith in the dealings with the Indians of which complaint is made, and that the legislative branch of the government exercised its best judgment in the premises. In any event, as Congress possessed full power in the matter, the judiciary cannot question or inquire into the motives which prompted the enactment of this legislation. If injury was occasioned, which we do not wish to be understood as implying, by the use made by Congress of its power, relief must be sought by an appeal to that body for redress and not to the courts.[12]

Lone Wolf implied that congressional legislation providing for the taking of recognized Aboriginal lands was not subject to judicial review either under the terms of the just compensation principle of the Fifth Amendment or under the terms of any other common law or constitutional principle. This radical and fundamentally inequitable view has been largely attenuated in subsequent decisions. Nevertheless, the inescapable conclusion to the *Lone Wolf* case was that the courts would not play a role in matters of compensation—even when recognized Aboriginal lands were taken—unless they were specifically mandated to do so by the United States Congress.

Fiduciary Obligations

The principles expressed in *Lone Wolf* were revisited in the 1937 case of *Shoshone Tribe* v. *United States*.[13] In *Shoshone Tribe,* the United States was sued for breach of treaty stipulations. The Shoshone Nation claimed it had been deprived of the possession and enjoyment of an undivided half-interest in tribal lands set aside by treaty. The United States had given an interest in the disputed lands to another Aboriginal nation over the protests of the Shoshone. Congress had granted the U.S. Court of Claims the jurisdiction to hear the case. Addressing the issue of congressional plenary powers over Aboriginal matters as expressed in *Lone Wolf,* Justice Cardozo stated:

> Power to control and manage the property and affairs of Indians in good faith for their betterment and welfare may be exerted in many ways and at times even in derogation of the provisions of a treaty. *Lone Wolf v. Hitchcock,* 187 U.S. 553, 564, 565, 566. The power does not extend so far as to enable the Government "to give the tribal lands to others, or to appropriate them to its own purposes, without rendering, or assuming an obligation to render, just compensation . . . for that 'would not be an exercise of guardianship, but an act of confiscation'" *United States v. Creek Nation, supra* [295 U.S. 103], p. 110; citing *Lane v. Pueblo of Santa Rosa,* 249 U.S. 110, 113; *Cherokee Nation v. Hitchcock,* 187 U.S. 294, 307-308. The right of the Indians to the occupancy of the lands pledged to them, may be one of occupancy only, but it is "as sacred as that of the United States to the fee" *United States v. Cook, supra* [19 Wall. 591], p. 593; *Lone Wolf v. Hitchcock, supra; Choate v. Trapp,* 224 U.S. 665, 671; *Yankton Sioux Tribe v. United States, supra* [272 U.S. 351]. Spoliation is not management.[14]

The apparently contradictory decisions of the Supreme Court of the United States in *Lone Wolf* and *Shoshone Tribe* were reconciled to some degree in the 1980 case of *United States* v. *Sioux Nation of Indians*.[15] There, the Supreme Court of the United States relied on the reasoning of the U.S. Court of Claims in *Fort Berthold Reservation*.[16] This reconciliation was achieved through reference to the fiduciary obligations of the United States in managing recognized Aboriginal lands.

In *Fort Berthold Reservation,* the U.S. Court of Claims concluded that Congress could not, in the same transaction involving recognized Aboriginal lands, act as a trustee for the benefit of the concerned Aboriginal nation and at the same time exercise its sovereign power of eminent domain. The sovereign power of eminent domain is the power of the United States to take the lands of its territory for public purposes. Accordingly, the U.S. Court of Claims set out a guideline to distinguish between congressional trust action and congressional eminent domain action in relation to Aboriginal proprietary interests. The guideline provides that where Congress has made an effort in good faith to give the concerned Aboriginal Peoples the full value of the land— and thus merely transmutes the property from land to money—there is no taking. In such circumstances, Congress is deemed to have acted in its trust capacity. Insofar as such a good-faith effort has been made by Congress, the courts will not interfere with the determination of compensation. However, where such good-faith effort has not been made, the courts may then intervene and order the payment of compensation to relieve the aggrieved Aboriginal Peoples.

In *Sioux Nation,* the Supreme Court of the United States expressly discarded the presumption underlying the *Lone Wolf* case that relations between the United States and the Aboriginal Peoples located on its territory were political matters in which the judiciary played no role.[17] The Court noted that the *Lone Wolf* case was decided at a time when Congress had not authorized litigation against the United States based on such claims, thus waiving the sovereign immunity of the United States against claims from Aboriginal Peoples. The Supreme Court of the United States concluded that the decisions in that case had thus lost much of their force. The Court therefore substituted principles closely related to fiduciary relationships:

> More significantly, *Lone Wolf*'s presumption of congressional good faith has little to commend it as an enduring principle for deciding questions of the kind presented here. In every case where a taking of treaty-protected property is alleged, a reviewing court must recognize that tribal lands are subject to Congress' power to control and manage the tribe's affairs. But the court must also be cognizant that "this power to control and manage [is] not absolute.

> While extending to all appropriate measures for protecting and advancing the tribe, it [is] subject to limitations inhering in . . . a guardianship and to pertinent constitutional restrictions." *United States v. Creek Nation,* 295 U.S., at 109-110. *Accord: Menominee Tribe v. United States,* 391 U.S. 404, 413 (1968); *FPC v. Tuscarora Indian Nation,* 362 U.S. 99, 122 (1960); *United States v. Klamath Indians,* 304 U.S. 119, 123 (1938); *United States v. Shoshone Tribe,* 304 U.S. 111, 115-116 (1938); *Shoshone Tribe v. United States,* 299 U.S. 476, 497-498 (1937).[18]

The Court approved the guideline set out in *Fort Berthold Reservation,* noting, however, that this guideline must be properly understood as deriving from trust relationships. Therefore the principal inquiry in a particular case is not to determine if the government acted in good faith, but rather to determine the adequacy of the consideration given by the government for the taking of recognized Aboriginal lands, it being understood that the issue of adequate compensation is a judicial and not a legislative question.[19]

In conclusion on this matter, in the United States, the judiciary cannot interfere with issues pertaining to compensation and taking of land subject to Aboriginal title unless such lands have been recognized through some instrument, including recognition by treaty, agreement, or statute. In the cases where recognized Aboriginal land is taken without proper Aboriginal consent, the courts may intervene if little effort to compensate the concerned Aboriginal Peoples has been made or if the level of compensation is clearly inadequate. If a careful review of the historical records and of the consideration paid reveals that the United States provided the concerned Aboriginal Peoples with payment for the full value of the land taken, the test is satisfied and the courts will not interfere. If the test is not satisfied, then the taking of the recognized land will give rise to an implied undertaking to make just compensation to the Aboriginal Peoples, an undertaking that will be enforced by the judiciary. Congress may, however, deny fair compensation or restrict access to the courts if it adopts clear legislation for this purpose.

Adequate Compensation

We now move to the issue of what constitutes adequate consideration or just compensation for the taking of recognized Aboriginal lands in the United States.

First, the land will normally be valued as if the Aboriginal Peoples held the fee simple to it. For instance, in *United States v. Shoshone Tribe,*[20] when the trial court valued the Aboriginal lands, it included the value of the timber and minerals on and in the land. On appeal, the Supreme Court of the United States rejected the government's contention that the interest of the Aboriginal

Peoples in the land amounted to less than a fee simple interest, and that consequently the inclusion of timber and minerals in the assessment of the Aboriginal interest was wrong. The Supreme Court held that "[t]he right of perpetual and exclusive occupancy of the land is not less valuable than full title in fee."[21]

Second, in most cases, the valuation is determined from the date of taking of the land.[22] This will generally be deemed to be when the United States formally deprived the concerned Aboriginal Peoples of their possession of the concerned land. The date at which third parties may have encroached on the land prior to formal government taking is not normally taken into account. Moreover, if the land taken was held by the Aboriginal Peoples under instruments, including treaties, either granting the land to them in fee simple or confirming a fee simple tenure in the land, the date of taking will be the date actual title to the land was transferred to a third party through letters patent.[23] The date of taking is not always easy to ascertain and can often be determined only through a detailed review of the historical record.

Third, the courts must determine the actual value of the land. This determination is usually based on considerations of market value in which the Aboriginal interest in the land is largely ignored. Market value was considered in *Miami Tribe of Oklahoma* v. *United States*,[24] where a decision of the Indian Claims Commission was cited with approval:

> Fair market value was defined by the Indian Claims Commission in the *Osage Nation of Indians* v. *United States,* 3 Ind. Cl. Comm. 231, as follows: Market price is the highest price in terms of money which land will bring if exposed for sale in the open market with a reasonable time allowed to find a purchaser buying with knowledge of all the uses and purposes to which it is best adapted and for which it is capable of being used.[25]

This is, of course, analogous to the concept of market value often used in cases of expropriation unrelated to Aboriginal rights.

This notion of market value when assessing land subject to a recognized Aboriginal interest was developed partly in opposition to the subsistence approach to valuation. The subsistence approach limits the value of the Aboriginal interest in the land to what economic value could be ascribed to traditional Aboriginal activities, generally reducing the level of compensation owed to the affected Aboriginal Peoples. In *Otoe & Missouria Tribe of Indians* v. *United States*,[26] the government argued that as there was no market value for the land being discussed, compensation for the taking of the land should be based on the value of the Aboriginal subsistence activities on the land. The U.S. Court of Claims rejected this approach and reiterated that even if no market existed for the lands, "this does not mean that such land was worth no more than the value of the subsistence it provided for the Indians."[27] The Court outlined the method of valuation to be used in order to properly determine the value of the land subject to the Aboriginal interest in the absence of evidence of market value in the conventional sense:

> This method of valuation takes into consideration whatever sales of neighboring lands are of record. It considers the natural resources of the land ceded, including its climate, vegetation, including timber, game and wildlife, mineral resources and whether they are of economic value at the time of cession, or merely of potential value, water power, its then or potential use, markets and transportation—considering the ready market at that time and the potential market.[28]

When determining the value of land subject to recognized Aboriginal interests, the courts must go beyond a simple assessment of the economic value of the Aboriginal activities carried out on the land. Rather, the fair value of the land is to be ascertained by taking into account all pertinent factors, including its mineral, timber, hydroelectric, and agricultural potential.[29]

Natural resources are of prime importance when considering the economic potential of any given tract of land. The compensation value of such resources may be considered when determining fair market value. Insofar as the potential uses of the land or its resources are sufficiently clear at the time of taking, they must be taken into account when ascertaining proper levels of compensation. For example, consideration must be given for the value of standing timber and minerals, even if the concerned Aboriginal Peoples are not actively pursuing the commercial exploitation of these resources.[30] The natural resources must be deemed as having some economic value at the time of taking, even though that value may be as-yet unrealized. The mere speculative chance of potential value, however, is insufficient. A reasonable expectation of exploiting the resource must be present at the time of taking in order for its value to be taken into account.

In *Alcea Band of Tillamooks* v. *United States*,[31] the evidence showed that the timber on the concerned land was of good quality and, given the state of the lumber industry in the United States at the time of taking in 1855, the exploitation of this resource could be reasonably foreseen. Consequently, the U.S. Court of Claims took into account the potential value of the timber when it valued the land. The Court applied the same reasoning when it found that the land also held agricultural value, as well as potential mineral value. Similar reasoning was used regarding the timber value of the land in *Rogue River Tribe of Indians* v. *United States*.[32]

Conversely, if the evidence discloses that the economic value of the natural resources of the land was highly speculative at the time of taking, this speculative value will not be considered. This rule applies even when reviewing historical land transactions with the benefit of hindsight. Thus, even if the natural resources of the land turn out to be of great value, this value will not normally be taken into account unless it was sufficiently clear at the time of taking. Values attributable purely to hindsight are not normally considered unless there is some evidence of fraud or other forms of sharp dealing. The application of this rule may lead to injustice, particularly in cases where the dispossession of Aboriginal Peoples was carried out with the purpose of acquiring lands with great mineral potential, albeit unrealized at the time of taking.[33]

Conclusion

Using market values to determine compensation for land compulsorily taken from Aboriginal Peoples fails to take into account the spiritual, cultural, and social values of the land for Aboriginal Peoples. Market values thus perpetuate the dispossession of Aboriginal Peoples by limiting the value given to the land to those factors of interest to the dominant society, and by ascribing little or no value to the factors of primary interest to the Aboriginal Peoples. From the Aboriginal perspective, the market value approach is deficient because it considers only one side of the equation.

The American experience with compensation shows that the rules of the game are often stacked against Aboriginal claimants. Aboriginal Peoples are confronted by a series of legal rules and precedents that make it very difficult not only to access the courts for the redress of their claims, but also to prosecute such claims. Many cases drag on for decades.

A review of the American case law leads to the conclusion that the prosecution of Aboriginal claims for compensation is an arduous exercise that requires years of sustained effort. The resolution of such claims is hampered by principles of compensation that often limit the debate to narrow concepts of market value that are foreign to the Aboriginal experience. These concepts ignore the spiritual, cultural, and social aspects of the relationship of Aboriginal Peoples with the land, and fail to provide them with the full measure of the future economic value of their lands. The very notion of forcible taking implies that the Aboriginal Peoples are severed from the decision-making process and, consequently, they are placed in a position that ensures that the value of their Aboriginal lands for uses unrelated to traditional Aboriginal activities will be enjoyed largely by others.

Chapter 8

A Proposal for
Principles of Compensation

Introduction

The previous chapters provide us with the background we need to discuss the general legal principles that should guide compensation in cases of infringements of Aboriginal or treaty rights. This chapter suggests broad and basic legal principles to determine compensation in such cases. In light of the state of the law in this regard, these principles are tentative suggestions.

As noted in *Delgamuukw*,[1] the determination of appropriate compensation in cases involving infringements of Aboriginal rights raises difficult questions. The framework I suggest attempts to answer these questions in a manner consistent with the doctrine of Aboriginal rights. Though certainly not exhaustive, the principles are specifically adapted to cases of infringements of Aboriginal and treaty rights, yet set out sufficiently broad parameters to fit the varied circumstances in which such infringements occur.

There are two principal sets of circumstances in which compensation may be required in cases of infringements of Aboriginal or treaty rights. First, there are infringements that are not justified under section 35 of the *Constitution Act, 1982* and the *Sparrow* test.[2] Second, there are infringements that are justified but that nevertheless warrant compensation under the common law and the *Sparrow* test. The principles to be applied in each category of circumstances are somewhat different, and in the discussion below, I attempt to distinguish between both sets of circumstances.

A. Compensation is to be determined in accordance with a methodology that takes into account the principles of fiduciary law

The first question to be resolved is the general legal framework in which compensation is to be determined.

The framework of private property law is inappropriate, since infringements of Aboriginal or treaty rights are not wrongs in a tort-law sense and are not governed by private property law principles. The doctrine of Aboriginal rights is tied to history and to the process of nation building. Infringements of Aboriginal and treaty rights must be viewed in this historical context and in the context of the underlying public-law concepts surrounding Crown interactions with Aboriginal Peoples. The application of the rules of private property law to the relationship between the Crown and Aboriginal Peoples is inappropriate, and this approach is to be discarded as inapplicable and wrong. As the Supreme Court of Canada has repeatedly stated, it is simply not possible to transpose to Aboriginal title, and to Aboriginal and treaty rights generally, concepts of private property law.[3]

When Aboriginal land rights, including Aboriginal title, are justifiably infringed, some may argue that the principles of expropriation law could govern compensation. Indeed, as discussed in chapter six, expropriation law has developed many principles that might be useful when discussing compensation in the context of Aboriginal rights. Certainly, determinations of compensation in cases of expropriation have influenced determinations of compensation in cases involving the taking of Aboriginal land in the United States. However, although expropriation law is to some extent part of public law, at least in the sense that the expropriating authority is acting on Crown authority, the main thrust of expropriation law is to compensate private parties for the forcible taking of their property. Expropriation law is somewhat at a loss when dealing with property that is not subject to a normal market environment.

When expropriation law deals with cases that do not fit traditional concepts of fair market value, it often does so through the concept of equivalent reinstatement. It is, however, difficult to apply this concept in the context of justifiable infringements of Aboriginal and treaty rights since, in most Aboriginal cases, reinstatement would be difficult or impossible in light of the particularities of the concerned rights. This is especially true of infringements of Aboriginal land and resource rights, where even when replacement is physically feasible, it cannot compensate for the spiritual, cultural, and social impacts that result from interfering with the Aboriginal Peoples' relationship with the land and its resources. For instance, the loss of an Aboriginal or treaty right to fish cannot be adequately compensated by providing the concerned group with an identical quantity of fish acquired at a fish market. Such a scheme of replacement and reinstatement completely ignores the social and spiritual dimensions of the Aboriginal right. In light of the definition of Aboriginal rights used by the Supreme Court of Canada—an integral practice, custom, or tradition of the Aboriginal culture of the concerned Aboriginal community[4]—the social and spiritual dimensions would probably render illusory most reinstatement schemes related to Aboriginal rights.

Moreover, the collective dimension of Aboriginal and treaty rights would be lost in the framework of expropriation law, because expropriation law deals mainly with individual property owners. It is thus difficult to imagine how Aboriginal rights could be governed by the same principles as those used when private property is expropriated. The collective dimension of Aboriginal and treaty rights and the special *sui generis* nature of these rights would be lost if expropriation principles were applied without modification in cases of infringements of such rights.

Finally, the principles of compensation developed under expropriation law generally suppose the existence of a market through which a fair and proper value may be ascertained. The very nature of Aboriginal rights takes them outside any market: "Aboriginal rights cannot be sold, mortgaged or be otherwise alienated to third parties. They are not marketable."[5] The fact that Aboriginal rights are outside the mainstream market leads to the conclusion that pure market valuations of such rights are inherently inappropriate.

Expropriation law can serve as a reference point from which to consider compensation in cases of justifiable infringements of Aboriginal or treaty rights, but it cannot serve as the governing legal framework in such cases.

The courts have understood that compensation in cases of infringements of Aboriginal and treaty rights should be governed by principles of fiduciary law. Fiduciary principles are appropriate to ensure that the honour of the Crown is preserved when compensation is required to alleviate the consequences of infringements of Aboriginal and treaty rights. As Justice La Forest stated in *Delgamuukw* v. *B.C.*:

> It must be emphasized, nonetheless, that fair compensation in the present context is not equated with the price of a fee simple. Rather, compensation must be viewed in terms of the right and in keeping with the honour of the Crown. Thus, generally speaking, compensation may be greater where the expropriation relates to a village area as opposed to a remotely visited area. I add that account must be taken of the interdependence of traditional uses to which the land was put.
>
> In summary, in developing vast tracts of land, the government is expected to consider the economic well being of *all* Canadians. But the aboriginal peoples must not be forgotten in this equation. Their legal right to occupy and possess certain lands, as confirmed by s. 35(1) of the *Constitution Act, 1982*, mandates basic fairness commensurate with the honour and good faith of the Crown.[6] [Emphasis in original]

This excerpt confirms that normal principles of expropriation law are inadequate to deal properly with infringements of Aboriginal title, and, by extension, with infringements of all Aboriginal and treaty rights. The words of Justice La Forest require that compensation be determined using a methodology that ensures Aboriginal Peoples are treated fairly when their lands or rights must be set aside. The yardstick against which this concept of fairness is to be measured is the "honour and good faith of the Crown," a yardstick that can be understood only in the context of the fiduciary relationship that binds the Crown and Aboriginal Peoples and that entails fiduciary duties on the part of the Crown. As stated by then Chief Justice Dickson in *Sparrow:*

> The relationship between the Government and aboriginals is trust-like, rather than adversarial, and contemporary recognition and affirmation of aboriginal rights must be defined in light of this historic relationship.[7]

Chief Justice Lamer also stressed the fiduciary relationship when he discussed compensation in the context of an infringement of common law Aboriginal title in *Delgamuukw:*

> Indeed, compensation for breaches of fiduciary duty are a well-established part of the landscape of aboriginal rights: *Guerin*. In keeping with the duty of honour and good faith of the Crown, fair compensation will ordinarily be required when aboriginal title is infringed.[8]

In proceeding with or authorizing an infringement of an Aboriginal or treaty right, the Crown is exercising a discretion that it alone has the authority to carry out, namely assenting to the infringement of an Aboriginal or treaty right without Aboriginal consent. This discretion transforms the fiduciary relationship of the Crown into a judicially enforceable fiduciary duty to provide, in appropriate circumstances, just compensation for these infringements.

In these regards, the standards set out in *Guerin* must be considered. In that case, the standards that the Crown was called upon to answer to were those of a fiduciary. As stated by Justice (later Chief Justice) Dickson:

> The Crown's fiduciary obligation to the Indians is therefore not a trust. To say as much is not to deny that the obligation is trust-like in character. As would be the case with a trust, the Crown must hold surrendered land for the use and benefit of the surrendering Band. The obligation is thus subject to principles very similar to those which govern the law of trusts concerning, for example, the measure of damages for breach.[9]

Using principles of fiduciary law when Aboriginal title or other Aboriginal or treaty rights are infringed allows the courts to develop flexible remedies that can be made to fit the particular facts of each case to ensure that the honour of the Crown is preserved in all circumstances. The remedies available in cases of breach of a fiduciary duty are far more numerous and much more flexible than those normally available at common or civil law. Remedies governed by fiduciary law vary with the nature of the relationship, with the extent of the breach, and with the particular fiduciary duty.[10]

In fiduciary cases, the courts go beyond the narrow confines of the common law and "look to the harm suffered from the breach of the given duty, and apply the appropriate remedy."[11] As L.I. Rotman noted:

> The nature of the wrong and the nature of the loss, not the nature of the cause of action, will dictate the scope of the remedy.
>
> Potential remedies which may be invoked upon a finding of a breach of fiduciary obligation include restitutionary, personal, proprietary, and deterrent remedies. These may include equitable remedies—such as constructive trust, injunctions, declarations, prohibitions, rescission, accounting for profits, repayment of improperly used moneys (plus interest), equitable liens, equitable damages, and *in rem* restitution—and/or liability based on negligence, fraud, coercion, undue influence, profiteering, economic duress, negligent misrepresentation, or third party liability. A court may also grant interest on financial proceeds awarded to remedy a breach of fiduciary duty which is payable from the date of the breach. Interest awarded may be ordinary or compounded.[12]

The nature of Aboriginal and treaty rights (as discussed in chapters one and two), the fiduciary relationship between the Crown and Aboriginal Peoples (as discussed in chapter three), and the *sui generis* nature of the doctrine of Aboriginal rights and its operation within the sphere of federal common law (as discussed in chapter four), all lead to the conclusion that the remedies available in cases of unlawful or unjustified violations of Aboriginal and treaty rights include those of fiduciary law. In fact, the application of remedies from fiduciary law in cases of unlawful or unjustified interference with Aboriginal rights is now well established.[13] These remedies are those developed to properly address fiduciary breaches, including the remedies of restitution and constructive trust.

In cases of unlawful or unjustifiable interference with Aboriginal or treaty rights, there can be compensation in addition to or in lieu of the remedies of restitution and constructive trust. The determination of compensation is made by taking into account the principles that apply in cases of breach of fiduciary duty. These principles ensure compensation equivalent to full restitution and disgorgement of benefits, compensation for lost opportunities, and compensation for injurious affection and consequential damages. The full scheme of remedies at fiduciary law can be used in cases of unlawful or unjustifiable infringements of Aboriginal or treaty rights.

In cases where the infringements of Aboriginal or treaty rights are carried out lawfully and are justified in accordance with the terms of section 35 of the *Constitution Act, 1982,* fiduciary principles are also to be taken into account. As stated by Justice (later Chief Justice) Dickson, "It is the nature of the relationship, not the specific category of actor involved that gives rise to the fiduciary duty. The categories of fiduciary like those of negligence, should not be considered closed."[14] Likewise, it is the nature of the relationship that governs the remedies available when the relationship is breached. Thus, the special fiduciary relationship between the Crown and Aboriginal Peoples, the overall constitutional responsibility of the Crown for Aboriginal Peoples and Aboriginal lands, the large discretion afforded to the Crown in authorizing lawful infringements of Aboriginal or treaty rights, the lack of alternatives available to Aboriginal Peoples when the infringements of their rights are deemed lawful and justifiable, and the historical vulnerability of Aboriginal Peoples all militate in favour of applying fiduciary principles to determine compensation in cases involving lawful and justified infringements of Aboriginal and treaty rights.

These fiduciary principles need, however, to be adapted to take into account the fact that the infringements of Aboriginal and treaty rights in such cases are being carried out in a lawful and justifiable manner. This does not mean that fiduciary remedies should be discarded. Rather, they should be adapted to take into account the particular circumstances in which the lawful and justified infringements are being carried out. These adaptations are discussed further below.

Thus, principles developed under expropriation law are inadequate as a framework for compensation in cases involving Aboriginal and treaty rights, and principles developed under fiduciary law serve as more appropriate guides.

B. Relevant factors in determining compensation include the impacts on the affected Aboriginal community and the benefits derived by the Crown and third parties from the infringement

Aboriginal rights require a special approach that ensures that the reconciliation of Aboriginal and mainstream Canadian societies can be achieved in a context of fairness and justice for both societies. Moreover, the honour of the Crown must be maintained at all times when Aboriginal interests are affected.

Aboriginal rights have been found to be unique *sui generis* rights. They require a special approach to the treatment of evidence in Aboriginal cases and a unique approach in determining the content of the rights themselves.[15] This special approach extends to the measure of compensation in cases of infringement. However, the extent to which the approach needs to be unique in order to achieve the noble purposes of reconciliation and of preservation of

Crown honour must not be such as to completely discard traditional Canadian legal concepts. The special approach taken with Aboriginal rights must not strain the Canadian legal and constitutional structure.[16]

In cases of unlawful or unjustified infringements of Aboriginal or treaty rights, this special approach is best served by applying remedies that find some analogy in fiduciary law. In cases where compensation is appropriate, it is to be determined in accordance with fiduciary principles.

In cases of lawful and justified infringements, fiduciary principles are difficult to apply without extensive adaptation to take into account the fact that the infringements are permissible. Here, the principles related to compensation in cases of expropriation can provide guidance as to how the principles of fiduciary compensation are to be adapted to fit the particular circumstances. Thus, though it is impossible to ever properly compensate Aboriginal Peoples for forcible infringements of their Aboriginal lands or rights, a proper melding of compensation principles applicable in cases of breach of fiduciary duty with compensation principles applicable in cases of expropriation can lead to compensation schemes that afford Aboriginal Peoples an acceptable measure of relief and that promote the reconciliation of both societies while preserving the honour of the Crown.

In expropriation, an attempt is made to fully compensate the affected party by providing the monetary equivalent of the expropriated property calculated *as of the time of taking*. Compensation is thus usually calculated based on the market value of the property at the time it is expropriated. This market value includes the value of the best use that may be made of the property and of the adaptability of the property for special purposes. In special cases where market value is inappropriate, reinstatement costs can be substituted. To this basic compensation is added compensation for injurious affection to the remaining property, if any, and compensation for consequential damages, including, in appropriate circumstances, compensation for the legal and other professional fees associated with the expropriation, for the costs of relocating, for business loss resulting from relocation, for general overall disturbance, as well as for stress and aggravation.

Fiduciary remedies attempt to fully compensate the aggrieved party by providing full restitution in kind, thus ensuring that the remedy compensates *for both the past breach and for the future consequences of the breach*. In other words, the remedy must ensure that the aggrieved party is restored to the situation the party would have been in had the breach of fiduciary duty never occurred. In consequence, restitution in kind is favoured over equivalent monetary compensation where such restitution is possible. The remedies of restitution, specific execution, tracing and constructive trust are thus favoured where the circumstances allow them to be applied. When such restitution is not possible, the full monetary value of the property must be provided as compensation, including any increases in value that occurred between the breach and the date on which compensation was actually made. In addition, in both cases where either restitution in kind is achieved or the monetary equivalent is provided, additional compensation must also be supplied to achieve the objective of full restitution, including, in appropriate cases, disgorgement of benefits and compensation for lost opportunities, for injurious affection, and for all consequential damages.

As set out previously in this chapter, the application of expropriation principles in cases where Aboriginal or treaty rights are infringed cannot adequately compensate the affected Aboriginal Peoples. Conversely, many of the fiduciary remedies, though appropriate and often necessary when the infringement is unlawful or unjustified, are clearly incongruous when the infringement is both lawful and justified. Indeed, when the infringement is justified, restitution in kind cannot be effected. The very cornerstone of fiduciary remedies is thus inapplicable in such cases.

In cases of lawful and justified infringements of Aboriginal or treaty rights, principles of fiduciary and expropriation compensation should be melded in such a way as to capture both the present and future values of the affected rights or properties for the concerned Aboriginal Peoples, as well as a portion of the future value gained by others in proceeding with the infringement. The objective is to capture, to a reasonable extent, both the notion of the *full present value* found in expropriation cases and the notion of *future value* that is inherent in fiduciary remedies.

When Aboriginal or treaty rights are infringed, particularly in cases where land subject to Aboriginal title or necessary for the exercise of an Aboriginal right is taken, the issue of future value is particularly important. By their very nature, many Aboriginal and treaty rights require a land base sufficient to ensure their proper exercise. The examples of hunting, fishing, and trapping come readily to mind. The taking of the land base for other purposes often results in a permanent and definitive diminution of the exercise of the right, and, in extreme cases, can lead to the demise of the Aboriginal activity the right is intended to protect. In many cases, infringements affect not only those Aboriginal Peoples exercising the right at the time the infringements are first carried out, but also future generations who could have benefited from the exercise of the right. The *sui generis* character of Aboriginal title and of Aboriginal and treaty rights generally, and particularly the collective, cultural, and historical nature of these rights, strongly suggest that the loss of the exercise of the right and the lost land base should be compensated not only in terms of present value, but also in terms that take into account the loss of the future uses of the land and the consequential long-term impacts on the affected Aboriginal society.

In this context, expropriation law, with its principles of market value at the time of taking, appears inadequate when determining appropriate compensation for the justified infringement of an Aboriginal or treaty right. In the rare cases where reinstatement is possible, this alternative should be pursued. However, in most cases, reinstatement will not be possible and it will be necessary to determine appropriate compensation in a manner that fully takes into account the loss of the future use of the concerned rights or lands. In such cases, fiduciary principles intervene to ensure that account is taken of all the impacts and of all aspects of the infringement.

I submit that three principal factors should be taken into consideration in such circumstances:

1. The present as well as the future impacts of the infringement on the affected Aboriginal or treaty right and on the Aboriginal Peoples themselves, on their society, on their distinct culture, and on their other rights and interests.
2. The present and reasonably foreseeable future benefits derived from the infringement by the Crown and by third parties generally.
3. In cases where land or property subject to Aboriginal title or otherwise used or required in the pursuance of an Aboriginal or treaty right is taken or otherwise infringed upon, the present and reasonably foreseeable future value of the land or property.

I further submit that these three factors should be assessed using a three-step process.

At the first stage, the market value of the right, land, or property should be ascertained. However, contrary to the principles applied in cases of expropriation, this valuation exercise should not be limited to the value of the best use at the time of taking. A just reconciliation of Aboriginal and mainstream Canadian societies requires that full account also be taken of the foreseeable future benefits derived from the infringement, as well as the foreseeable future value the affected lands or property will gain through the infringement.[17] In this manner, the value derived from the infringement should be fully considered.

At the second stage, this valuation, which measures both present market values as well as future benefits and additional future values (including those resulting from the infringement), should be compared with the value of the concerned right or land to the Aboriginal Peoples. It is at this second stage that the present as well as the future impacts of the infringement are to be taken into account. The impacts considered at this stage include those affecting the exercise of the Aboriginal or treaty right and extend to the impacts on the Aboriginal Peoples themselves, on their society, on their distinct culture, and on their other rights and interests. The past infringements of the rights and lands of the concerned Aboriginal Peoples should also be taken into account at this stage. An apparently minor infringement can have a huge impact when it is added to past encroachments. The impact of the infringement is thus to be assessed in light of the history of the relationship between the affected Aboriginal Peoples and the rest of Canadian society, and compensation valuations should include a consideration of the cumulative impacts resulting from a history of past infringements.

Throughout this exercise, the Aboriginal perspective on these matters should be given full consideration. In most cases, the Aboriginal perspective on the spiritual, cultural, and social dimensions of the affected right or land will render monetary valuations impossible. It is usually futile to attempt to place monetary or market values on a way of life or on the spiritual, cultural, and social dimensions of Aboriginal and treaty rights. Nevertheless, the exercise of considering these factors from an Aboriginal and historical perspective will greatly assist in proceeding to the next stage of the valuation process.

At the third stage, the interests of Aboriginal and mainstream Canadian societies must be balanced in such a way as to ensure full and complete compensation for the affected Aboriginal Peoples in terms that ensure that the honour of the Crown is preserved and that favours the reconciliation of both societies. In *Delgamuukw,* the Chief Justice, referring to cases of justified infringements of Aboriginal title in British Columbia, speaks of the need for "governments [to] accommodate the participation of aboriginal peoples in the development of the resources of British Columbia."[18] Adequate value must be transferred to the Aboriginal party to ensure that the affected Aboriginal Peoples may pursue their collective existence as a society and grow as a distinct culture despite the loss represented by the infringement.

In many cases, achieving this balance will entail providing the affected Aboriginal Peoples with a monetary award based on the value of the right, land, or property as determined under the principles of expropriation law. To this compensation is added a reasonable portion of the future benefits and additional future values derived from or attributable to the infringement in an amount sufficient to maintain the honour of the Crown. Where appropriate, and particularly when Aboriginal Peoples themselves request it, this monetary compensation should not take the form of a one-time payment. Preference should be given to structured remedial measures and compensation schemes that repair the impacts of the infringement while at the same time ensuring the participation of the affected Aboriginal Peoples in the economic benefits derived from the infringement. It is here that fiduciary restitution remedies can be useful, and the constructive trust may be a vehicle particularly well suited to achieving such structured remedial measures and compensation schemes.

Where the infringement does not give rise to reasonably foreseeable future economic benefits—for example, when a military installation infringes upon Aboriginal or treaty rights—then the comparative exercise described above should still be carried out, even if the economic component does not carry as much weight. In such cases, the compensation should include expropriation market valuations that factor in the value of future potential uses of the lost lands or resources. It should also include remedial measures to ensure proper compensation for the impacts of the infringement on present and future generations. In appropriate cases, the cost of alternatives to using Aboriginal lands could also be taken into account.

This method for determining compensation, even in cases where there are no reasonably foreseeable future economic benefits, ensures that Aboriginal Peoples are not shortchanged or unduly victimized. For example, if the cost of building a military installation outside the area subject to Aboriginal rights is higher, the savings realized by using lands subject to Aboriginal rights could, in appropriate circumstances, be taken into account in the valuation process. Provisions requiring the return of the lands to the affected Aboriginal Peoples after their use by the Crown should also be part of the overall valuation process.

In determining compensation, one should, where feasible, consider the circumstances and conditions under which a reasonable, well-informed, and properly counselled Aboriginal community would in good faith voluntarily agree to the infringement.

Once the basic level of compensation has been determined, additional compensation could be added for injurious affection to the remaining Aboriginal or treaty rights and, in cases involving land, to the remaining Aboriginal lands, insofar as this injurious affection has not already been taken into account in the determination of basic compensation.

Compensation for lost opportunities is also to be considered, but only insofar as these lost opportunities have not already been captured in the determination of the basic compensation. In addition, in appropriate circumstances, consequential damages could also be provided, including compensation for the legal and other professional fees incurred as a result of the proposed infringement, compensation for general disturbance resulting from the infringement, and generally, compensation for any additional expense or loss that may reasonably be attributable to the infringement.

In closing, it is appropriate to stress once again that the special compensation principles suggested above concern cases where the infringement of Aboriginal or treaty rights is both lawful and justified. In cases where the infringement is either unlawful or unjustified, the full scheme of fiduciary remedies is available, and compensation in such cases is to be determined largely in accordance with the principles of fiduciary law.[19]

C. Compensation is to be determined in accordance with federal common law and will thus be governed by rules that apply uniformly throughout Canada

The doctrine of Aboriginal rights is an integral component of federal common law. As such, it is closely related to public law and it operates uniformly across Canada within the federal sphere of constitutional authority.[20]

This aspect of the doctrine of Aboriginal rights is particularly relevant when discussing compensation for infringements of Aboriginal or treaty rights. Compensation in such cases must ensure that the honour of the Crown is preserved. It is difficult to reconcile the honour of the Crown with principles of compensation that would vary according to the province or territory in which the affected Aboriginal Peoples happen to reside. Likewise, it is difficult to ensure that the honour of the Crown is preserved if the method used to determine compensation is subject to the variations of provincial legislation. The honour of the Crown cannot be governed by different principles in British Columbia, New Brunswick, or Quebec.[21] There is but one honour to which the Crown is bound, and the concept of multiple and variable Crown honours is difficult to sustain.

Moreover, provincial legislatures have no primary constitutional authority when it comes to Aboriginal and treaty rights.[22] Infringements of Aboriginal and treaty rights go to the core of such rights. Consequently, provincial laws of general application do not govern the determination of compensation in cases of infringements of such rights. Provincial laws of general application do not displace the doctrine of Aboriginal rights, which is governed by federal common law. Any law that would displace federal common law in this regard would be in relation to "Indians" or to "Lands reserved for the Indians," and such laws are beyond the constitutional powers of the provinces. Provincial laws that purport to displace the doctrine of Aboriginal rights are not contemplated by section 88 of the *Indian Act,* since this section concerns laws that have only an incidental impact on "Indians." Provincial legislation cannot therefore regulate infringements of Aboriginal title or of other Aboriginal rights.[23]

In certain circumstances, the provinces may infringe on Aboriginal rights. However, when compensation is owed by the provinces pursuant to such infringements, the principles that determine the level and type of compensation are normally to be established in accordance with the doctrine of Aboriginal rights.

These concepts have been extensively reviewed in chapter four of this book and need not be repeated here. Reference may thus be made to chapter four for a further discussion of these issues.

D. Compensation is generally the responsibility of the Crown but may, in appropriate circumstances, be assumed by third parties

The rules governing compensation in cases of infringements of Aboriginal or treaty rights are rooted in the doctrine of Aboriginal rights, which incorporates general remedies and principles of compensation applicable in cases of breach of fiduciary duties. The remedies vary according to the nature of the infringement. In cases of unlawful or unjustified infringement, the full scheme of fiduciary remedies is available in order to rectify the infringement. In cases of lawful and justifiable infringement where compensation is appropriate, it will be determined in accordance with principles of fiduciary law adapted to fit the particular circumstances in a manner that ensures that the honour of the Crown is preserved.

The principles of compensation discussed in this book are tied to the concept of a fiduciary relationship between the Crown and Aboriginal Peoples. This may lead to the view that these principles do not find application when third parties infringe on Aboriginal or treaty rights. If fiduciary remedies are available when a fiduciary relationship exists, how can these remedies be made applicable to third parties who are not Crown agents but who nevertheless infringe on Aboriginal or treaty rights? The answer to this question lies in the special constitutional and common law framework in which Aboriginal and treaty rights evolved.

There are three basic sets of legal circumstances in which a third party who is not a Crown agent could be involved in determinations of compensation subsequent to the infringement of an Aboriginal or treaty right carried out by that third party: (1) where the infringement is made without Crown or statutory authorization or pursuant to an otherwise unlawful authorization; (2) where the infringement is otherwise lawfully authorized but is not justified under the *Sparrow* test; and (3) where the infringement is lawfully authorized and otherwise justified but where compensation is nevertheless required under the doctrine of Aboriginal rights and to meet the justification test.

The first set of circumstances captures the cases where a third party that is not an agent of the Crown acts on its own to infringe on an Aboriginal or treaty right. This could occur when a third party attempts to appropriate Aboriginal lands or interferes with an Aboriginal right, such as a right to fish for food, without any authorization. In these cases, the non-governmental third party is responsible for these infringements and, in appropriate circumstances, will be required to provide compensation to the affected Aboriginal community.

The second set of circumstances captures those cases where the infringement is carried out by a non-governmental third party pursuant to an otherwise valid Crown authorization, but where the infringement is not justified. This could occur when an individual diverts, for purposes of irrigation, a waterway subject to an Aboriginal right to fish. The individual could have obtained the required permits to do so from the Crown, but this may not meet a compelling and substantial legislative objective sufficient to justify the infringement or may not meet the minimal impairment criteria or the other standards set out under the justification test. In these cases, it is submitted that both the Crown authorizing the unjustified infringement and the non-governmental third party carrying out the infringement are to be held responsible for the compensation owed.

The third set of circumstances captures those cases when the infringement carried out by the non-governmental third party is both validly authorized and otherwise justified, but where compensation is owed under common law and in order to properly meet the justification test. This could occur when a private corporation is justifiably required to use Aboriginal lands, such as reserve lands, for the purpose of an access road to its facilities having sought Crown authorization to do so. In these cases, it is submitted that, as a matter of policy, the third party should be made to assume the financial liabilities resulting from the infringement by means of appropriate licensing requirements and conditions. It is also submitted that, as a matter of law, the courts may, in appropriate circumstances, order that the compensation owed in such circumstances be assumed by the third party that benefits from the justified infringement or, in appropriate circumstances, may apportion this compensation between the third party and the Crown.

Having set out our argument, let us review the principles touching on third-party infringement that can be gathered from the case law.

Where the infringement is carried out by a third party without authorization or pursuant to an otherwise unlawful authorization, there is no cogent reason not to hold the third party responsible for the infringement. This is the position generally held in the United States:

> Ordinary trespass remedies are available to Indian tribes to prevent trespasses upon their land and to recover damages for injuries arising out of such trespasses. Actions have been maintained for ejectment, for injunctions against intrusions, and for damages for trespass on, or injury to, tribal land. State courts may entertain trespass or ejectment actions brought against non-Indians on behalf of Indians.[24]

In *County of Oneida* v. *Oneida Indian Nation,* the question was raised whether tribes of the Oneida Indians could bring a suit for damages against third parties (here the Counties of Oneida and Madison in the State of New York) for the occupation and use of tribal lands allegedly conveyed unlawfully in 1795. In upholding the right to bring the action, Justice Powell stated that numerous decisions of the Supreme Court of the United States recognize that

Indians have a federal common law right to sue to enforce their Aboriginal land rights, including a common law right of action for an accounting of all rents, issues, and profits against trespassers on their land. The Oneida Indians could therefore bring a common law action against third parties to vindicate their Aboriginal land rights.[25]

The position in Canada is essentially the same.[26] In *Fairford First Nation* v. *Canada,* claims were made against Canada based on alleged breaches of the Crown's fiduciary duties in regard to the construction of a water-control structure by the Government of Manitoba. Although he rejected on various grounds many of the fiduciary duty claims against Canada, Justice Rothstein stated the following as to the capacity of Aboriginal Peoples to sue third parties that interfere with any of their rights, including their Aboriginal and treaty rights:

> Except where the Indian Act imposes restrictions, Indians may sue for negligence, trespass, or I think, any other interference with their interest in their land or any other rights recognized by statute, common law or, indeed, the Constitution.[27]

Where the infringement is carried out by a third party without any Crown authorization, compensation will be owed by that party directly for the resulting infringement of the Aboriginal or treaty right at issue.[28] Where the infringement is carried out by a third party pursuant to an unlawful Crown authorization, there is no cogent reason to exclude that party from the liability for the compensation owed as a result of the infringement.[29] An analogy can be made with the case of *St.Catharines Milling* discussed in chapter one. In that case, a lumber company harvested timber on Crown lands under an authorization from the federal government. The Government of Ontario sought judicial redress against the lumber company, including damages.[30] The conclusions sought, including the damages claimed, were awarded to Ontario.[31] The action was upheld in all appeal courts, including the Privy Council.[32] The fact that the lumber company was acting under an authorization from the federal government was not a bar to damages being awarded to Ontario for breaches of its property rights protected by the Constitution. If this is the case for provincial property rights, there is no cogent reason to find differently where Aboriginal rights are affected.

Infringements may, however, arise from activities of non-governmental third parties authorized under some form of otherwise valid federal or provincial permit, approval, or other authorization.[33] Such an authorization may be found not to meet the *Sparrow* justification test.

Where a third party carries out an infringement under government authority, and that infringement is found to be unjustified, the infringing party may assume certain of the liabilities resulting from the infringement jointly with the Crown authority that authorized the unjustified infringement. The simple fact that the infringement is deemed unjustified places that infringement in the same category as if it was carried out without authorization. The same principles as those expounded above thus apply here also. An analogy used in an unrelated context by Justice Robertson of the Federal Court of Appeal in *Canadian Pacific Ltd.* v. *Matsqui Indian Band* seems apposite here:

> Assume that the government and citizen X are squabbling over who is the true owner of the infamous "blackacre" and that they agree to resolve their differences in the following manner: the government provides a deed to citizen X "absolutely" relinquishing its interest in blackacre for $100. It is trite law that if blackacre is subject to a mortgage vested in a third party, citizen X takes blackacre subject to that security interest. Citizen X may have a cause of action against the government for breach of contract or covenant, but that does not affect the rights of the third party. It is equally trite law that you cannot sell what you do not own (*nemo dat quod non habet*). In the present case, the appellants are the third party, and they are entitled to the "use and benefit" of reserve lands and the protections provided under the *Indian Act*.[34]

As noted by the Supreme Court of Canada in the seminal case of *Sparrow,* for many years the rights of Aboriginal Peoples to their Aboriginal lands were virtually ignored as legal rights, even though these rights existed at common law.[35] In consequence, the treatment afforded Aboriginal Peoples in Canada cannot be the object of much pride.[36] It would be contrary to the nature of Aboriginal rights to ignore or tolerate third-party interferences with them or not to hold third parties accountable for infringing on these rights. This is particularly relevant when such rights are affirmed and recognized in the supreme law of the nation.[37] If Aboriginal and treaty rights are to be taken seriously, then third-party responsibilities for the unjustified infringement of these rights is a necessary corollary to the existence of these rights at common law and to the affirmation and recognition of these rights under the Constitution. There is no reason to believe that this would not also be the case even if the third party is acting under government authorization.[38]

However, should the non-governmental third party be held to the same standards as the government that authorizes it to proceed with activities that result in the unjustified infringement of Aboriginal interests?

Governments are required, in appropriate cases, to provide compensation when lawful and justified infringements of Aboriginal or treaty rights are carried out. Governments are also held accountable in cases of unlawful or unjustified infringements, and in these circumstances the available remedies extend well beyond the determination of compensation. Various equitable and common law remedies are thus available in order to seek and obtain appropriate redress from governments. These remedies flow in large part from the fiduciary relationship. Although third parties are not usually bound by this fiduciary relationship, it seems logical that the rules governing their responsibilities should be similar. It would be inappropriate and unprincipled to burden Aboriginal Peoples with different legal rules, depending on whether the infringement resulted from the operations of a third party acting on government authorization or from direct government action. From the Aboriginal perspective, the infringement is the same.[39] The fact that Aboriginal and treaty rights receive constitutional affirmation and recognition reinforces the view that infringements of such rights should be governed by one set of legal principles.

In circumstances where the unjustified infringement results from third-party activities carried out pursuant to Crown authorization, there appears no reason not to hold both the Crown and the third party accountable for the unjustified infringement. This approach has the added advantage of fitting the well-known rule that holds, both at common and civil law, that plaintiffs need not attribute liability among joint wrongdoers.[40] Moreover, in cases where the third party is aware that the activity involves an infringement of an Aboriginal or treaty right, this approach is congruent with the concept recognized at common law that, in certain circumstances, third parties are subject to a constructive trust when they knowingly deal with trust property or assist in a breach of a trust duty.[41] It is equity and not tort or contract that governs whether a person shall be liable in equity as a constructive trustee.[42] Moreover, remedies depend on the substance of the right at hand, not on whether they can be fitted into a particular framework.[43]

The issue of the liabilities of third parties acting in good faith in regard to an unlawful interference with Aboriginal lands was dealt with in the case of *Chippewas of Sarnia Band* v. *Canada (A.G.)*.[44] In that case, the Chippewas of Sarnia were seeking to cancel a nineteenth-century transaction involving land that had been reserved to them under a treaty. The disputed lands had long since been sold to third parties and constituted a large portion of modern urban Sarnia. Although the Ontario Court of Appeal rejected the Chippewas' claim for restitution of the land from the present land owners, it recognized that in appropriate circumstances there were remedies available to Aboriginal Peoples for third-party infringements of their land rights, including remedies involving the actual restitution of land. In certain circumstances, remedies are to be enforced even against parties who purchased Aboriginal lands in good faith. In this particular case involving the Chippewas, however, the remedies involving the restitution of the land were deemed unavailable against the specific landowners involved in the litigation. The Court of Appeal reached this finding in light of the discretionary nature of the recourse and the circumstances of the case, as well as in light of various principles of equity, including the equitable doctrines of laches and acquiescence, which the Court of Appeal deemed applicable notwithstanding the special status of Aboriginal land rights.

The equitable doctrines of laches and acquiescence provide that certain rights may not be pursued before the courts in circumstances where a party has "slept" on rights or acquiesced implicitly the rights of another party. The circumstances in which these doctrines apply are complex and will not be delved into here, save to state that these doctrines may result in a court refusing to sanction an otherwise valid right even if no statute of limitations has precluded the court from recognizing the right. It is interesting to note that in *County of Oneida* v. *Oneida Indian Nation,*[45] Justice Powell, in delivering the majority opinion of Supreme Court of the United States in that case, did not recognize any statutory limitation of claim period for third-party breaches of Aboriginal land rights and, absent congressional legislation in this regard, the majority held that the existence of an Aboriginal right of action was not otherwise subject to any time limitations. Justice Powell did, however, leave open in that case the applicability of the equitable doctrine of laches. Likewise, in the case of *Chippewas of Sarnia Band,* the Ontario Court of Appeal found that no statutory limitation of claim period was applicable to Aboriginal claims against third parties requesting the return of land said to have never been surrendered.[46] In that case, in light of the 150 years that had elapsed between the breach and the action, the Ontario Court of Appeal did apply various principles of equity to deny restitution of the land from third parties, including the equitable doctrine of laches.[47]

However, in *Chippewas of Sarnia Band,* both the Court of Appeal and the judge who first adjudicated the case placed the issue of third-party responsibilities in cases of unjustified infringements of Aboriginal rights squarely within the context of the reconciliation of Aboriginal societies with the rest of Canadian society. This objective is deemed of primary importance by the Supreme Court of Canada. The Ontario Court of Appeal stated:

> We fully accept that courts do not have an open-ended discretion to enforce or deny aboriginal property rights as seems to suit the convenience of the case. In particular, it would be plainly wrong to deny a remedy to vindicate a valid claim to aboriginal title purely on the grounds that recognition of the claim would be troublesome to others: see *R. v. Marshall I,* [1999] 3 S.C.R. 533 at 565.
>
> On the other hand, aboriginal rights are an integral aspect of the Canadian legal landscape. Their shape, definition and enforcement do not and cannot exist in a vacuum. In the Canadian legal tradition, no right is absolute, not even constitutionally protected aboriginal rights: see *R. v. Nikal,* [1996] 1

S.C.R. 1013 at 1057-1058; *R. v. Agawa* (1988), 65 O.R. (2d) 505 at 524
(C.A.). As the Supreme Court of Canada has made clear, aboriginal rights
"must be directed towards the reconciliation of the pre-existence of aboriginal
societies with the sovereignty of the Crown" (*R. v. Van der Peet,* [[1996] 2
S.C.R. 507] at 539) and "with the rest of Canadian society" (*R. v. Gladstone,*
[1996] 2 S.C.R. 723 at 775).[48]

In the *Chippewas of Sarnia Band* case, the trial judge found, and the
Ontario Court of Appeal assumed, that a proper reconciliation of Aboriginal
and mainstream Canadian societies requires the recognition of third-party
responsibilities for infringements of Aboriginal land rights. The responsibilities
of third parties are, however, to be determined in a manner that does not
offend the fundamental sense of justice for both the Aboriginal and mainstream
Canadian societies and that promotes the reconciliation of both societies. In
the specific instance of the Sarnia land transactions, the Ontario Court of
Appeal determined that a period of some 150 years without complaint from
the concerned Aboriginal Peoples was a bar to the recovery of unlawfully
transferred Aboriginal land from third-party purchasers who had acquired it
in good faith. This determination was made in a context where the monetary
compensation claim of the Aboriginal Peoples against the Crown for the
unlawful taking of their lands in the nineteenth century could nevertheless
proceed.

The Ontario Court of Appeal noted the following:

> In our view the imposition of a strict sixty year "equitable limitation period",
> extending the time within which the Chippewas could assert their claim to
> the lands unaffected by the operation of a good faith purchaser for value
> defence, is not supported in law. . . . On the other hand, we accept that the
> factors that motivated the creation of the sixty year "equitable limitation
> period", namely the need to reconcile Aboriginal title and treaty claims with
> the rights of innocent purchasers, are factors that should be considered on a
> case-by-case basis. It may well be that where the denial of the Aboriginal
> right is substantial or egregious, a rigid application of the good faith purchaser
> for value defence would constitute an unwarranted denial of a fundamental
> right.[49]

The recognition of third-party responsibilities has the advantage of
allowing the courts, in appropriate circumstances, to provide restitution to
Aboriginal Peoples who have been deprived of their lands or of their rights
contrary to the principles of the doctrine of Aboriginal rights or in a manner
that cannot be justified under section 35 of the *Constitution Act, 1982.* Full
restitution can thus be achieved in appropriate circumstances notwithstanding

that the title to the Aboriginal lands may have been formally but unlawfully transferred to a third party or may have been otherwise formally but unlawfully burdened.

Moreover, from a policy perspective, the concept of third-party responsibilities is extremely useful in setting the standards for compensation in cases of lawful and justified infringements of Aboriginal and treaty rights. Indeed, many major infringements of these rights occur in the context of forestry, mining, hydroelectric development, and other economic activities. The burden of providing adequate compensation in such circumstances need not necessarily fall on the shoulders of all taxpayers but, in appropriate circumstances, it could also be assumed by those who most benefit from the infringement of the concerned Aboriginal or treaty right. This is clearly the approach favoured under the *Indian Act* when Aboriginal lands reserved under that act are required to be taken by a third party for a public purpose.[50]

Thus, in authorizing justified infringements, governments may condition these infringements in a manner that ensures that appropriate remedial measures and compensation schemes are provided to the affected Aboriginal Peoples by those who promote the infringement or largely benefit from it. In assessing the justification of the infringement, the courts should consider these government-sponsored remedial measures and the compensation provided thereunder.

The Supreme Court of Canada has made it clear that Aboriginal rights must be directed towards the reconciliation of pre-existing Aboriginal societies *both* with the sovereignty of the Crown *and* with the rest of Canadian society.[51] Though the Supreme Court of Canada has not as yet addressed the issue directly, the general approach of reconciliation favoured by the Court leads to the conclusion that where the remedial measures and compensation schemes are inadequate in the framework of justifiable infringements, the courts may consider both the underlying obligations of the Crown and the responsibilities of those who most benefit from the infringement.

Where the infringement requires compensation in order to be deemed justified, a judicial consideration of all these issues and of all relevant factors could lead, in appropriate circumstances, to remedies involving both the infringing third party and the Crown. Insofar as a court determines that an infringement is otherwise justified save the level of compensation provided, that infringement nevertheless remains legally unjustified until adequate compensation is provided. The infringing third party would thus be acting without legal justification until adequate compensation is made. In appropriate circumstances, it may thus be fitting to require the third party to assume in whole or in part the compensation required to ensure that the infringement is justified and that the affected Aboriginal Peoples are treated fairly.

In this manner, a true reconciliation of Aboriginal and mainstream

Canadian societies can be achieved by laying at least part of the financial burdens for justified infringements of Aboriginal or treaty rights on the shoulders of those who most benefit from these infringements. However, depending on all the surrounding circumstances, and particularly on the terms of the legislation under which the third-party infringement was carried out, the liability for the compensation may fall entirely upon the Crown.[52] The courts are thus to consider each case on its particular facts without, however, closing any options. In cases of justified infringements of Aboriginal or treaty rights, all the circumstances are to be factored in to ascertain the proper method of achieving the required reconciliation.

E. Compensation may be provided through structured compensation schemes or through a global monetary award

As discussed in the section B of this chapter, in cases of lawful and justified infringements of Aboriginal or treaty rights, structured remedial measures and compensation schemes should be preferred. In cases of unlawful and unjustified infringements of such rights, fiduciary restitution should be preferred through various fiduciary remedies such as the constructive trust.

Although, as discussed in section B, structured remedial measures and compensation schemes are to be preferred, it may be necessary, in appropriate circumstances, to provide compensation through a global or comprehensive monetary award. In such circumstances, there is no need to distinguish between the various components that constitute the award.[53] The amount of compensation must be just and reasonable in the circumstances, but it need not be determined with mathematical accuracy.

For example, in *Guerin,* Justice Collier of the Federal Court Trial Division awarded a global amount of $10 million to the Aboriginal claimants in accordance with certain compensation guidelines derived from equity and strongly influenced by the principles of fiduciary law.[54] In the Supreme Court of Canada, the appropriateness of proceeding to a global award was questioned. Justice Wilson and Justice (subsequently Chief Justice) Dickson both approved of the global award and reiterated that mathematical accuracy was not the object of the exercise.[55]

In *Semiahmoo Indian Band* v. *Canada,*[56] the Federal Court Appeal Division used the remedy of constructive trust to return certain *Indian Act* reserve land that had been inappropriately taken by the Crown. The court also ordered that additional compensation be provided to the concerned band under the principles of fiduciary law, including compensation for injurious affection and consequential damages. The compensation issue was returned to the Federal Court Trial Division for determination, but the Federal Court Appeal Division provided guidelines under which such determination was to be carried out. These guidelines were derived from the compensation principles of fiduciary law. The Federal Court Appeal Division emphasized that compensation in such cases was not driven by mathematical formulas but rather by the principles of equity:

> There is no perfectly accurate formula for calculating the equitable damages required in order to provide full restitution to the Band in this case. Rather, it is a task which we can only ask the referee to perform the best that he or she can.[57]

The concept of a comprehensive award that does not require mathematical accuracy or specific attribution to various heads of claims is consistent with the approach followed by the courts in expropriation and fiduciary cases, and there does not appear to be any cogent reason to discard this approach in cases involving Aboriginal rights.[58]

F. Compensation is normally to be awarded for the benefit of the affected Aboriginal community as a whole

Aboriginal and treaty rights are collective rights held by the members of the concerned Aboriginal nations. This was explicitly recognized in regard to Aboriginal title in *Delgamuukw,* where Chief Justice Lamer stated:

> A further dimension of aboriginal title is the fact that it is held *communally.* Aboriginal title cannot be held by individual aboriginal persons; it is a collective right to land held by all members of an aboriginal nation. Decisions with respect to that land are also made by that community. This is another feature of aboriginal title which is *sui generis* and distinguishes it from normal property interests.[59] [Emphasis in original]

Likewise, by their very nature, Aboriginal rights are also collective rights held by the members of the concerned Aboriginal nation.[60] As a general rule, treaty rights are also collective rights,[61] though the terms of a particular treaty may, under certain circumstances, provide for individual treaty entitlements.

Insofar as Aboriginal and treaty rights are collective rights, compensation resulting from infringements of such rights is normally to be paid to the collectivity that holds the rights. This issue was dealt with by the British Columbia Court of Appeal in *Oregon Jack Creek Indian Band et al.* v. *Canadian National Railway.*[62] In that case, various Aboriginal chiefs had initiated a claim requesting, among other remedies, monetary compensation for what was stated to be an unlawful infringement of lands subject to Aboriginal title. The action was subsequently amended to add as plaintiffs the concerned Aboriginal nations and *Indian Act* bands. In dealing with a preliminary motion to determine which parties were entitled to pursue the claim, the British Columbia Court of Appeal noted that any payment eventually made to compensate the infringement would "form a common fund or pool of money which will stand in place of the last rights. The common pool will be enjoyed by all the plaintiffs in the place of their enjoyment of the communal rights."[63] This decision was confirmed in the Supreme Court of Canada, but in its decision the Court did not directly address the issue of compensation.[64] The Court rather took the view that the issue of the personal entitlement of the members of an *Indian Act* band or of an Aboriginal nation in such claims should be determined through an analysis of the specific facts of each case and was best decided within the context of a full hearing rather than as a preliminary matter.

Despite this argument, numerous decisions rendered by the Supreme Court since the *Oregon Jack* case lead to the conclusion that, in principle, compensation for infringements of Aboriginal rights should be provided to the collectivity that holds the rights rather than to the individual members of that collectivity. Logically, if the rights are collective, then the compensation for infringements of those rights should be provided to the collectivity. Similarly, if fundamental decisions relating to the concerned rights can be made only by the collectivity holding the rights, then fundamental decisions relating to the use or distribution of the compensation provided in cases of infringement should also be made by this collectivity. The collective dimension of compensation in such cases is confirmed to some extent by the provisions for land surrender set out in the *Indian Act,* which stipulate that compensation received pursuant to the surrender of land reserved under that act must be held for the benefit of the band as a whole.[65]

However, even though these rights are held collectively, they are exercised by individuals. It is, therefore, quite possible that certain individuals may be affected more seriously than others when such rights are infringed. The collective nature of the rights requires that the issue of compensation between the Aboriginal community and the parties responsible for the infringement be dealt with on a collective basis. The issue of individual compensation for particular individualized impacts can be dealt with as an internal matter of the concerned Aboriginal nation, subject to court supervision in appropriate circumstances. Individual claims based on infringements of Aboriginal or treaty rights can nevertheless be entertained by the courts in appropriate circumstances, particularly where the Aboriginal group holding the right refuses or neglects to uphold the right to the detriment of those who actually exercise the right.[66]

The questions of whether these compensation monies should be distributed among the individual members of the group and how such a distribution should be carried out are best decided on a case-by-case basis. A case-by-case approach also appears appropriate to the management of collective compensation monies. The wishes of the members of the community should be given considerable weight, but these views must be balanced against the rights and needs of future generations. The rules governing the management and distribution of compensation payments should take into account the present and future interests of the affected Aboriginal community as a whole.

The *Blueberry River Indian Band* case (also known as *Apsassin*) provides a case in point. Pursuant to the decision of the Supreme Court of Canada in this case,[67] Canada had been held liable for various breaches of its fiduciary obligations in regard to certain *Indian Act* reserve land transactions. The Supreme Court of Canada remitted the matter to the Federal Court for assessment of damages. A settlement was reached between the parties and, on March 2, 1998, pursuant to the settlement, Justice Hugessen of the Federal Court Trial Division ordered that the settlement proceeds of $147 million be paid to the bands.[68] Of this amount, the bands were required to set aside $12 million in trust to deal with individual claims. Individualized compensation was to be determined through a distribution process supervised by the court. The *sui generis* rights required a *sui generis* solution to address the issues of compensation that flowed from the Crown's breach of its fiduciary duties.

Thus, though compensation in cases of infringements of Aboriginal or treaty rights is normally to be provided to the collectivity holding the right, the courts may exercise a supervisory role in ensuring that the individual members of the affected Aboriginal community are provided with fair access to the compensation. This will generally be achieved through structured compensation schemes, of which the model in *Blueberry River Indian Band* is but one example among many. Throughout this process, the use of the compensation monies and any rules related to its distribution should be consistent with the preservation of the honour of the Crown and with the interests of both present and future generations of the affected Aboriginal Peoples. Full consideration should be given to the Aboriginal perspective, and measures should be taken to ensure that the decisions made are consistent with the long-term interests of the concerned Aboriginal community and with its survival as a viable, distinct culture and society.

Conclusion

The issue of compensation in cases of infringements of Aboriginal and treaty rights raises numerous complex legal issues that go to the heart of the doctrine of Aboriginal rights. In this book, I suggest simple but comprehensive legal principles for determining compensation. Six basic principles arise out of this study:

A. compensation is to be determined in accordance with a methodology that takes into account the principles of fiduciary law;
B. relevant factors in determining compensation include the impacts on the affected Aboriginal community and the benefits derived by the Crown and third parties from the infringement;
C. compensation is to be determined in accordance with federal common law and will thus be governed by rules that apply uniformly throughout Canada;
D. compensation is generally the responsibility of the Crown but may, in appropriate circumstances, be assumed by third parties;
E. compensation may be provided through structured compensation schemes or through a global monetary award;
F. compensation is normally to be awarded for the benefit of the affected Aboriginal community as a whole.

This discussion is but a first step in what will certainly be a complex process of sorting out the appropriate legal principles applicable in cases of compensation for infringements of Aboriginal and treaty rights.

It has been a long and difficult struggle for Aboriginal Peoples to achieve full recognition of their Aboriginal and treaty rights. After such a struggle for recognition, it is essential not to leave these rights sitting on a theoretical fence. The true content and impact of these rights will be ascertained through the treatment afforded in cases where they are infringed, particularly when such infringements are deemed justified in order to satisfy the economic development imperatives of mainstream Canadian society. It is in this context hat Canadian society as a whole, and the judiciary specifically, will be called upon to make good on the promise to take these rights seriously. The methods used to determine compensation, the levels of compensation provided, and the legal mechanisms through which compensation will be managed and distributed will all determine whether Aboriginal Peoples in Canada will be afforded fair treatment and recognition in a manner that ensures the true reconciliation of Aboriginal and mainstream Canadian societies.

Notes

Notes to Introduction

1 *Delgamuukw* v. *B.C.,* [1997] 3 S.C.R. 1010.
2 *Constitution Act, 1982,* being Schedule B to the *Canada Act 1982* (U.K.), 1982, c. 11, reprinted in R.S.C. 1985, app. II, no. 44.
3 As Professor Brian Slattery has pointed out in reviewing the recent case law of the Supreme Court of Canada: "We now know broadly what is *terra firma* and what is not, and the monsters have been largely tamed or banished to the decorative margins. Nevertheless, the first fruits of the Court's labours amount to a series of explorer's charts, enlightening so far as they go, but covering different areas, drawn in varying projections, and sometimes bearing an uncertain relation to one another." B. Slattery, "Making Sense of Aboriginal and Treaty Rights" (2000) 79 Can. Bar Rev. 196 at 197.
4 *Delgamuukw, supra* note 1 at 1114 (para. 169).
5 *R.* v. *Sparrow,* [1990] 1 S.C.R. 1075.
6 K. Roach, *Constitutional Remedies in Canada* (Aurora, Ontario: Canada Law Book, 1998) at 15-1.

Notes to Chapter I

1 See generally R.A. Williams, Jr., *The American Indian in Western Legal Thought* (New York: Oxford University Press, 1990); L.C. Green & Olive P. Dickason, *The Law of Nations and the New World* (Edmonton: University of Alberta Press, 1989); J.S. Youngblood Henderson, M.L. Benson, & I.M. Findlay, *Aboriginal Tenure in the Constitution of Canada* (Toronto: Carswell, 2000); M. Morin, *L'usurpation de la souveraineté autochtone* (Montréal: Les Éditions du Boréal, 1997); A. Lajoie *et al., Le statut juridique des peuples autochtones au Québec et le pluralisme* (Cowansville, Québec: Les Éditions Yvon Blais, 1996); B. Slattery, "Aboriginal Sovereignty and Imperial Claims" (1991) 29 Osgoode Hall L.J. 1; B. Slattery, "Did France Claim Canada on 'Discovery'?" in J.M. Bumsted, ed., *Interpreting Canada's Past,* vol. 1 (Toronto: Oxford University Press, 1986).
2 See generally K. McNeil, *Common Law Aboriginal Title* (Oxford: Clarendon Press, 1989); K. McNeil, "The Meaning of Aboriginal Title," in Michael Ash, ed.,

Aboriginal and Treaty Rights in Canada (Vancouver: U.B.C. Press, 1997); K. McNeil, "Aboriginal Title and Aboriginal Rights: What's the Connection" (1997) 36 Alta. L. Rev. 117; B. Slattery, "Understanding Aboriginal Rights" (1987) 66 Can. Bar. Rev. 727; B. Slattery, "The Hidden Constitution: Aboriginal Rights in Canada" (1984) 32 Am. J. Comp. L. 361; B. Slattery, *The Land Rights of Indigenous Canadian Peoples* (Doctoral thesis, Oxford University, 1979), available from University of Saskatchewan, Native Law Centre; R.H. Bartlett, "Aboriginal Land Claims at Common Law" [1984] 1 C.N.L.R. 1; K. Lysyk, "The Unique Constitutional Position of the Canadian Indian" (1967) 45 Can. Bar Rev. 513; K. Lysyk, "The Indian Title Question in Canada: An Appraisal in Light of Calder" (1973) 51 Can. Bar Rev. 450; P. Macklem, "Aboriginal Rights and State Obligations" (1997) 36 Alta. L. Rev. 97; B. Clark, *Indian Title in Canada* (Toronto: Carswell, 1987); D.W. Elliott, "Aboriginal Title," in B.W. Morse, ed., *Aboriginal Peoples and the Law* (Ottawa: Carleton University Press, 1989); H. Brun, "Les Droits des Indiens sur le territoire du Québec" (1969) 10 C. de D. 415; H. Brun, *Le territoire du Québec* (Québec: Les Presses de l'Université Laval, 1974); N. Rouland, S. Pierré-Caps, & J. Poumarède, *Droits des minorités et des peuples autochtones* (Paris: Presses Universitaires de France, 1996).

3   *Tito v. Waddell (No. 2)*, [1977] 3 All. E.R. 129 (Ch.), provides a striking example of this reluctance. In that case, the Banabans, who had inhabited Ocean Island in the western Pacific Ocean, sued in Chancery for relief against the British Phosphate Commissioners and the Attorney-General as representing the Government of the United Kingdom in regard to phosphate mining operations carried out on the island. The court refused to recognize a judicially enforceable fiduciary duty on the Crown in regard to its dealings with the Banabans, stating that relationships of trust between the Crown and colonized peoples generally fell within the political realm: "A trust in the higher sense, or governmental obligation, on the other hand lacks this characteristic [of judicial enforcement]; and where the primary obligation itself is one that the courts will not enforce, then I do not think that it can itself give rise to a secondary obligation which will be enforceable by the courts. To hold otherwise would be to give some legal force or effect to a relationship which has none" (at 228).

4   *Connolly v. Woolrich* (1867), 17 R.J.R.Q. 75; 11 L.C. Jur. 197; conf'd: *Johnstone et al. v. Connolly* (1867), 17 R.J.R.Q. 266; 1 R.L.O.S. 253.

5   *Johnson v. M'Intosh,* 21 U.S. (8 Wheat.) 543 (1823).

6   *Cherokee Nation v. Georgia, 30 U.S. (5 Pet.) 1 (1831).*

7   *Worcester v. Georgia,* 31 U.S. (6 Pet.) 515 (1832).

8   *The Royal Proclamation,* October 7, 1763, reprinted in S.C.R. 1985, app. II, no. 1. In regard to this proclamation, see generally *Campbell v. Hall* (1774), 1 Cowp. 204, 98 E.R. 1045; *R. v. Lady McMaster,* [1926] Ex. C.R. 68; *St. Catherine's Milling & Lumber Company v. The Queen* (1888), 14 App. Cas. 46; *R. v. White and Bob* (1964), 50 D.L.R. (2d) 613 (B.C.C.A.); aff'd [1965] S.C.R. vi; (1965), 52 D.L.R. (2d) 481 (S.C.C.); *Johnson v. M'Intosh, supra* note 5; *Mitchell v. United States* (1835), 9 Law Ed. 89.

9   *Johnson v. M'Intosh, ibid.*

10   *Ibid.* at 588.

11 *Ibid.* at 572–74.

12 *Cherokee Nation* v. *Georgia, supra* note 6.

13 *Worcester* v. *Georgia, supra* note 7.

14 *Cherokee Nation* v. *Georgia, supra* note 6.

15 *Worcester* v. *Georgia, supra* note 7 at 544.

16 *Ibid.* at 555.

17 *Ibid.* at 560–61.

18 J. Hurley, "Aboriginal Rights, the Constitution and the Marshall Court" (1982–83) 17 R.J.T. 403.

19 In *Delgamuukw* v. *B.C.,* [1997] 3 S.C.R. 1010, the Supreme Court of Canada did not address the issue of self-government. This issue was also avoided in *R.* v. *Pamajewon,* [1996] 2 S.C.R. 821. See, however, *Delgamuukw* v. *B.C.* (1993), 104 D.L.R. (4th) 470 (B.C.C.A.); *Campbell* v. *British Columbia (A.G.)* (2000), 189 D.L.R. (4th) 333 (B.C.S.C.).

20 *Amodu Tijani* v. *Southern Nigeria (Secretary),* [1921] 2 A.C. 399 (P.C.).

21 *St. Catharines Milling and Lumber Co.* v. *The Queen* (1887), 13 S.C.R. 577; aff'd *St. Catherine's Milling & Lumber Company* v. *The Queen, supra* note 8.

22 *Quebec Act* (1774), 14 Geo. 3, c. 83.

23 *Regina* v. *St. Catharines Milling Co.* (1885), 10 O.R. 196 at 197.

24 *Constitution Act, 1867* (U.K.), 30 & 31 Vict., c. 3, reprinted in R.S.C., 1985, app. II, no. 5.

25 *St. Catharines Milling and Lumber Co.* v. *The Queen, supra* note 21.

26 It is interesting to note that Justice Taschereau sided with Justices Strong and Gwynne in finding that the terms of the *Quebec Act* (1774) 14 Geo. 3 c. 83 had not affected the rights of Aboriginal Peoples conferred by the *Royal Proclamation, 1763* should such rights be deemed to have been conferred by the said proclamation. The effect of the *Quebec Act* (1774) on the *Royal Proclamation* was reviewed by the Ontario Court of Appeal in the case of *Ontario (A.G.)* v. *Bear Island Foundation* (1989), 68 O.R. (2d) 394 (Ont. C.A.), in which that court found that the substantive rights of Aboriginal Peoples as provided for in the *Royal Proclamation* had not been affected by the *Quebec Act* (1774), though the procedural aspects relating to the surrender of Aboriginal title found in the said proclamation had been repealed by the said act. The Ontario Court of Appeal further found in *Chippewas of Sarnia Band* v. *Canada (A.G.)* (C.A.), [2001] 1 C.N.L.R. 56 (Ont. C.A.) at paras. 19, 198–99, 206–19 that these procedural surrender requirements were nevertheless applicable in Ontario since they had been incorporated at common law as a result of the established protocol between the Crown and Aboriginal Peoples that Aboriginal title could be lost only by surrender to the Crown.

27 *St. Catharines Milling and Lumber Co.* v. *The Queen, supra* note 21 at 674. In this regard, Justice Gwynne was simply reiterating the common understanding of the importance of this proclamation for the Aboriginal Peoples of North America. The common recognition of this proclamation as a "charter of rights" was also noted by the Chancery Division of Ontario in its decision in the case of *Regina* v. *St. Catharines Milling Co., supra* note 23 at 226.

28 *St. Catherine's Milling & Lumber Company* v. *The Queen, supra* note 8.

29 *Ibid.* at 55.

30 Similar conclusions were drawn by the Privy Council in relation to reserve lands located within the province of Quebec in *A.G. for Quebec* v. *A.G. for Canada* *("Star Chrome" case)*, [1921] 1 A.C. 401. See also *Ontario Mining Company* v. *Seybold*, [1903] A.C. 73; *Smith* v. *R.*, [1983] 1 S.C.R. 554.

31 *Calder* v. *A.G. of British Columbia*, [1973] S.C.R. 313. See also K. Lysyk, "The Indian Title Question in Canada: An Appraisal in Light of Calder," *supra* note 2.

32 For a brief history of the long-standing efforts of the Nisga'a in pursuit of their Aboriginal rights, see *Campbell* v. *British Columbia (A.G.)*, *supra* note 19.

33 *Calder* v. *A.G. of British Columbia*, *supra* note 31 at 328.

34 *Ibid.* at 390.

35 *Delgamuukw* v. *B.C.*, *supra* note 19.

36 *Guerin* v. *The Queen*, [1984] 2 S.C.R. 335.

37 *Ibid.* at 365.

38 *Indian Act*, R.S.C., 1985, c. I-5.

39 *Guerin* v. *The Queen*, *supra* note 36 at 379. This statement of the law was reiterated by Chief Justice Lamer in *Delgamuukw* v. *B.C.*, *supra* note 19 at 1085 (para. 120).

40 *Guerin* v. *The Queen*, *ibid.* at 376 (Dickson J.). See also the comments of Wilson J. at 348–49.

41 "The principle that a change in sovereignty over a particular territory does not in general affect the presumptive title of the inhabitants was approved by the Privy Council in *Amodu Tijani* v. *Southern Nigeria (Secretary)*, [1921] 2 A.C. 399 (P.C.). That principle supports the assumption implicit in *Calder* that Indian title is an independent legal right which, although recognized by the *Royal Proclamation, 1763*, nonetheless predates it." *Ibid.* at 378.

42 *Ibid.* at 382. See also *Opetchesaht Indian Band* v. *Canada*, [1997] 2 S.C.R. 119 at paras. 37–39, where the characteristics of Aboriginal title as described in the reasons of Dickson J. in *Guerin* are reiterated.

43 *R.* v. *Van der Peet*, [1996] 2 S.C.R. 507.

44 *Ibid.* at 538 (paras. 28–29), 579 (para. 116), and 642–48 (paras. 263–75).

45 See K. Lysyk, "The Rights and Freedoms of the Aboriginal Peoples of Canada," in W.S. Tarnopolsky and G.-A. Beaudoin, eds., *The Canadian Charter of Rights and Freedoms: Commentary* (Toronto: Carswell, 1982). See also K. McNeil, "The Constitutional Rights of the Aboriginal Peoples of Canada" (1982) 4 Supreme Court L.R. 255.

46 *R.* v. *Van der Peet*, *supra* note 43.

47 *R.* v. *Adams*, [1996] 3 S.C.R. 101.

48 *Delgamuukw* v. *B.C.*, *supra* note 19.

49 *Ibid.* at 1094–95 (para. 138).

50 *R.* v. *N.T.C. Smokehouse Ltd.*, [1996] 2 S.C.R. 672.

51 *R.* v. *Gladstone*, [1996] 2 S.C.R. 723.

52 *Fisheries Act*, R.S.C. 1970, c. F-14.

53 *British Columbia Fishery (General) Regulations*, SOR/84-248.

54 *R.* v. *Van der Peet*, *supra* note 43 at 538 (paras. 28–29).

55 *Ibid.* at 538–39 (paras. 30–31).

56 *Ibid.* at 548 (para. 44).

57 This raises interesting evidence issues, which were partially addressed in *Delgamuukw* v. *B.C.*, *supra* note 19 at 1070–79.

58 See the dissenting opinions in *R.* v. *Van der Peet*, *supra* note 43, particularly L'Heureux-Dubé J. at 596–603 and McLachlin J. at 633–36. As we note, it may be argued that Aboriginal practices, customs, and traditions that arose from contact with the Europeans may still be recognized at common law, although they may not receive the constitutional protection of s. 35 of the *Constitution Act, 1982*.

59 It also raises issues in relation to the Aboriginal rights of the Métis, who, by definition, were born as a people after contact between Aboriginal nations and Europeans. There is some indication that, in the case of the Métis, the concept of "time of contact" could be replaced by the concept of "time of effective Crown sovereignty" or of "time when effective control of the area was taken over by the European based culture." *R.* v. *Powley* (February 23, 2001), Docket C34065 (Ont. C.A.) at paras. 93–97, aff'g [1999] 1 C.N.L.R. 153 (Ont. C.J.) at paras. 87–91, and [2000] 2 C.N.L.R. 233 (Ont. S.C.). See also *R.* v. *Horse,* [2000] 3 C.N.L.R. 228 (B.C. Prov. Ct.).

60 See in this regard J. Webber, "Relations of Force and Relations of Justice" (1995) 33 Osgoode Hall L.J. 623.

61 *Constitution Act, 1982*, s. 25, being Schedule B to the *Canada Act 1982* (U.K.), 1982, c. 11.

62 See *R.* v. *Côté*, [1996] 3 S.C.R. 139 at 174–75 (paras. 52–53) and *Delgamuukw* v. *B.C.*, *supra* note 19 at 1093 (para. 136).

63 *R.* v. *Gladstone*, *supra* note 51.

64 *R.* v. *N.T.C. Smokehouse Ltd.*, *supra* note 50.

65 *Delgamuukw* v. *B.C.*, *supra* note 19 at 1066 (para. 82). See also *R.* v. *Sparrow,* [1990] 1 S.C.R. 1075 at 1112; *St. Mary's Indian Band* v. *Cranbrook*, [1997] 2 S.C.R. 657 at 666–67 (para. 14).

66 *Delgamuukw* v. *B.C.*, *supra* note 19.

67 *Delgamuukw* v. *British Columbia* (1991), 79 D.L.R. (4th) 185 (B.C.S.C.); [1991] 5 C.N.L.R. xiii.

68 *Delgamuukw* v. *B.C.* (B.C.C.A.), *supra* note 19.

69 *Delgamuukw* v. *B.C.*, *supra* note 19.

70 *R.* v. *Van der Peet*, *supra* note 43.

71 *Delgamuukw* v. *B.C.*, *supra* note 19 at 1083 (para. 117).

72 *Ibid.* at 1086–87 (para. 122). See also *Haida Nation* v. *British Columbia (Minister of Forests)* (1997), 153 D.L.R. (4th) 1 (B.C.C.A.) at 4–5 (paras. 5–6).

73 *Delgamuukw* v. *B.C.*, *supra* note 19 at 1090 (para. 130).

Notes to Chapter 2

1 In *R.* v. *Sioui*, [1990] 1 S.C.R. 1025, for example, the treaty there discussed concerned the peace of 1760 between the Hurons and the British forces invading New France.

2 For example, Treaty 11 of 1921 provides as one of its considerations that the Aboriginal signatories "have been notified and informed by His Majesty's said commissioner that it is His desire to open for settlement, immigration, trade,

travel, mining, lumbering and such other purposes as to His Majesty may seem meet, a tract of country bounded and described as hereinafter set forth, and to obtain the consent thereto of His Indian subjects inhabiting the said tract, and to make a treaty, so that there may be peace and goodwill between them and His Majesty's other subjects."

3 For example, the treaty reviewed in *R. v. Marshall*, [1999] 3 S.C.R. 456, concerned peace between the Mi'kmaq and the Crown, as well as trade relations between the parties.

4 See generally on the issue of treaties, S. Grammond, *Les traités entre l'État canadien et les peuples autochtones* (Cowansville, Québec: Les Éditions Yvon Blais, 1995); S. Grammond, "Aboriginal Treaties and Canadian Law" (1994) 20 Queen's L.J. 57; S. Aronson, "The Authority of the Crown to Make Treaties with Indians" [1993] 2 C.N.L.R. 1; A. Morris, *The Treaties of Canada with the Indians of Manitoba and the North-West Territories* (Toronto: Belfords, Clarke and Co., 1880; reprint, Saskatoon: Fifth House, 1991); Royal Commission on Aboriginal Peoples, *Treaty Making in the Spirit of Co-existence: An Alternative to Extinguishment* (Ottawa: Minister of Supply and Services, 1995); J. Woodward, *Native Law* (Toronto: Carswell, 1994) particularly chap. 21; B.H. Wildsmith, "Pre-Confederation Treaties," in B.W. Morse, ed., *Aboriginal Peoples and the Law* (Ottawa: Carleton University Press, 1989); N.K. Zlotkin, "Post-Confederation Treaties," in B.W. Morse, ed., *Aboriginal Peoples and the Law* (Ottawa: Carleton University Press, 1989); K. Lysyk, "Indian Hunting Rights: Constitutional Considerations and the Role of Indians Treaties in British Columbia" (1966) 2 U.B.C. L. Rev. 401; D. Knoll, "Treaty and Aboriginal Hunting and Fishing Rights" [1979] 1 C.N.L.R. 1; I. Brownlie, *Treaties and Indigenous Peoples* (Oxford: Clarendon Press, 1992).

5 *R. v. Sioui, supra* note 1 at 1043. Self-government provisions may also form part of a treaty: *Campbell v. British Columbia (A.G.)* (2000), 189 D.L.R. (4th) 333 (B.C.S.C.) at 367–68 (paras. 137–43).

6 *Cree School Board v. Canada (A.G.)*, [1998] 3 C.N.L.R. 24 (Que. S.C.) (appeal pending in Que. C.A. #500-09-006312-987) at 49, 51 (paras. 104–08, 118).

7 *A.G. for Quebec v. A.G. for Canada ("Star Chrome"case)*, [1921] 1 A.C. 401 at 410–11; *Guerin v. The Queen*, [1984] 2 S.C.R. 335 at 375; *Delgamuukw v. B.C.*, [1997] 3 S.C.R. 1010 at 1085 (para. 120).

8 *R. v. White and Bob* (1964), 50 D.L.R. (2d) 613 (B.C.C.A.) at 616 (Davey J.A.); aff'd [1965] S.C.R. vi; (1965), 52 D.L.R. (2d) 481 (S.C.C.) and the opinion of Norris J. in that case. See also *Cree School Board v. Canada (A.G.), supra* note 6 at 56 (para. 155).

9 *Campbell v. British Columbia (A.G.), supra* note 5 at 340 (para. 9). Compare with *B.C. (Minister of Forests) v. Okanagan Indian Band* (2000), 187 D.L.R. (4th) 664, where a claim of Aboriginal rights without further evidence was deemed insufficient as a bar to an interlocutory injunction against the pursuit of the activity said to be subject to the right. Such evidence requirements are significantly reduced when the concerned Aboriginal right is recognized by treaty.

10 *R. v. White and Bob, supra* note 8; *Simon v. R.*, [1985] 2 S.C.R 387, in particular at 404, 410; *R. v. Sioui, supra* note 1, in particular at 1038–44, 1063; *R. v. Badger,*

[1996] 1 S.C.R. 771, in particular at 813–14 (paras. 78–79); *R.* v. *Sundown,* [1999] 1 S.C.R. 393 at 406–07 (paras. 24–25); *R.* v. *Marshall, supra* note 3.

11 Professor B. Slattery put it this way: "It seems clear that historic treaties are governed, neither by English common law nor aboriginal customary law, but by a unique body of treaty law that forms a branch of the doctrine of aboriginal rights." B. Slattery, "Making Sense of Aboriginal and Treaty Rights" (2000) 79 Can. Bar Rev. 196 at 207.

12 See, amongst other cases, *R.* v. *White and Bob, supra* note 8; *R.* v. *Taylor and Williams* (1982), 34 O.R. (2d) 360; *Simon* v. *R., supra* note 10; *Saanichton Marina Ltd.* v. *Tsawout Indian Band* (1989), 57 D.L.R. (4th) 161 (B.C.C.A.); *R.* v. *Sioui, supra* note 1; *R.* v. *Badger, supra* note 10; *R.* v. *Sundown, supra* note 10; *R.* v. *Marshall, supra* note 3 at 496–99, 511–13 (paras. 49–52, 78).

13 *Calder* v. *A.G. of British Columbia,* [1973] S.C.R. 313 at 402–04; *Guerin* v. *The Queen, supra* note 7 at 377; *R.* v. *Sparrow,* [1990] 1 S.C.R. 1075 at 1099; *R.* v. *Gladstone,* [1996] 2 S.C.R. 723 at 750–51 (para. 34); *Delgamuukw* v. *B.C.,* [1997] 3 S.C.R. 1010 at 1122–23 (para. 183); *Watt* v. *Canada (Minister of Citizenship and Immigration),* [1999] 2 C.N.L.R. 326 (F.C.A.) at 334–36 (paras. 13–16); *R.* v. *Jacob,* [1999] 3 C.N.L.R. 239 (B.C.S.C.) at 266–67 (paras. 107–09); and B. Slattery, "Understanding Aboriginal Rights" (1987) 66 Can. Bar Rev. 727 at 748–49, 765–66.

14 *Indian Act,* R.S.C., 1985, c. I-5, s. 88.

15 *R.* v. *Badger, supra* note 10 at 812–14 (paras. 77–82). See also *R.* v. *Bombay,* [1993] 1 C.N.L.R. 92 (Ont. C.A.) and *R.* v. *Sundown, supra* note 10 at 415, 417 (paras. 43, 46).

16 Justice Lamer stated the following in this regard in *R.* v. *Sioui, supra* note 1 at 1052–53: "I consider that, instead, we can conclude from the historical documents that both Great Britain and France felt that the Indian nations had sufficient independence and played a large enough role in North America for it to be good policy to maintain relations with them very close to those maintained between sovereign nations."

17 See generally on this matter B. Slattery, "Aboriginal Sovereignty and Imperial Claims" (1991) 29 Osgoode Hall L.J. 1; B. Slattery, "Making Sense of Aboriginal and Treaty Rights," *supra* note 11 at 209.

18 *R.* v. *White and Bob, supra* note 8.

19 *Ibid.* at 649.

20 *Simon* v. *R., supra* note 10.

21 A further detailed discussion of s. 88 of the *Indian Act* and its application can be found in chapter four.

22 *Simon* v. *R., supra* note 10 at 410. See also *R.* v. *Sioui, supra* note 1 at 1043.

23 *R.* v. *Sioui, ibid.*

24 *Ibid.* at 1031.

25 *Simon* v. *R., supra* note 10.

26 See the discussion in chapter one.

27 *R.* v. *Sioui, supra* note 1 at 1038.

28 *R.* v. *Taylor and Williams, supra* note 12.

29 *R.* v. *Sioui, supra* note 1 at 1045.

30 *Ibid.* at 1071.
31 *R.* v. *Sundown, supra* note 10.
32 *Constitution Act, 1930,* R.S.C., 1985, app. II, no. 26.
33 In regard to the impact on treaties of the Natural Resources Transfer Agreements see generally *Cardinal* v. *A.G. of Alberta,* [1974] S.C.R. 695; *Frank* v. *R.,* [1978] 1 S.C.R. 95; *R.* v. *Sutherland,* [1980] 2 S.C.R. 451 at 460; *Moosehunter* v. *R.,* [1981] 1 S.C.R. 282; *R.* v. *Horseman,* [1990] 1 S.C.R. 901, particularly at 933, and *R.* v. *Badger, supra* note 10 at 794–97 (paras. 43–48). See also *R.* v. *Wesley,* [1932] 2 W.W.R. 337 (Alta. S.C. App. Div.) at 344.
34 *Simon* v. *R., supra* note 10 at 403; cited with approval in *R.* v. *Sundown, supra* note 10 at 408–09 (para. 27).
35 *Ibid.* at 412 (paras. 35, 36).
36 See amongst other cases, *R.* v. *Marshall, supra* note 3 at 511–13 (para. 78); *R.* v. *Sundown, supra* note 10 at 406–07 (para. 24); *R.* v. *Badger, supra* note 10 at 813 (para. 78); *R.* v. *Sioui, supra* note 1 at 1043; *Simon* v. *R., supra* note 10 at 404.
37 *R.* v. *Taylor and Williams, supra* note 12.
38 *Ibid.* at 367.
39 *R.* v. *Badger, supra* note 10.
40 *Ibid.* at 781–82 (para. 9). See also *Nowegijick* v. *R.,* [1983] 1 S.C.R. 29; *Mitchell* v. *Peguis Indian Band,* [1990] 2 S.C.R. 85; *Osoyoos Indian Band* v. *Oliver (Town),* (1999), 172 D.L.R. (4th) 589 (B.C.C.A.) at 629 (para. 92).
41 *R.* v. *Marshall, supra* note 3.
42 *Simon* v. *R., supra* note 10.
43 *R.* v. *Marshall, supra* note 3 at 468 (para. 5).
44 *Ibid.* at 492–93 (para. 43).
45 *Ibid.* at 501–02 (paras. 58–59).
46 Justice (now Chief Justice) McLachlin summarized in her own words these principles at para. 78 of the *Marshall* decision, *supra* note 3: (a) "[t]reaties should be liberally construed and ambiguities or doubtful expressions should be resolved in favour of the Aboriginal signatories"; (b) "[t]he goal of treaty interpretation is to choose from among the various possible interpretations of common intention the one which best reconciles the interests of both parties at the time the treaty was signed"; (c) "[i]n searching for the common intention of the parties, the integrity and honour of the Crown is presumed"; (d) "[i]n determining the signatories' respective understanding and intentions, the court must be sensitive to the unique cultural and linguistic differences between the parties"; (e) "[t]he words of the treaty must be given the sense which they would naturally have held for the parties at the time"; (f) "[a] technical or contractual interpretation of treaty wording should be avoided"; (g) "[w]hile construing the language generously, courts cannot alter the terms of the treaty by exceeding what is possible on the language or realistic"; (h) "[t]he treaty rights of aboriginal peoples must not be interpreted in a static or rigid way. They are not frozen at the date of signature. The interpreting court must update treaty rights to provide for their modern exercise. This involves determining what modern practices are reasonably incidental to the core treaty right in its modern context."
47 *R.* v. *Marshall, supra* note 3 at 513–14 (para 81).

48 *Ibid.* at 514–15 (paras. 82–83).

49 *Ibid.* at 526 (para. 102).

50 *Ibid.* at 499 (para. 52).

51 *R.* v. *Sioui, supra* note 1 at 1063; *Simon* v. *R., supra* note 10 at 401; *R.* v. *Badger, supra* note 10 at 793–94, 796–97 (paras. 41, 47); *R.* v. *Sundown, supra* note 10 at 406–07 (para. 24).

52 *R.* v. *Taylor and Williams, supra* note 12 at 367; *R.* v. *Sparrow, supra* note 13 at 1107–08; *R.* v. *Badger, supra* note 10 at 793–94, 813 (paras. 41, 78); *R.* v. *Marshall, supra* note 3 at 496–97, 511–13 (paras. 49, 78); *Ontario* v. *Dominion of Canada and Quebec: In Re Indian Claims* (1895), 25 S.C.R. 434, at 511–12; *R.* v. *Powley* (February 23, 2001), Docket C34065 (Ont. C.A.) at para. 80.

53 *R.* v. *Badger, supra* note 10 at 799–800, 803–04 (paras. 55–58); *R.* v. *Taylor and Williams, supra* note 12 at 365; *R.* v. *Marshall, supra* note 3 at 472–73 (para. 12).

54 *R.* v. *Marshall, supra* note 3 at 472–75, 511–13 (paras. 12–14, 78); *R.* v. *Badger, supra* note 10 at paras. 14, 41, 52; *Simon* v. *R., supra* note 10 at 402; *R.* v. *Sioui, supra* note 1 at 1035; *Guerin* v. *The Queen, supra* note 7 at 388; *R.* v. *Horseman, supra* note 33 at 906–07, 930; *Halfway River First Nation* v. *B.C. (Ministry of Forests)*, [1999] 4 C.N.L.R. 1 (B.C.C.A.) at 32–34 (paras. 105–09).

55 *R.* v. *Taylor and Williams, supra* note 12 at 367; *R.* v. *Sioui, supra* note 1 at 1045; *R.* v. *Badger, supra* note 10 at 798–99 (para. 52); *Simon* v. *R., supra* note 10 at 401–03; *R.* v. *Sundown, supra* note 10 at 406–08 (paras. 24–25); *R.* v. *Marshall, supra* note 3 at 471–72, 511–13 (paras. 9–11, 78, 81); *R.* v. *Horseman, supra* note 33 at 907; *Delgamuukw* v. *B.C., supra* note 7 at para. 87.

56 *R.* v. *Sioui, supra* note 1 at 1068–69; *R.* v. *Marshall, supra* note 3 at 511–13 (para. 78).

57 *R.* v. *Marshall, supra* note 3 at 492–93 (paras. 42, 43); *R.* v. *Sioui, supra* note 1 at 1067; *Simon* v. *R., supra* note 10 at 403; *R.* v. *Sundown, supra* note 10 at 409–11 (paras. 30–33).

58 *Simon* v. *R., supra* note 10 at 402; *R.* v. *Sundown, supra* note 10 at 410–11 (para. 32); *R.* v. *Marshall, supra* note 3 at 499, 511–13 (paras. 53, 78).

59 *Nowegijick* v. *R., supra* note 40 at 36; *Mitchell* v. *Peguis Indian Band, supra* note 40 at 142–43; *R.* v. *Lewis*, [1996] 1 S.C.R. 921 at para. 66; *Opetchesaht Indian Band* v. *Canada*, [1997] 2 S.C.R. 119 at paras. 76, 77.

60 *Simon* v. *R., supra* note 10 at 406; *R.* v. *Sioui, supra* note 1 at 1061; *R.* v. *Badger, supra* note 10 at 793–94, 796–97 (paras. 41, 47).

61 *R.* v. *Marshall, supra* note 3 at 513 (para. 80).

62 *R.* v. *Badger, supra* note 10 at 812 (para. 76). See also *Ontario (A.G.)* v. *Bear Island Foundation*, [1991] 2 S.C.R. 570; *Ontario* v. *Dominion of Canada and Quebec: In Re Indian Claims, supra* note 52 at 504–05, 511–12; *R.* v. *Marshall, supra* note 3 at 497 (para. 50); *Campbell* v. *British Columbia (A.G.), supra* note 5 at 355 (para. 84); B. Slattery, "Making Sense of Aboriginal and Treaty Rights," *supra* note 11 at 209–10.

63 *Dreaver* v. *R.* (1935), 5 C.N.L.C. 92 (Exch. C.).

64 *Ibid.* at 115–16.

65 *Sikyea* v. *R.*, [1964] S.C.R. 642; *R.* v. *George*, [1966] S.C.R. 267; *Moosehunter* v. *R., supra* note 33; *R.* v. *Horseman, supra* note 33 at 936.

66 *Sikyea* v. *R., ibid.*
67 *Migratory Birds Convention Act,* 1952, R.S.C., chap. 179.
68 *Migratory Birds Convention Act,* 1917 (Can.), c. 18.
69 *Sikyea* v. *R.* (1964), 43 D.L.R. (2d) 150 (N.W.T.C.A.) at 154. This decision of the Northwest Territories Court of Appeal was subsequently appealed to the Supreme Court of Canada. This conclusion of the Court of Appeal was subsequently affirmed by the Supreme Court of Canada in *Sikyea* v. *R., supra* note 65 at 646.
70 *R.* v. *Badger, supra* note 10 at 814 (para. 82).

Notes to Chapter 3

1   Reference may be made in this regard, amongst other cases, to *R.* v. *Sparrow,* [1990] 1 S.C.R. 1075 at 1108; *Guerin* v. *The Queen,* [1984] 2 S.C.R. 335 at 375–76; *R.* v. *Van der Peet,* [1996] 2 S.C.R. 507 at 536–37 (para. 24); *Quebec (A.G.)* v. *Canada (N.E.B.),* [1994] 1 S.C.R 159 at 183; *Delgamuukw* v. *B.C.,* [1997] 3 S.C.R. 1010 at 1125–26. See generally L.I. Rotman, *Parallel Paths: Fiduciary Doctrine and the Crown-Native Relationship in Canada* (Toronto: University of Toronto Press, 1996); J. Hurley, "The Crown's Fiduciary Duty and Indian Title: Guerin v. The Queen" (1985) 30 McGill L.J. 559; R.H. Bartlett, "The Fiduciary Obligation of the Crown to the Indians" (1989) 53 Sask. L. Rev. 301; R.H. Bartlett "You Can't Trust the Crown: The Fiduciary Obligation of the Crown to the Indians: Guerin v. The Queen" (1984–85) 49 Sask. L. Rev. 367; W.R. McMurtry & A. Pratt, "Indians and the Fiduciary Concept, Self-Government, and the Constitution: Guerin in Perspective" [1986] 3 C.N.L.R. 19; D.P. Owen, "Fiduciary Obligations and Aboriginal Peoples: Devolution in Action" [1994] 3 C.N.L.R. 1; B. Slattery, "First Nations and the Constitution: A Question of Trust" (1992) 71 Can. Bar Rev. 261; B. Slattery, "Understanding Aboriginal Rights" (1987) 66 Can. Bar Rev. 727; E.J. Weinrib, "The Fiduciary Obligation" (1975) 25 U.T.L.J. 1; P. Hutchins *et al.,* "When Do Fiduciary Obligations to Aboriginal Peoples Arise?" (1995) 59 Sask. L. Rev. 97.
2   *R.* v. *Badger,* [1996] 1 S.C.R. 771 at 782 (para. 9). See also *Ontario* v. *Dominion of Canada and Quebec: In Re Indian Claims* (1895), 25 S.C.R. 434 at 534–35; *Nowegijick* v. *R.,* [1983] 1 S.C.R. 29 at 36; *Mitchell* v. *Peguis Indian Band,* [1990] 2 S.C.R. 85 at 142–43.
3   *R.* v. *Sparrow, supra* note 1 at 1108.
4   B. Slattery, "Understanding Aboriginal Rights," *supra* note 1 at 753.
5   *Guerin* v. *The Queen, supra* note 1. For a detailed summary of the facts applicable and a further review of the *Guerin* case, see the discussion of this case in chapter one.
6   *Kinlock* v. *Secretary of State for India in Council* (1882), 7 App. Cas. 619.
7   *Tito* v. *Waddell (No. 2),* [1977] 3 All. E.R. 129 (Ch.).
8   See *Guerin* v. *The Queen, supra* note 1 at 384. See also *Semiahmoo Indian Band* v. *Canada,* [1998] 1 F.C. 3 (C.A.); *Lord* v. *Canada,* [2000] 3 C.N.L.R. 69 (Que. C.A.) at 73 (para. 13).
9   See *R.* v. *Sparrow, supra* note 1; *R.* v. *Adams,* [1996] 3 S.C.R. 101; *Delgamuukw* v. *B.C., supra* note 1; *Cree Regional Authority* v. *Canada,* [1992] 1 F.C. 440

(T.D.); *Samson Indian Nation and Band* v. *Canada*, [1996] 2 F.C. 528 (F.C.T.D.); *Union of Nova Scotia Indians* v. *Canada (A.G.)*, [1997] 1 F.C. 325 (F.C.T.D.); *Nunavik Inuit* v. *Canada*, [1998] 4 C.N.L.R. 68 (F.C.T.D.); *Gitanyow First Nation* v. *Canada*, [1999] 3 C.N.L.R. 89 (B.C.S.C.); *Halfway River First Nation* v. *B.C. (Ministry of Forests)*, [1999] 4 C.N.L.R. 1 (B.C.C.A.); *B.C. Native Women's Society* v. *Canada*, [2000] 3 C.N.L.R. 4 (F.C.T.D.) at 10–11 (paras. 19–21).

10 Decisions where a legally enforceable fiduciary duty was not found to be incumbent on the Crown in the particular circumstances of these cases include *Boyer* v. *R.*, [1986] 2 F.C. 393; [1986] 4 C.N.L.R. 53 (F.C.A.); *Quebec (A.G.)* v. *Canada (N.E.B.)*, supra note 1; *Fairford First Nation* v. *Canada (A.G.)*, [1999] 2 F.C. 48 (T.D.); *Scrimbitt* v. *Sakimay Indian Band Council*, [2000] 1 C.N.L.R. 205 (F.C.T.D.); *Tsartlip Indian Band* v. *Canada (Minister of Indian Affairs and Northern Development)* (C.A.), [2000] 2 F.C. 314 (C.A.); *Chippewas of Nawash First Nation* v. *Canada*, [2001] 1 C.N.L.R. 20.

11 *Blueberry River Indian Band* v. *Canada*, [1995] 4 S.C.R. 344.

12 *Ibid.* at para. 16.

13 *Semiahmoo Indian Band* v. *Canada*, supra note 8.

14 *Ibid.* at 25–26 (para. 45).

15 *Ibid.* at 32–33 (para. 59).

16 *Seminole Nation* v. *United States*, 316 U.S. 286 (1942).

17 *Ibid.* at 296–97. See also *Carlo* v. *Gustafson*, 512 F. Supp. 833 (1981) at 838.

18 *Ontario (A.G.)* v. *Bear Island Foundation*, [1991] 2 S.C.R. 570.

19 *Ibid.* at 575. See also *Cree Regional Authority* v. *Canada*, supra note 9 at 463–64; *Cree School Board* v. *Canada (A.G.)*, [1998] 3 C.N.L.R. 24 (Que. S.C.) (appeal pending in Que. C.A. #500-09-006312-987) at 46, 51 (paras. 78, 116).

20 *Ontario* v. *Dominion of Canada and Quebec: In Re Indian Claims*, supra note 2 at 511–12.

21 *R.* v. *Marshall*, [1999] 3 S.C.R. 456 at 497 (para. 50).

22 See *R.* v. *Sparrow*, supra note 1 at 1105; *Ontario (A.G.)* v. *Bear Island Foundation*, supra note 18; *R.* v. *Côté*, [1996] 3 S.C.R. 139 at 185; *R.* v. *Badger*, supra note 2 at 820–21 (para. 96); *Côté* v. *R.*, [1993] R.J.Q. 1350 (Que. C.A.) at 1371–72; *Cree Regional Authority* v. *Canada*, supra note 19 at 470; *R.* v. *Secretary of State*, [1981] 4 C.N.L.R. 86 (Eng. C.A.) at 97, 117; *Gitanyow First Nation* v. *Canada*, supra note 9 at 100–02 (paras. 45–53); *Halfway River First Nation* v. *B.C. (Ministry of Forests)*, supra note 9; *R.* v. *Young*, [2000] 3 C.N.L.R. 286 (Que. S.C.) at 300–02 (paras. 69–75).

23 See the James Bay and Northern Quebec Agreement, reprinted as *James Bay and Northern Quebec Agreement and Complementary Agreements*, 1998 ed. (Sainte-Foy: Les Publications du Québec, 1998). The James Bay and Northern Quebec Agreement was approved, given effect, and declared valid by the *James Bay and Northern Quebec Native Claims Settlement Act*, S.C. 1976–77, c. 32, and the *Act approving the Agreement concerning James Bay and Northern Quebec*, 1976 S.Q., c. 46. See also the Nisga'a Final Agreement which was approved, given effect and declared valid by the *Nisga'a Final Agreement Act*, S.C. 2000, c. 7.

24 *Cree School Board* v. *Canada (A.G.)*, supra note 19 at 46, 51 (paras. 78, 116).

25 *Halfway River First Nation* v. *B.C. (Ministry of Forest)*, supra note 9; *Perry* v.

Ontario, [1998] 2 C.N.L.R. 79 (Ont. C.A.); *Gitanyow First Nation* v. *Canada, supra* note 9 at 100–02 (paras. 45–53). However, see *Bear Island Foundation* v. *Ontario,* [2000] C.N.L.R. 13 (Ont. C.A.) at 23–24 (paras. 34–35).

26   B. Slattery, "Understanding Aboriginal Rights," *supra* note 1 at 755. See also Manitoba, *Report of the Aboriginal Justice Inquiry of Manitoba,* vol. 1 (Winnipeg: Queen's Printer Province of Manitoba, 1991) at 155.

Notes to Chapter 4

1   *R.* v. *White and Bob* (1964), 50 D.L.R. (2d) 613 (B.C.C.A.) at 617, 652–655; aff'd [1965] S.C.R. vi; (1965), 52 D.L.R. (2d) 481 (S.C.C.).

2   *Campbell* v. *British Columbia (A.G.)* (2000), 189 D.L.R. (4th) 333 (B.C.S.C.) at 351 (para. 70).

3   *Reference re Secession of Quebec,* [1998] 2 S.C.R. 217 at 262–63 (para. 82).

4   *Roberts* v. *Canada,* [1989] 1 S.C.R. 322.

5   J.M. Evans & B. Slattery, "Federal Jurisdiction-Pendant Parties-Aboriginal Title and Federal Common Law-Charter Challenges-Reform Proposals: *Roberts* v. *Canada*" (1989) 68 Can. Bar Rev. 817 at 832. See also B. Slattery, "Understanding Aboriginal Rights" (1987) 66 Can. Bar Rev. 727 at 732, 736–41, 777; Royal Commission on Aboriginal Peoples, *Partners in Confederation: Aboriginal Peoples, Self-Government and the Constitution* (Ottawa: Minister of Supply and Services, 1993) at 20.

6   *R.* v. *Côté,* [1996] 3 S.C.R. 139 at 170, 172–75 (paras. 45, 46, 49–54).

7   *R.* v. *Adams,* [1996] 3 S.C.R. 101 at 120–22 (paras. 31–33).

8   *Ibid.*

9   *R.* v. *Côté, supra* note 6.

10   *R.* v. *Sparrow,* [1990] 1 S.C.R. 1075.

11   *Roberts* v. *Canada, supra* note 4.

12   *R.* v. *Côté, supra* note 6 at 173 (para. 49). See also *Cree School Board* v. *Canada (A.G.),* [1998] 3 C.N.L.R. 24 (Que. S.C.) (appeal pending in Que. C.A. #500-09-006312-987) at 49 (para. 102).

13   *Delgamuukw* v. *B.C.,* [1997] 3 S.C.R. 1010 at 1118–19 (paras. 176, 179).

14   Since both Aboriginal and treaty rights are part of the federal common law and fall under the federal sphere of constitutional authority, it follows logically that the constitutional position of treaty rights is similar to that of Aboriginal rights.

15   *St. Catherine's Milling & Lumber Company* v. *The Queen* (1888), 14 App. Cas. 46.

16   Though the Judicial Committee of the Privy Council based its decision on the premise that the Aboriginal interest in the land derived from the *Royal Proclamation, 1763,* common law Aboriginal title also falls under s. 91(24) of the *Constitution Act, 1867: Delgamuukw* v. *B.C., supra* note 13 at 119; *Guerin* v. *The Queen,* [1984] 2 S.C.R. 335 at 379; *A.G. of Quebec* v. *A.G. of Canada ("Star Chrome" case),* [1921] 1 A.C. 401.

17   See also *"Star Chrome" case, ibid.* at 406; *Smith* v. *R.,* [1983] 1 S.C.R. 554 at 580–81.

18   *Delgamuukw* v. *B.C., supra* note 13.

19   *Ibid.* at 1121 (paras. 180–81).

20 See in general P.W. Hogg, *Constitutional Law of Canada*, 4th ed., vol. 1 (looseleaf) (Toronto: Carswell, 1997), particularly chap. 27; K. Lysyk, "The Unique Constitutional Position of the Canadian Indian" (1967) 45 Can. Bar Rev. 513; K. McNeil, "Aboriginal Title and the Division of Powers" (1998) 61 Sask. L. Rev. 431; J. Woodward, *Native Law* (Toronto: Carswell, 1994) particularly chaps. 3, 4; B. Slattery, "Understanding Aboriginal Rights" (1987) 66 Can. Bar Rev. 727; M. Patenaude, *Le droit provincial et les terres indiennes* (Montréal: Les Éditions Yvon Blais, 1986); N. Lyon, "Constitutional Issues in Native Law," in B.W. Morse, ed., *Aboriginal Peoples and the Law* (Ottawa: Carleton University Press, 1989); D. Sanders, "The Application of Provincial Laws," in B.W. Morse, ed., *Aboriginal Peoples and the Law* (Ottawa: Carleton University Press, 1989); B. Slattery, "The Hidden Constitution: Aboriginal Rights in Canada" (1984) 32 Am. J. Comp. L. 361.

21 Some of the relevant Supreme Court of Canada cases decided prior to *Delgamuukw* v. *B.C., supra* note 13, and dealing with the application of provincial laws in regard to the first branch of the federal jurisdiction, namely "Indians," are *Cardinal* v. *A.G. of Alberta*, [1974] S.C.R. 695; *Natural Parents* v. *Superintendent of Child Welfare*, [1976] 2 S.C.R 751; *Kruger* v. *R.*, [1978] 1 S.C.R. 104; *Four B Manufacturing Ltd.* v. *United Garment Workers of America*, [1980] 1 S.C.R. 1031; *R.* v. *Sutherland*, [1980] 2 S.C.R. 451; *Dick* v. *R.*, [1985] 2 S.C.R. 309; *Derrickson* v. *Derrickson*, [1986] 1 S.C.R. 285; *R.* v. *Francis*, [1988] 1 S.C.R. 1025.

22 See *Derrickson* v. *Derrickson, ibid.* Compare *Oka (Municipality)* v. *Simon*, [1999] 2 C.N.L.R. 205 (Que. C.A.) (leave to appeal to S.C.C. refused October 21, 1999, file 27124) with *Surrey* v. *Peace Arch Ent. Ltd.* (1970), 74 W.W.R. 380 (B.C.C.A.) and *Morin* v. *Canada*, [2000] 4 C.N.L.R. 218 (F.C.T.D.). See also *R.* v. *Young*, [2000] 3 C.N.L.R. 286 (Que. S.C.) at 298 (paras. 40–41).

23 *R.* v. *Sutherland, supra* note 21.

24 *Kruger* v. *R., supra* note 21; *Four B Manufacturing Ltd.* v. *United Garment Workers of America, supra* note 21; *Kitkatla Band* v. *British Columbia*, [2000] 2 C.N.L.R. 36 (B.C.C.A.).

25 See *R.* v. *Alphonse*, [1993] 4 C.N.L.R. 19 (B.C.C.A.).

26 *Delgamuukw* v. *B.C., supra* note 13 at 1121 (para. 181). This statement of the law was reiterated in the unanimous decision of the Supreme Court of Canada in *Lovelace* v. *Ontario*, [2000] 1 S.C.R. 950 at 1012–13 (para. 110).

27 In *R.* v. *Badger*, [1996] 1 S.C.R. 771 at 809 (para. 69), it was noted that "the regulation of Indian hunting rights would ordinarily come within the jurisdiction of the Federal government and not the Province." See also *St. Catherine's Milling & Lumber Company* v. *The Queen, supra* note 15 at 60.

28 *R.* v. *White and Bob* (1964), 50 D.L.R. (2d) 613 (B.C.C.A.) at 618, 647; aff'd [1965] S.C.R. vi; (1965), 52 D.L.R. (2d) 481 (S.C.C.).

29 *Derrickson* v. *Derrickson, supra* note 21.

30 *Ibid.* at 296. The Court added at 301–04 that compensation could, however, be ordered under the terms of the provincial legislation relating to the division of family assets to take into account the fact that reserve lands held by the spouses could not be divided under the terms of the provincial legislation.

31 *Delgamuukw* v. *B.C., supra* note 13 at para. 173; *R.* v. *Young, supra* note 22 at

294–95 (paras. 37–38); *A.G. of Quebec* v. *A.G. of Canada ("Star Chrome" case), supra* note 16.

32   *Indian Act,* R.S.C., 1985, c. I-5, s. 88.

33   This legislative prohibition in regard to provincial legislation affecting treaties has far-reaching implications. In particular, the justification test laid out by the Supreme Court of Canada in application of s. 35 of the *Constitution Act, 1982* when provincial laws purport to infringe on Aboriginal rights may not be fully applicable to treaty rights because of the operation of s. 88 of the *Indian Act.* Though the issue is not finally settled, it can be forcefully argued that s. 88 may afford a special and paramount statutory protection for the terms of treaties against any potentially conflicting provincial law. See generally *Kruger* v. *R., supra* note 21 at 114–15; *Simon* v. *R.,* [1985] 2 S.C.R. 387; *R.* v. *Sioui,* [1990] 1 S.C.R. 1025; *R.* v. *Côté, supra* note 6 at 191 (para. 86); *R.* v. *Sundown,* [1999] 1 S.C.R. 393 at 417–18 (para. 47).

34   When Parliament incorporates the law of another legislative jurisdiction by reference in its own legislation, the law so incorporated becomes federal law and is to be applied as such, provided that all the conditions precedent to incorporation have been satisfied. See *Roberts* v. *Canada,* [2000] 3 C.N.L.R. 303 (F.C.A.) at 311–12 (para. 28); *R.* v. *Alphonse, supra* note 25; *A.G. for Ontario* v. *Scott,* [1956] S.C.R. 137; *Coughlin* v. *Ontario Highway Transport Board et al.,* [1968] S.C.R. 569.

35   See generally *Derrickson* v. *Derrickson, supra* note 21 at 293–96, 299–303; *Delgamuukw* v. *B.C., supra* note 13 at 1116–23 (paras. 174–83); *Surrey* v. *Peace Arch Ent. Ltd., supra* note 22; *Matsqui Indian Band* v. *Bird,* [1993] 3 C.N.L.R. 80 (B.C.S.C.); *Stoney Creek Indian Band* v. *British Columbia,* [1999] 1 C.N.L.R. 192 (B.C.S.C.) at 201–10, set aside on procedural grounds; *Stoney Creek Indian Band* v. *Alcan Aluminium Ltd.,* [2000] 2 C.N.L.R. 345 (B.C.C.A.). See also Hon. D. Lambert, *"Van der Peet* and *Delgamuukw:* Ten Unresolved Issues" (1998) 32:2 U.B.C. L. Rev. 249 at 266–67; N. Barnes, *"Delgamuukw,* Division of Powers and Provincial Land and Resource Laws: Some Implications for Provincial Resource Rights" (1998) 32:2 U.B.C. L. Rev. 318.

36   Compare *Oka (Municipality)* v. *Simon, supra* note 22, with *Surrey* v. *Peace Arch Ent. Ltd., supra* note 22, and *Morin* v. *Canada, supra* note 22.

37   See *Dick* v. *R., supra* note 21, and *Delgamuukw* v. *B.C., supra* note 13 at 1121–22 (para. 182).

38   *R.* v. *Horseman,* [1990] 1 S.C.R. 901 at 936.

39   *Delgamuukw* v. *B.C., supra* note 13 at 1113 (para. 168).

40   Like all other federal legislation, since 1982 provincial legislation referentially incorporated under the terms of the *Indian Act* is also subject to certain constitutional constraints, which flow, *inter alia,* from the provisions of s. 35 of the *Constitution Act, 1982.*

41   See our discussion in the next chapter concerning the infringement of Aboriginal and treaty rights.

42   See *Blueberry River Indian Band* v. *Canada,* [1995] 4 S.C.R. 344 at 358, 387 (paras. 6, 72); *Canadian Pacific* v. *Paul,* [1988] 2 S.C.R. 654 at 678; *St. Mary's*

Indian Band v. *Cranbrook*, [1997] 2 S.C.R. 657 at 666–67 (para. 14); *Delgamuukw* v. *B.C.*, *supra* note 13 at 1090 (para. 130).

43 *R.* v. *Côté*, *supra* note 6 at 173 (para. 49); *Reference re Secession of Quebec*, *supra* note 3 at 262–63 (para. 82).

Notes to Chapter 5

1 *Calder* v. *A.G. of British Columbia*, [1973] S.C.R. 313 at 402–04.

2 *Ibid.* at 404. See also in this regard *Guerin* v. *The Queen*, [1984] 2 S.C.R. 335 at 377; *R.* v. *Sparrow*, [1990] 1 S.C.R. 1075 at 1099; *R.* v. *Gladstone*, [1996] 2 S.C.R. 723 at 750–51 (para. 34); *Delgamuukw* v. *B.C.*, [1997] 3 S.C.R. 1010 at 1122–23 (para. 183); *Delgamuukw* v. *B.C.* (1993), 104 D.L.R. (4th) 470 (B.C.C.A.); *Watt* v. *Canada (Minister of Citizenship and Immigration)*, [1999] 2 C.N.L.R. 326 (F.C.A.) at 334–36 (paras. 13–16); *R.* v. *Jacob*, [1999] 3 C.N.L.R. 239 (B.C.S.C.) at 266–67 (paras. 107–09); and B. Slattery, "Understanding Aboriginal Rights" (1987) 66 Can. Bar Rev. 727 at 748–49, 765–66.

3 *Delgamuukw* v. *B.C.*, *supra* note 2 at 1116 (para. 173).

4 *R.* v. *White and Bob* (1964), 50 D.L.R. (2d) 613 (B.C.C.A.) at 662; aff'd [1965] S.C.R. vi; (1965) 52 D.L.R. (2d) 481 (S.C.C.); B. Slattery, "Understanding Aboriginal Rights," *supra* note 2 at 766.

5 In this regard, reference may be made to the mixed opinions of Justices Judson and Hall in *Calder* v. *A.G. of British Columbia*, *supra* note 1, and to the mixed opinions delivered in the decision of the British Columbia Court of Appeal in *Delgamuukw* v. *B.C.* (1993), 104 D.L.R. (4th) 470 (B.C.C.A.).

6 The case that comes to mind is the federal legislation that purported to extinguish certain land rights in the territory contemplated by the James Bay and Northern Quebec Agreement, including certain land rights pertaining to those Aboriginal Peoples who were not signatories to that agreement: *James Bay and Northern Quebec Native Claims Settlement Act*, S.C. 1976–77, c. 32, s. 3(3), 4(1)b. On post-1867 extinguishments in relation to the building of the trans-continental railway, see *Canadian Pacific Ltd.* v. *Matsqui Indian Band* (1999), 176 D.L.R. (4th) 35 (F.C.A.).

7 *Sikyea* v. *R.*, [1964] S.C.R. 642; *R.* v. *George*, [1966] S.C.R. 267; *Frank* v. *R.*, [1978] 1 S.C.R. 95; *Moosehunter* v. *R.*, [1981] 1 S.C.R. 282 at 293; *R.* v. *Horseman*, [1990] 1 S.C.R. 901 at 936; *R.* v. *Badger*, [1996] 1 S.C.R. 771 at 795–97 (paras. 45–48), 812–13 (paras. 74, 77); *R.* v. *Marshall*, [1999] 3 S.C.R. 456 at 496 (para. 48).

8 See *Chippewas of Sarnia Band* v. *Canada (A.G.)* (April 30, 1999), Carswell Ont. 1244 (Ont. S.C.) at paras. 562–70; rev'd in part in *Chippewas of Sarnia Band* v. *Canada (A.G.)* (C.A.), [2001] 1 C.N.L.R. 56 (Ont. C.A.) (in regard to the extinguishment of treaty rights, see paras. 238–40).

9 B. Slattery, "Making Sense of Aboriginal and Treaty Rights" (2000) 79 Can. Bar Rev. 196 at 209.

10 *R.* v. *Sioui*, [1990] 1 S.C.R. 1025 at 1063.

11 *R.* v. *Marshall*, *supra* note 7 at 496 (para. 48); *Halfway River First Nation* v. *B.C. (Ministry of Forests)*, [1999] 4 C.N.L.R. 1 (B.C.C.A.) at 39–40 (para. 133). See

also the following cases for examples of treaty rights being modified unilaterally albeit through the operation of constitutional documents: *R. v. Horseman, supra* note 7, and *R. v. Badger, supra* note 7.

12 *Delgamuukw* v. *B.C., supra* note 2 at 1116 (para. 113); *R.* v. *White and Bob, supra* note 4 at 618, 663.

13 See amongst other cases, *Watt* v. *Canada (Minister of Citizenship and Immigration), supra* note 2 at 335 (para. 15).

14 E.C.E. Todd, *The Law of Expropriation and Compensation in Canada*, 2d ed. (Toronto: Carswell, 1992) at 24–25. However, see *Manitoba Fisheries Ltd.* v. *R.,* [1979] 1 S.C.R. 101; *R. (B.C.)* v. *Tener,* [1985] 1 S.C.R. 533 at 549–52, 557; *Casamiro Resource Corp.* v. *British Columbia (A.G.)* (1991), 80 D.L.R. (4th) 1 (B.C.C.A.); *Cream Silver Mines Ltd.* v. *British Columbia* (1991), 85 D.L.R. (4th) 269 (B.C.S.C.); B. Barton, "Comment" (1987) 66 Can. Bar Rev. 145.

15 *Kruger* v. *R.,* [1978] 1 S.C.R. 104 at 108.

16 See *R.* v. *Sundown,* [1999] 1 S.C.R. 393 at 414–15 (paras. 41–42).

17 See *Delgamuukw* v. *B.C., supra* note 2 at 1114, 1133–34 (paras. 169, 203); *Guerin* v. *The Queen, supra* note 2; *Calder* v. *A.G. of British Columbia, supra* note 1, in particular the reasons of Hall J.; *Oyekan* v. *Adele,* [1957] 2 All E.R. 785 (P.C.) at 788; *Amodu Tijani* v. *Southern Nigeria (Secretary),* [1921] 2 A.C. 399 (P.C.); *Tamaki* v. *Baker,* [1901] A.C. 561; *R.* v. *Symonds* , [1847] N.Z.P.C.C. 387.

18 See *R.* v. *Van der Peet,* [1996] 2 S.C.R. 507 at 538 (paras. 28, 29); *Delgamuukw* v. *B.C., supra* note 2 at 1092 (para. 134-135).

19 See generally D. Sanders, "The Rights of the Aboriginal Peoples of Canada" (1983) 61 Can. Bar. Rev. 314; J. O'Reilly, "La Loi constitutionnelle de 1982, droit des autochtones" (1984) 25 C. de D. 125; B. Slattery, "The Constitutional Guarantee of Aboriginal and Treaty Rights" (1982–83) 8 Queen's L.J. 232.

20 *R.* v. *Sparrow, supra* note 2 at 1110. See M. Asch & P. Macklem, "Aboriginal Rights and Canadian Sovereignty: An Essay on R. v. Sparrow" (1991) 26:2 Alta. L. Rev. 502; W.I.C. Binnie, "The Sparrow Doctrine: Beginning of the End or End of the Beginning?" (1991) 15 Queen's L.J. 217; L.I. Rotman, "Defining Parameters: Aboriginal Rights, Treaty Rights, and the Sparrow Justificatory Test" (1997) 36 Alta. L. Rev. 149; S. Grammond, "La protection constitutionnelle des droits ancestraux des peuples autochtones et l'arrêt Sparrow" (1991) 36 McGill L.J. 1382.

21 *R.* v. *Sparrow, supra* note 2.

22 *Ibid.* at 1099.

23 *R.* v. *Van der Peet, supra* note 18. See our discussion in this regard in chapter one.

24 *R.* v. *Sparrow, supra* note 2 at 1109.

25 *Ibid.* at 1110.

26 *Prima facie* means at first sight or at first view.

27 *R.* v. *Badger, supra* note 7 at 814–15 (para. 82). See also *Halfway River First Nation* v. *B.C. (Ministry of Forests), supra* note 11 at 38 (para. 127).

28 *R.* v. *Sparrow, supra* note 2 at 1111.

29 *Ibid.* at 1112.

30 *R.* v. *Gladstone, supra* note 2 at 757 (para. 43).

31 *Ibid.* This was further reiterated in *R.* v. *Côté,* [1996] 3 S.C.R. 139 at 185–86 (para. 75).

32 *R.* v. *Adams,* [1996] 3 S.C.R. 101 at 131–32 (paras. 53–54). See also *R.* v. *Côté, supra* note 31 at 186–87 (para. 76) and *R.* v. *Marshall, supra* note 7 at 504–05 (para. 64).

33 *R.* v. *Nikal,* [1996] 1 S.C.R. 1013 at 1065 (para. 110).

34 *Ibid.* at 1065–1066 (para. 111); *R.* v. *Badger, supra* note 7 at 822 (para. 98).

35 *R.* v. *Sparrow, supra* note 2 at 1113. See also *R.* v. *Côté, supra* note 31 at 189 (para. 89) and *R.* v. *Adams, supra* note 32 at 133 (para. 56); See *R.* v. *Powley* (February 23, 2001), Docket C34065 (Ont. C.A.) at paras. 168–69 for examples of how public-interest arguments are now presented under the guise of social and economic benefit or fairness arguments.

36 *R.* v. *Sparrow, supra* note 2 at 1113–14.

37 *R.* v. *Gladstone, supra* note 2 at 774–75 (paras. 73, 75).

38 *Delgamuukw* v. *B.C., supra* note 2 at 1111, 1132–33 (paras. 165, 202).

39 *R.* v. *Sparrow, supra* note 2 at 1119.

40 *R.* v. *Badger, supra* note 7 at 822 (para. 98).

41 *R.* v. *Sparrow, supra* note 2 at 1116. See also *R.* v. *Jack,* [1980] 1 S.C.R. 294.

42 *R.* v. *Gladstone, supra* note 2.

43 *R.* v. *Van der Peet, supra* note 18.

44 Justice L'Heureux-Dubé, in her concurring opinion in *R.* v. *Gladstone, supra* note 2, specifically discarded the approach to extinguishment applicable in the United States as set out in the *Santa Fe Pacific Railroad* case at 809 (para. 149): "In the case at bar, the respondent argues that the test is met when the aboriginal right and the activities contemplated by the legislation cannot co-exist. Such an approach, based on the view adopted by the United States Supreme Court in United States v. Santa Fe Pacific Railroad Co., 314 U.S. 339 (1941), is irreconcilable with the 'clear and plain intention' test favoured in Canada."

45 *R.* v. *Gladstone, supra* note 2 at 766–67 (para. 62).

46 See *R.* v. *Sparrow, supra* note 2 at 1119; *R.* v. *Badger, supra* note 7 at 821–22 (para. 97); *R.* v. *Nikal, supra* note 33 at 1064–65 (para. 109); *R.* v. *Côté, supra* note 31 at 189 (para. 81); *Delgamuukw* v. *B.C., supra* note 2 at 1111–14 (paras. 165–69).

47 *R.* v. *Sparrow, supra* note 2 at 1119; *Delgamuukw* v. *B.C., supra* note 2 at para. 168; *R.* v. *Marshall (No. 2),* [1999] 3 S.C.R. 533 at 564 (para. 43); *Halfway River First Nation* v. *B.C. (Ministry of Forests), supra* note 11; *TransCanada Pipeline Limited* v. *Beardmore (Township)* (2000), 186 D.L.R., (4th) 403 (Ont. C.A.) at 452–54 (paras. 113–20); *Westbank First Nation* v. *British Columbia (Minister of Forests),* [2001] 1 C.N.L.R. 361 at paras. 84–85; *Liidlii Kue First Nation* v. *Canada,* [2000] 4 C.N.L.R. 123 (F.C.T.D.) at 137–38 (paras. 47–50). Sonia Lawrence and Patrick Macklem argue that when the Crown seeks to engage in an action that adversely affects Aboriginal interests, the duty to consult requires it to make good-faith efforts to negotiate an agreement specifying the rights of the parties. S. Lawrence & P. Macklem, "From Consultation to Reconciliation: Aboriginal Rights and the Crown's Duty to Consult" (2000) 79 Can. Bar Rev. 252.

48 *Delgamuukw* v. *B.C., supra* note 2 at 1113; *Liidlii Kue First Nation* v. *Canada, supra* note 47 at 138–42 (in particular paras. 52, 62).

49 *R.* v. *Nikal, supra* note 33 at 1065 (para. 110): "[T]he need for the dissemination of information and a request for consultations cannot simply be denied"; *Halfway River First Nation* v. *B.C. (Ministry of Forests), supra* note 11 at 44 (para. 160); *Liidlii Kue First Nation* v. *Canada, supra* note 47 at 143 (para. 65).

50 The issue of Aboriginal leadership is complex since there may often exist various power structures within a given Aboriginal community, including traditional leadership structures at odds with *Indian Act* band council leadership. It is beyond the scope of this book to address this matter further.

51 *Delgamuukw* v. *B.C., supra* note 2 at 1113 (para. 168).

52 *R.* v. *Côté, supra* note 31 at 191–92 (paras. 86–87).

53 See *Delgamuukw* v. *B.C. supra* note 2 at 1114, 1133–34 (paras. 169, 203); *Guerin* v. *The Queen, supra* note 2; *Calder* v. *A.G. of British Columbia, supra* note 1, in particular the reasons of Hall J.; *Oyekan* v. *Adele, supra* note 17 at 788; *Amodu Tijani* v. *Southern Nigeria (Secretary), supra* note 17; *Tamaki* v. *Baker, supra* note 17; *R.* v. *Symonds, supra* note 17.

54 Though this right to compensation flows from the common law and, since 1982, from the *Constitution Act, 1982,* it may also be available, in certain circumstances, pursuant to the terms of the *Canadian Bill of Rights,* R.S.C., 1985, app. III, in particular subsections 1(a) and (b). Indeed, the right to compensation for extinguishment of Aboriginal title in Australia is deemed to result, *inter alia,* from the application of human rights legislation: *Mabo* v. *Queensland (No. 1)* (1988), 166 C.L.R. 186 (Aust. H.C.). Insofar as compensation is generally awarded for the forcible taking of non-Aboriginal property, it can be argued that it would be discriminatory under the *Canadian Bill of Rights* not to provide an equivalent right to compensation for the forcible taking of Aboriginal property. It should, however, be noted that the availability of compensation under the *Canadian Bill of Rights* in cases relating to the taking of property is a complex and controversial issue: Walter S. Tarnopolsky, *The Canadian Bill of Rights,* 2d rev. ed. (McClelland & Stewart, 1975) at 218–35. However, the argument here is not that the *Canadian Bill of Rights* protects property rights, but rather that where compensation is available in cases of the taking of property, it would be discriminatory to refuse such compensation in cases where the proprietary interest is Aboriginal.

Notes to Chapter 6

1 See *A.G.* v. *de Keyser Royal Hotel Ltd.,* [1920] A.C. 508 (H.L.) at 542; *Newcastle Breweries Ltd.* v. *R.,* [1920] 1 K.B. 854 at 866; *Montreal* v. *Montreal Harbour Commission,* [1926] A.C. 299 at 313; *Burmah Oil Company* v. *Lord Advocate,* [1965] A.C. 75 at 167–68; *Manitoba Fisheries Ltd.* v. *R.,* [1979] 1 S.C.R. 101; *R. (B.C.)* v. *Tener,* [1985] 1 S.C.R. 533 at 547, 559; *Toronto Area Transit Operating Authority* v. *Dell Holdings Ltd.,* [1997] 1 S.C.R. 32; E.C.E. Todd, *The Law of Expropriation and Compensation in Canada,* 2d ed. (Toronto: Carswell, 1992) at 31–38.

2 *R.* v. *Quebec Gas* (1917), 17 Ex. C.R. 386, 42 D.L.R. 61; aff'd 49 D.L.R. 692, 59

S.C.R. 677; *Vyricheria* v. *Revenue Divisional Officer*, [1939] A.C. 302.

3 *Vyricheria* v. *Revenue Divisional Officer, ibid.* at 312.

4 *R.* v. *Quebec Improvement Company* (1913), 18 Ex. C.R. 35; *R.* v. *Carrière de Beauport*, [1915] 17 Ex. C.R. 414; *R.* v. *Fowlds* (1893), 4 Ex. C.R. 1.

5 *Vyricheria* v. *Revenue Divisional Officer, supra* note 2 at 313.

6 *Dau* v. *Murphy Oil*, [1970] S.C.R. 861; *Pointe Gourde Quarrying & Transport Company* v. *Sub-Intendant of Crown Lands*, [1947] A.C. 565 (P.C.); *Re Lucas Chesterfield Gas and Water Board*, [1909] 1 K.B. 16 (C.A.) at 25; *R.* v. *Beech*, [1930] Ex. C.R. 133 at 142; *Fraser* v. *Fraserville (City)*, [1917] A.C. 187 at 192–94; *Gough & The Aspatria, Silloth & District Joint Water Board*, [1904] 1 K.B. 417 (C.A.) at 423; *Vyricheria* v. *Revenue Divisional Officer, supra* note 2 at 313.

7 *Cedar Rapids Manufacturing and Power Company* v. *Lacoste*, [1914] A.C. 569 at 576–77; *Re Lucas Chesterfield Gas and Water Board, ibid.* at 28; *R.* v. *Elgin Realty Company Ltd.*, [1943] S.C.R. 49 at 52; *R.* v. *Fraser*, [1963] S.C.R. 455; *C.N.R.* v. *Palmer*, [1965] 2 Ex. C.R. 305; *Lamb* v. *Manitoba Hydro-Electric Board*, [1966] S.C.R. 229; *Saint John Priory* v. *City of Saint John*, [1972] S.C.R. 746.

8 *Cedar Rapids Manufacturing and Power Company* v. *Lacoste, ibid.* at 576. See also *R.* v. *Woods Manufacturing Company Ltd.*, [1951] S.C.R. 504 at 506–07.

9 *R.* v. *Beech, supra* note 6 at 142; *Brown* v. *Commissioner for Railways* (1890), 15 A.C. 240 (P.C.); *Bailey* v. *Isle of Thanet Light Railways*, [1900] 1 Q.B. 722; *Montreal* v. *Brown et al.*, [1876–77] 2 App. Cas. 168 at 184; *Trent Stoughton* v. *Barbados Water Supply Co.*, [1893] A.C. 502 at 504; *Morrison* v. *Montreal*, [1877–78] 3 App. Cas. 148 at 156; *Fitzpatrick* v. *New Liskeard* (1909), 13 O.W.R. 806 (C.A.); *Re Ridell & Newcastle Gateshead Water Company* (1879), 90 L.T. 44n.

10 *Re Lucas Chesterfield Gas and Water Board, supra* note 6 at 25; *Vyricheria* v. *Revenue Divisional Officer, supra* note 2 at 315–18, 323; *Gough & The Aspatria, Silloth & District Joint Water Board, supra* note 6 at 423.

11 *St. Michael's College* v. *City of Toronto*, [1926] S.C.R. 318 at 324.

12 *R.* v. *Sisters of Charity of Rockingham*, [1924] Ex. C.R. 79.

13 *Ibid.* at 83.

14 G.S. Challies, "Quelques problèmes d'expropriation" (1961) 21 R. du B. 165 at 165–81. See also E. Picard, *Traité général de l'expropriation pour utilité publique* (Bruxelles: F. Larcier, 1875) at 237–49.

15 J. Forgues & J. Prémont, *Loi sur l'expropriation annotée* (Cowansville, Québec: Les Éditions Yvon Blais, 1998) at 77–80.

16 See Ontario Law Reform Commission, *Report on the Basis for Compensation on Expropriation*, Toronto: Attorney General for the Province of Ontario, 1967, at 19–20.

17 See generally *Toronto Area Transit Operating Authority* v. *Dell Holdings Ltd., supra* note 1; Ontario Law Reform Commission, *Report on the Basis for Compensation on Expropriation, ibid.* at 34–43; E.C.E. Todd, *The Law of Expropriation and Compensation in Canada, supra* note 1 at 274–327; G.S. Challies, *The Law of Expropriation* (Montreal: Wilson et Lafleur, 1963).

18 *Canadian Pacific Railway Company* v. *Albin* (1919), 59 S.C.R. 151 at 160. See also *Cowper Essex* v. *Local Board for Acton* (1889), 14 App. Cas. 153 at 162. One explanation given for the rule is that a "willing seller will only sell a portion

of his land at a price that takes into account not only the market value of the portion sold but also any diminution in value caused to the remaining land by reason of the construction or use of the works by the purchaser or his successor in title on the portion sold." E.C.E. Todd, *The Law of Expropriation and Compensation in Canada, supra* note 1 at 334.

19 Ontario Law Reform Commission, *Report on the Basis for Compensation on Expropriation, supra* note 16 at 47. This statement of the law was itself taken from Angers J. in *Autographic Register Systems* v. *C.N.R.,* [1933] Ex. C.R. 152 at 155–56.

20 *R.* v. *Woods Manufacturing Company Ltd., supra* note 8 at 515; Ontario Law Reform Commission, *Report on the Basis for Compensation on Expropriation supra* note 16 at 14–15; G.S. Challies, *The Law of Expropriation, supra* note 1 at 94.

Notes to Chapter 7

1 *R.* v. *Sparrow,* [1990] 1 S.C.R. 1075 at 1103.

2 Reference in this regard may be made to D.E. Wilkins, *American Indian Sovereignty and the U.S. Supreme Court—The Masking of Justice* (Austin: University of Texas Press, 1997). See J. Hurley, "Aboriginal Rights in Modern American Case Law" [1983] 2 C.N.L.R. 9; F.S. Cohen, *Felix S. Cohen's Handbook of Federal Indian Law,* Rennard Strickland *et al.,* eds. (Charlottesville, Virginia: The Michie Company, 1982); R.N. Clinton, N.J. Newton, & M.E. Price, *American Indian Law* (Charlotteville, Virginia: The Michie Company, 1991); G.A. Wilkinson "Indian Tribal Claims Before the Court of Claims" (1966) 55 Georgetown L.J. 511; S.P. McSloy, "Revisiting the 'Courts of the Conqueror': American Indian Claims against the United States" (1994) 44 American University L.R. 537.

3 *Norton* v. *Cobell* (February 23, 2001), files no. 00-5081 and 00-5084, U.S. Court of Appeals for the District of Columbia.

4 *United States* v. *Alcea Band of Tillamooks et al.,* 341 U.S. 48 (1951); *Tee-Hit-Ton Indians* v. *United States,* 348 U.S. 272 (1955). As noted by N.J. Newton: "[T]he courts have developed two doctrinal strains limiting fifth amendment protection for Indian lands. First, the Supreme Court has held that aboriginal Indian land is not 'property' for the purposes of the fifth amendment, in Tee-Hit-Ton. Second, the courts have, in effect, held that not all takings are takings; some acquisitions of Indian land by the federal government are outside the scope of the fifth amendment." N.J. Newton, "The Judicial Role in Fifth Amendment Takings of Indian Land: An Analysis of the *Sioux Nation* Rule" (1982) 61 Oregon L.R. 245 at 248.

5 *Tee-Hit-Ton Indians* v. *United States, ibid.*

6 See among other cases, *Cherokee Nation* v. *Georgia,* 30 U.S. (5 Pet.) 1 (1831); *Worcester* v. *Georgia,* 31 U.S. (6 Pet.) 515 (1832).

7 *Tee-Hit-Ton Indians* v. *United States, supra* note 4 at 290–91.

8 *Santa Clara Pueblo* v. *Martinez,* 436 U.S. 49 (1978); *Elk* v. *Wilkins,* 112 U.S. 94 (1884).

9 See *Delgamuukw* v. *B.C.,* [1997] 3 S.C.R. 1010 at 1114, 1133–34 (paras. 169,

203); *Guerin* v. *The Queen,* [1984] 2 S.C.R. 335; *Calder* v. *A.G. of British Columbia,* [1973] S.C.R. 313, in particular the reasons of Hall J.

10 *R.* v. *Symonds,* [1847] N.Z.P.C.C. 387; *Tamaki* v. *Baker,* [1901] A.C. 561; *Amodu Tijani* v. *Southern Nigeria (Secretary),* [1921] 2 A.C. 399; *Oyekan* v. *Adele,* [1957] 2 All. E.R. 785 (P.C.) at 788. In Australia, the issue of the right to compensation at common law in cases of extinguishment of Aboriginal title remains uncertain in light of the divided opinions on this matter in *Mabo* v. *Queensland (No. 2),* [1992] 5 C.N.L.R. 1 at 11–12, 90. However, that issue is somewhat moot in Australia since the right to compensation in cases of infringement or extinguishment of Aboriginal title flows in any event from the operation of the *Racial Discrimination Act, 1975* of the Commonwealth of Australia as interpreted in *Mabo* v. *Queensland (No. 1)* (1988), 166 C.L.R. 186 (Aust. H.C.).

11 *Lone Wolf* v. *Hitchcock,* 187 U.S. 553 (1903) at 568.

12 *Ibid.* at 568.

13 *Shoshone Tribe* v. *United States,* 299 U.S. 476 (1937).

14 *Ibid.* at 497–98.

15 *United States* v. *Sioux Nation of Indians,* 448 U.S. 371 (1980).

16 *Fort Berthold Reservation* v. *United States,* 390 F.2d 686 (Ct. Cl., 1968).

17 See also *Delaware Tribal Business Comm.* v. *Weeks,* 430 U.S. 73 (1977) at 84.

18 *United States* v. *Sioux Nation, supra* note 15 at 414–15. See N.J. Newton, "The Judicial Role in Fifth Amendment Takings of Indian Land: An Analysis of the *Sioux Nation* Rule," *supra* note 4.

19 *United States* v. *Sioux Nation, supra* note 15 at 416–17.

20 *United States* v. *Shoshone Tribe,* 304 U.S. 111 (1938).

21 *Ibid.* at 116. See also *United States* v. *Klamath and Moadoc Tribe of Indians,* 304 U.S. 119 (1938); *Otoe & Missouria Tribe of Indians* v. *United States,* 131 F. Supp. 265 (Ct. Cl., 1955), cert. denied, 350 U.S. 848 (1955); *Miami Tribe of Oklahoma* v. *United States,* 175 F. Supp. 926 (Ct. Cl., 1959) at 942.

22 *Fort Berthold Reservation* v. *United States, supra* note 16 at 698; *United States* v. *Cherokee Nation,* 474 F.2d 628 (Ct. Cl., 1973); *Pillager Bands of Chippewa Indians, Minn.* v. *United States,* 428 F.2d 1274 (Ct. Cl., 1970) at 1277; *Sac and Fox Tribes of Indians of Okla.* v. *United States,* 383 F.2d 991 (Ct. Cl., 1967) at 1001, cert. denied, 389 U.S. 90.

23 *Creek Nation* v. *United States,* 302 U.S. 620 (1938); *United States* v. *Cherokee Nation, ibid.* at 635.

24 *Miami Tribe of Oklahoma* v. *United States, supra* note 21.

25 *Ibid.* at 943.

26 *Otoe & Missouria Tribe of Indians* v. *United States, supra* note 21.

27 *Ibid.* at 290.

28 *Ibid.*

29 See generally *United States* v. *Shoshone Tribe, supra* note 20; *Alcea Band of Tillamooks* v. *United States,* 89 F. Supp. 938 (Ct. Cl., 1950), rev'd as to interest only 341 U.S. 48; *Rogue River Tribe of Indians* v. *United States,* 89 F. Supp. 798 (Ct. Cl., 1950), cert. denied, 341 U.S. 902; *Osage Nation of Indians* v. *United States,* 97 F. Supp. 381 (Ct. Cl., 1951), cert. denied, 342 U.S. 896 (1951); *Otoe & Missouria Tribe of Indians* v. *United States, supra* note 21; *Miami Tribe of*

Oklahoma v. *United States, supra* note 21 at 943–44.

30 See *United States* v. *Klamath and Moadoc Tribe of Indians, supra* note 21.

31 *Alcea Band of Tillamooks* v. *United States, supra* note 29.

32 *Rogue River Tribe of Indians* v. *United States, supra* note 29.

33 See *Sioux Tribe of Indians* v. *United States,* 146 F. Supp. 229 (Ct. Cl., 1956).

Notes to Chapter 8

1 *Delgamuukw* v. *B.C.,* [1997] 3 S.C.R. 1010 at 1114 (para. 169).

2 *R.* v. *Sparrow,* [1990] 1 S.C.R. 1075.

3 *R.* v. *Sundown,* [1999] 1 S.C.R. 393 at 412 (para. 35); *St. Mary's Indian Band* v. *Cranbrook,* [1997] 2 S.C.R. 657 at 666–67 (para. 14); *Delgamuukw* v. *B.C., supra* note 1 at 1081–83, 1090 (paras. 112–15, 117, 130); *R.* v. *Van der Peet,* [1996] 2 S.C.R. 507 at 580 (para. 119); *Blueberry River Indian Band* v. *Canada,* [1995] 4 S.C.R. 344 at 358, 387 (paras. 6, 72); *R.* v. *Badger,* [1996] 1 S.C.R. 771 at 813 (para. 78); *R.* v. *Sparrow, supra* note 2 at 1112; *Canadian Pacific* v. *Paul,* [1988] 2 S.C.R. 654 at 678; *Simon* v. *R.,* [1985] 2 S.C.R. 387 at 404; *Guerin* v. *The Queen,* [1984] 2 S.C.R. 335 at 379, 382.

4 See amongst other cases, *R.* v. *Van der Peet, supra* note 3, and our discussion in chapter one.

5 *Skeetchestn Indian Band* v. *British Columbia (Registrar of Land Titles),* [2000] 2 C.N.L.R. 330 (B.C.S.C.) at 338 (para. 24); aff'd [2001] 1 C.N.L.R. 310 (B.C.C.A.).

6 *Delgamuukw* v. *B.C., supra* note 1 at 1134 (paras. 203–04). See also *Nation Innu de Betsiamites* v. *Canada (P.G.),* [1999] R.J.Q. 1388 (Que. S.C.) at 1397–98.

7 *R.* v. *Sparrow, supra* note 2 at 1108.

8 *Delgamuukw* v. *B.C., supra* note 1 at 1113–14 (para. 169).

9 *Guerin* v. *The Queen, supra* note 3 at 386–87. See also 390, where Dickson J. adds that, in his opinion, "the quantum of damages is to be determined by analogy with the principles of trust law."

10 See generally *Lac Minerals* v. *International Corona Resources,* [1989] 2 S.C.R. 574 at 643–56, 668–80; *Canson Enterprises Ltd.* v. *Boughton & Co.,* [1991] 3 S.C.R. 534; *Norberg* v. *Wynrib,* [1992] 2 S.C.R. 226; *Hodgkinson* v. *Simms,* [1994] 3 S.C.R. 377 at 439–55.

11 *Hodgkinson* v. *Simms, ibid.* at 444, La Forest J.

12 L.I. Rotman, *Parallel Paths: Fiduciary Doctrine and the Crown-Native Relationship in Canada* (Toronto: University of Toronto Press, 1996) at 196.

13 See *Guerin* v. *The Queen, supra* note 3; *Delgamuukw* v. *B.C., supra* note 1 at 1113–14 (para. 169), 1133–34 (para. 203); *Semiahmoo Indian Band* v. *Canada,* [1998] 1 F.C. 3 (C.A.).

14 *Guerin* v. *The Queen, supra* note 3 at 384. See also *Frame* v. *Smith,* [1987] 2 S.C.R. 99 at 135–36; *Lac Minerals* v. *International Corona Resources, supra* note 10 at 643–56; *Hodgkinson* v. *Simms, supra* note 10 at 404–14.

15 *Delgamuukw* v. *B.C., supra* note 1 at 1065–67 (paras. 81–84).

16 *Ibid.* at 1066 (para. 82); *R.* v. *Van der Peet, supra* note 3 at 550–51 (para. 49).

17 See *Nation Innu de Betsiamites* v. *Canada (P.G.), supra* note 6 at 1397–98.

18 *Delgamuukw* v. *B.C., supra* note 1 at 1112 (para. 167).

19 See generally *Guerin* v. *The Queen, supra* note 3; *Delgamuukw* v. *B.C., supra* note 1 at 1113–14 (para. 169), 1133–34 (para. 203); *Semiahmoo Indian Band* v. *Canada, supra* note 13.

20 *Roberts* v. *Canada,* [1989] 1 S.C.R. 322; *R.* v. *Côté,* [1996] 3 S.C.R. 139 at 170, 172–75 (paras. 45, 46, 49–54); *R.* v. *Adams,* [1996] 3 S.C.R. 101 at 120–22 (paras. 31–33); J.M. Evans & B. Slattery, "Federal Jurisdiction-Pendant Parties-Aboriginal Title and Federal Common Law-Charter Challenges-Reform Proposals: *Roberts* v. *Canada*" (1989) 68 Can. Bar Rev. 817 at 832; B. Slattery, "Understanding Aboriginal Rights" (1987) 66 Can. Bar Rev. 727 at 732, 736–741, 777; B. Slattery, "Making Sense of Aboriginal and Treaty Rights" (2000) 79 Can. Bar Rev. 196 at 198–99; Royal Commission on Aboriginal Peoples, *Partners in Confederation: Aboriginal Peoples, Self-Government and the Constitution* (Ottawa: Minister of Supply and Services, 1993) at 20.

21 *R.* v. *Côté, supra* note 20 at 170, 172–75 (paras. 45, 46, 49–54); *R.* v. *Adams, supra* note 20 at 120–22 (paras. 31–33).

22 See the discussion in chapter four above and the case law there referred to, and in particular *Delgamuukw* v. *B.C, supra* note 1 at 1121 (para. 181); *St. Catherine's Milling & Lumber Company* v. *The Queen* (1888), 14 App. Cas. 46.

23 See the discussion in chapter four, as well as B. Slattery, "Understanding Aboriginal Rights," *supra* note 20 at 777.

24 F.S. Cohen, *Felix S. Cohen's Handbook of Federal Indian Law,* Rennard Strickland *et al.,* eds. (Charlottesville, Virginia: The Michie Company, 1982) at 524, referring in these regards to *Oneida Indian Nation* v. *County of Oneida,* 464 F.2d 916 (2d Cir. 1972), rev'd and remanded on other grounds, 414 U.S. 661 (1974); *Choctaw Nation* v. *Oklahoma I,* 397 U.S. 620 (1970); *United States* v. *Santa Fe Pacific Railroad Co.,* 314 U.S. 339 (1941); *United States ex rel. Whitehorse* v. *Briggs,* 555 F.2d. 283 (10th Cir., 1977).

25 *County of Oneida* v. *Oneida Indian Nation,* 470 U.S. 226 (1985) at 235–36.

26 *Joe* v. *Findlay,* [1981] 3 C.N.L.R. 58 (B.C.C.A); 122 D.L.R. (3d) 377; *Johnson* v. *B.C. Hydro and Power Authority,* [1981] 3 C.N.L.R. 63 (B.C.S.C.); *Shewish* v. *MacMillan Bloedel Ltd.,* [1990] 4 C.N.L.R. 93 (B.C.C.A.).

27 *Fairford First Nation* v. *Canada (A.G.),* [1999] 2 F.C. 48 (T.D.) at 88 (para. 66).

28 For examples of compensation awards pursuant to third-party infringements of Aboriginal lands and resources reserved under the terms of the *Indian Act,* see *Johnson* v. *B.C. Hydro and Power Authority, supra* note 26, and *Shewish* v. *MacMillan Bloedel Ltd., supra* note 26.

29 The third party may possibly have a recourse against the Crown authority that issued the authorization unlawfully; however, this is a complex issue that is not explored here. The Crown may also be liable to the Aboriginal Peoples for having issued an unlawful authorization affecting their Aboriginal or treaty rights.

30 *Regina* v. *St. Catharines Milling Co.* (1885), 10 O.R. 196 at 196.

31 *Ibid.* at 235.

32 *St. Catherine's Milling Lumber Company* v. *The Queen* (1888), 14 App. Cas. 46.

33 These types of situations are illustrated in a number of cases such as *Haida Nation* v. *British Columbia (Ministry of Forests)* (1997), 153 D.L.R. (4th) 1 (B.C.C.A.); *MacMillan Bloedel Limited* v. *Mullin,* [1985] 3 W.W.R. 577 (B.C.C.A.);

Saanichton Marina Ltd. v. *Tsawout Indian Band* (1989), 57 D.L.R. (4th) 161 (B.C.C.A.); *Stoney Creek Indian Band* v. *British Columbia,* [1999] 1 C.N.L.R. 192 (B.C.S.C.) at 201–10.

34 *Canadian Pacific Ltd.* v. *Matsqui Indian Band* (1999), 176 D.L.R. (4th) 35 (F.C.A.) at 93. See also the reasons of Desjardins J. at 57, supporting Robertson J. on this aspect of his dissident opinion.

35 *R.* v. *Sparrow, supra* note 2 at 1103.

36 *Ibid.*

37 *Constitution Act, 1982,* ss. 35 and 52, being Schedule B to the *Canada Act 1982* (U.K.), 1982, c. 11, reprinted in R.S.C. 1985, app. II, no. 44.

38 As is the case where the infringement is carried out pursuant to an unlawful authorization, the non-governmental third party may possibly have a recourse against the Crown authority that issued the unjustified authorization; however, as previously noted, this is a complex issue that is not reviewed in this book.

39 The Aboriginal perspective is to be afforded some importance in such matters. See, by analogy, *R.* v. *Van der Peet, supra* note 3 at 547, 550–51 (paras. 42, 49, 50). See also *Delgamuukw* v. *B.C., supra* note 1 at 1065–67 (paras. 81, 82, 84).

40 *Heydon's Case* (1613), 77 E.R. 1150, at 1151, 1154; *London Association for Protection of Trade* v. *Greenlands Limited,* [1916] 2 A.C. 15 at 32, 33; *Arneil* v. *Paterson,* [1931] A.C. 560 at 563–64; *Napierville Junction Railway Company* v. *Dubois,* [1924] S.C.R. 375 at 384; *Deguire Avenue Ltd.* v. *Adler,* [1963] B.R. 101 (Que. C.A.) at 111–12; *Pappadia* v. *St-Cyr,* [1959] B.R. 639 (Que. C.A.) at 640–41.

41 *Citadelle* v. *Lloyds Bank,* [1997] 3 S.C.R. 805; *Gold* v. *Rosenberg,* [1997] 3 S.C.R. 767; *Air Canada* v. *M & L Travel Ltd.,* [1993] 3 S.C.R. 787. See also *Gordon* v. *Winnipeg Canoe Club* (1999), 172 D.L.R. (4th) 423 (Man. C.A.); *McDonald* v. *Hauer,* [1977] 1 W.W.R. 51 (Sask. C.A.) at 60–66; *Imperial Bank* v. *Begley* (1936), 3 D.L.R. 1 (P.C.) at 4–5; *Ankcorn* v. *Stewart* (1920), 54 D.L.R. 74; 18 O.W.N. 204 (C.A.) at 205; *Taylor* v. *Davies* (1917), 41 D.L.R. 510 (Ont. S.C. App. Div.) at 514, 515 *per* Meredith C.J.O.; *London and Western Trust Company* v. *Dominion Savings and Investment Society* (1908), 12 O.W.R. 77 (C.A.) at 78; *Soar* v. *Ashwell,* [1891–4] All. E.R. Rep. 991 (C.A.) at 994 *per* Bowen L.J.; *Selangor United Rubber Estates Ltd.* v. *Cradock (No. 3),* [1968] 1 W.L.R. 1555 (Ch.) at 1578–91, in particular 1590E and F; *Karak Rubber Company* v. *Burden,* [1972] 1 W.L.R 602 (Ch.) at 632–37; *Nelson* v. *Larholt,* [1948] 1 K.B. 339; *G.L. Baker Ltd.* v. *Medway Building and Supplies Ltd.,* [1958] 1 W.L.R. 1216 (C.A.) at 1227; P.D. Maddaugh & J. McCamus, *The Law of Restitution* (Aurora, Ontario: Canada Law Book, 1990) at 84–85.

42 *Selangor United Rubber Estates Ltd.* v. *Cradock (No. 3), supra* note 41 at 1582C.

43 *Nelson* v. *Larholt, supra* note 41 at 343 *per* Denning J.

44 *Chippewas of Sarnia Band* v. *Canada (A.G.)* (C.A.), [2001] 1 C.N.L.R. 56 (Ont. C.A.), aff'g in part *Chippewas of Sarnia Band* v. *Canada (A.G.)* (April 30, 1999), Carswell Ont. 1244 (Ont. S.C.).

45 *County of Oneida* v. *Oneida Indian Nation, supra* note 25 at 240–45.

46 *Chippewas of Sarnia Band* v. *Canada (A.G.)* (C.A.), *supra* note 44 at paras. 220–42.

47　On the applicability of limitation of claim legislation to Aboriginal claims against third parties in Canada, see also *Stoney Creek Indian Band* v. *British Columbia*, *supra* note 33.

48.　*Chippewas of Sarnia Band* v. *Canada (A.G.)* (C.A.), *supra* note 44 at paras. 262–63; see also para. 267. On the issue of reconciliation, see *R.* v. *Gladstone*, [1996] 2 S.C.R. 723 at 775 (para. 74); *R.* v. *Van der Peet*, *supra* note 3 at 547–48, 550–51 (paras. 42, 49, 50); *Delgamuukw* v. *B.C.*, *supra* note 1 at 1065–67 (paras. 81–84).

49　*Chippewas of Sarnia Band* v. *Canada (A.G.)* (C.A.), *supra* note 44 at paras. 308–09.

50　*Indian Act*, R.S.C., 1985, c. I-5, s. 35.

51　*R.* v. *Gladstone*, *supra* note 48 at 775 (paras. 74–75); *R.* v. *Van der Peet*, *supra* note 3 at 539, 547–46, 550–51 (paras. 31, 42–43, 49–50).

52　Thus, in *Canadian Pacific* v. *Paul*, *supra* note 3, the pre-Confederation railroad legislation of New Brunswick was found to allow private railroad companies to use Aboriginal lands for railway purposes without transferring ownership interest in the land. This use was authorized without requiring the railway company to provide compensation to the affected Aboriginal Peoples. The Court nevertheless left open in that case (see 676) the question of whether the Government of New Brunswick had failed to carry out its obligations to the affected Aboriginal Peoples and whether these were entitled to compensation as a consequence. The Court strongly implied that such compensation would be available under the principles set out in *Guerin* v. *The Queen*, *supra* note 3.

53　*Nation Innu de Betsiamites* v. *Canada (P.G.)*, *supra* note 6; *McKenzie* v. *Quebec (A.G.)*, [1999] 3 C.N.L.R. 180 (Que. S.C.).

54　*Guerin* v. *The Queen*, [1982] 2 F.C. 385 (T.D.) at 441.

55　*Guerin* v. *The Queen*, *supra* note 3 at 359, 363 (Wilson J.) and 372–73, 390–91 (Dickson J.).

56　*Semiahmoo Indian Band* v. *Canada*, *supra* note 13.

57　*Ibid.* at 55–56 (para. 111). Reference may also be made to the decision of Teitelbaum J. of the Federal Court Trial Division in *Wewayakum Indian Band* v. *Canada and Wewayakai Indian Band* (1995), 99 F.T.R. 1 at 192 (para. 600).

58　*Calder* v. *A.G. of British Columbia*, [1973] S.C.R. 313 at 352; *Nation Innu de Betsiamites* v. *Canada (P.G.)*, *supra* note 6; *McKenzie* v. *Quebec (A.G.)*, *supra* note 53; *Woods Manufacturing Company Ltd.* v. *R.*, [1951] S.C.R. 504 at 506–07, 515; *Lac Minerals* v. *International Corona Resources*, *supra* note 10 at 623–56; *Hodgkinson* v. *Simms*, *supra* note 10 at 404–14.

59　*Delgamuukw* v. *B.C.*, *supra* note 1 at 1082–83 (para. 115).

60　*R.* v. *Van der Peet*, *supra* note 3; *R.* v. *N.T.C. Smokehouse Ltd.*, [1996] 2 S.C.R. 672; *R.* v. *Gladstone*, *supra* note 48; *R.* v. *Powley* (February 23, 2001), Docket C34065 (Ont. C.A.) at para. 90.

61　*R.* v. *Sundown*, *supra* note 3 at 412 (paras. 35–36).

62　*Oregon Jack Creek Indian Band et al.* v. *Canadian National Railway*, [1990] 2 C.N.L.R. 85. (B.C.C.A.), aff'd [1989] 2 S.C.R. 1069.

63　*Ibid.* at 94.

64　*Oregon Jack Creek Indian Band* v. *C.N.*, [1989] 2 S.C.R. 1069.

65　*Indian Act*, R.S.C., 1985 c. I-5, s. 62.

66 *McKenzie* v. *Quebec (A.G.),* [1998] 3 C.N.L.R. 112 (Que. C.A.).
67 *Blueberry River Indian Band* v. *Canada, supra* note 3.
68 *Apsassin et al.* v. *Canada* (March 2, 1998), T-4178-78 (F.C.T.D.).

Index

Page numbers for cases cited are to be found in the Table of Cases at the front of this book.

About the Author

In the course of a professional career spanning twenty-five years, the author of this book has been involved in major Aboriginal litigations and in numerous negotiations involving Aboriginal issues. Although he has practised principally in the field of Aboriginal law, representing mainly Aboriginal interests, Mr. Mainville's career has spanned administrative and constitutional law, labour law, and business law, and he has represented government and industry as well as Aboriginal groups. He has been actively involved in litigations and negotiations relating to treaty implementation and to comprehensive land claims. Mr. Mainville has been particularly involved in the impact of hydroelectric developments on Aboriginal Peoples, and he negotiated the first major Aboriginal-industry joint venture in this field. He holds degrees in law from the Université de Montréal and from McGill University, and he has lectured in Aboriginal law at both the McGill University Law Faculty and the Law Department of the Université du Québec à Montréal.